John Waters is an American filmmaker, actor, writer and visual artist best known for his cult films, including *Hairspray* (which was later turned into a blockbuster stage show and musical film), *Pink Flamingos* and *Cecil B. DeMented*. He lives in Baltimore, Maryland.

CARSICK

CARSICK

JOHN WATERS

corsair

CORSAIR

First published in the USA in 2014 by Farrar, Straus and Giroux

This edition published in 2014 by Corsair

A CIP catalogue record for this book
is available from the British Library.

ISBN 978-1-47211-892-9 (hardback)
ISBN 978-1-47211-613-0 (trade paperback)
ISBN: 978-1-47211-614-7 (ebook)

Printed and bound in Great Britain by
CPI Group (UK) Ltd, Croydon CR0 4YY

Corsair
is an imprint of
Constable & Robinson Ltd
100 Victoria Embankment
London EC4Y 0DY

An Hachette UK Company
www.hachette.co.uk

www.constablerobinson.com

TO MY SISTERS, KATHY AND TRISH,

AND IN MEMORY OF MY BROTHER, STEVE

CONTENTS

CARSICK

I haven't felt this excited or scared for a long time. Maybe ever. I just signed a book deal resulting from the shortest pitch ever. I, John Waters, will hitchhike alone from the front of my Baltimore house to my co-op apartment in San Francisco and see what happens. Simple, huh?

Am I fucking nuts? Brigid Berlin, Andy Warhol's most dangerous and glamorous sixties superstar, recently said to me, "How can I be bad at seventy?" She's got a point. I mean, yes, I'm "between pictures," as they say in Hollywood, but long ago I realized, as a so-called cult-film director, not only did I need a Plan B that was just as important to me as moviemaking, I needed a Plan C, D, and E. But Plan H, for "hitchhike"? I'm sixty-six years old, for chrissake.

"Why would a man who has worked so hard his whole life to reach the level of comfort you have, put yourself in such an *un*comfortable position?" Marianne Boesky, my New York art dealer, asked me when I told her of my "undercover travel adventure," as the publishers were calling my new book in trade announcements. A onetime actor in my early films who had a recent homeless past was even more alarmed when I hinted that I might do a hitchhiking book. "You'll never get a ride," he warned, telling me he had tried hitchhiking himself out of necessity in Florida last year. "No one picks up hitchhikers these days," he griped with disgust. *"No one!"*

Even successful hipsters seemed shocked when I confided my plans. "Nice knowing you," a California photographer buddy muttered with a laugh over dinner when he realized he wouldn't see me again until after my hobo-homo journey was scheduled to be completed. God, I wondered grandiosely, would I be like JFK on those recently released secret White House tapes, where he was heard planning his first day back from Dallas before anyone knew he'd be assassinated, commenting on what a "tough day" that would be. If he only knew.

What *am* I trying to prove here? I mean, I'm not bored. An ex-convict woman I recently met claimed her criminal past was not a result of a bad childhood but just because she "wanted an adventure." I do, too. Kicks. But hasn't writing and directing fifteen movies and penning six books made me feel complete? My career dreams *already* came true years ago and what I do now is all gravy. Shouldn't I be retiring rather than sticking out my thumb? Retiring to what, though? Insanity?

Will I be safe? I know serial killers routinely pick up hitchhikers and murder them, but aren't the victims, unfortunately, usually young female hookers? Yeah, yeah, I know about Herb Baumeister, "the I-70 Strangler," who choked at least sixteen gay men to death, but he picked them up in gay bars, not on exit ramps of truck stops. Yet I must admit even truckers I know are fairly nuts. One of them must have raised a few of my neighbors' eyebrows when he came over to visit and parked his eighteen-wheeler right on the small, quiet residential street in front of my house, taking up half the block. He's funny and sexy and straight but a real freak and likes to horrify me with his stories from the road. How he travels, high on speed, picking up teenage run-aways and screwing them in the back of the truck or driving full speed ahead in the night, carrying a bag of someone else's clean urine prepared for any random drug tests as he masturbates into a sock. He laughs when he admits sometimes illegally dumping huge loads of gravel in the middle of an unsuspecting suburbanite's lawn if he knows he's overloaded and a weigh station is coming up that will be open. Suppose someone like *this* guy picks me up?

Can I really give up the rigid scheduling I'm so used to in real life? Me? The ultimate control freak who plans, weeks ahead, the day I can irresponsibly eat candy? Sure, I've got all my interstate routes planned out for the trip and I think I know how many truck stops there are and how far apart they are, but so what? Will I really get out of the car if my ride strays from my route but is still headed west? I keep thinking beggars *can* be choosers, but I have to open my mind to the possibility I may be wrong.

WE ARE ALL BUMS, a radical left-wing poster boasted on the wall of my bedroom in my parents' house in the sixties. I remember the rage this particular slogan caused in my father. A bum. The worst thing you could be in his book. Now that he is, sadly, gone, can I finally become one? A vagabond? A freeloader? Is it possible to be a vagrant when you own three homes and rent another place in Provincetown for the summer? Will this book end up as a new spin on that now dated but incredibly influential 1961 nonfiction book *Black Like Me*, where the white author, John Howard Griffin, hitched and rode buses through the South disguised as a black man to see how it feels to be discriminated against?

I am afraid just the way the *Black Like Me* man was. But of different things. Like bad drivers. I'm amazed every person driving their car isn't killed every day. Riding along at high speeds in lanes just a few feet from each other. Texting, talking on the phone behind the wheel. Or just plain driving while stupid! Nobody is really a safe driver. I worry my own involuntary backseat driving will cause problems for anyone who picks me up. Will cries of "Slow down!" or slamming imaginary brakes from the passenger side cause bad will with my host drivers? I'm never in the front seat of a car if I'm not behind the wheel except when I take taxis in Australia, because I read the drivers there think you're snooty if you get in the back. Where I live in Baltimore, if you got in the front of the cab, they'd think you were robbing them and probably shoot you.

I've had a good history with hitchhiking. It's hard to imagine today, but in the early sixties my parents expected me to hitchhike home every day from high school. All the kids did. The roads were filled with preppy teenage boys, lacrosse sticks over their shoulders and their thumbs out. I'm sure just as many serial killers were behind the wheel then as now, but you never heard about them. Nobody warned us of the dangers of hitchhiking. Evil definitely did *not* seem to be lurking.

Of course perverts were out there, and I hitchhiked every day with a hard-on hoping one would pick me up and give me a blow job. Many did. On this trip, I guess I'll still technically be horny while hitchhiking, but I may be carrying a Viagra in my pocket instead of an erection. Is all hitchhiking gay? Aren't truck stops and Levi's-clad tough-guy hitchhikers staples of porn movies? My planned route is I-70 West, and if I'm lucky enough to get a ride going that way, I'll be able to find out if there really is such a place as the Kansas City Trucking Company—or was that just the title of a fictitious garage in that classic gay film directed by Joe Gage? I saw the real El Paso Wrecking Corp. on my drive from El Paso to Marfa, Texas, and almost drove off the road remembering this sequel. If there really is such a place, maybe I can get dropped off there and make friends.

I drove all five cross-country interstate routes in the United

States when I was a young man and loved it. We used to get "drive-away" cars, where the owner gave you the keys and you paid the gas and delivered the car to an address on the opposite coast. I even remember singing "America the Beautiful" stoned on hashish with my fellow travelers (David Lochary, Steve Butow, and David Hartman) as we drove toward a beautiful sunset in Minneapolis. Looking back, I'm amazed anyone trusted any of us considering how we looked at the time, but even though we violated the rules by taking other passengers (and drugs), we always did deliver the car in one piece. But come to think about it, we didn't ever pick up a hitchhiker *then*, and that was in the heyday of the hippie years. And in 2012, I expect someone to stop?

I still hitchhike in Provincetown to Longnook, the most beautiful beach in Truro (about ten miles away). I usually ask someone to go on a thumbing date with me. Author Philip Hoare, artist and singer Kembra Pfahler, the late and great art dealer Colin de Land, have all joined me alongside the highway. And we've never had any real trouble either. Once I was hitching with photographer Henny Garfunkel, whose extreme hairdo and stunning fashions can make children cry, and a man did a U-turn and picked us up—never a good sign. As usual, I got in the front and the woman hitchhiker got in the back. It smelled inside, like he was living in his car or something. I had a sudden flashback to the scene I wrote in *Pink Flamingos* where Mink Stole's character says to her husband, played by David Lochary, that she's tired of "just driving around . . . driving around" looking for female hitchhikers to pick up, kidnap, and then have raped and impregnated so the babies could be sold on the black market.

"See that safety sticker?" our vaguely creepy driver asked. "Yeah," I said hesitatingly, looking at the Massachusetts official emissions-test sticker on the inside of the windshield. "I drew that myself," he chuckled with a leer. I turned around to see

Henny's wide-eyed look of panic but it was all a false alarm; he dropped us off at the beach without incident.

But sometimes I go alone and I'm never sure if the drivers who pick me up recognize me. "Who is this man in the car?" a confused child who had never heard of hitchhiking once asked his mom and dad after I got in. "Why is he in *this* car?" he continued as I squirmed in embarrassment under the kid's hostile glare and tried to explain what hitchhiking was.

Another time, a handsome long-haired pirate type stopped to give me a ride in his pickup, and just as I was about to jump in the front, he smiled and said, "No, you'll have to ride in the back, my dog's up here in the front." Ha! Suddenly put in my proper place around such rugged hippie good looks, I laughed and happily climbed up into the open truck bed. I was thrilled to get a ride with such a sexy devil even if I could only see his beautiful long hair from the rear as he pulled off toward Provincetown.

Even weirder was the time the A&E *Biography* TV show was doing a segment on me and asked if they could shoot me hitchhiking in Provincetown and I reluctantly said yes. The crew hid in the bushes, and when I got a ride, they jumped in their van and followed. The nice local fisherman who picked me up not only didn't recognize me, he didn't see the crew either. Nervously eyeing the cameramen hanging out their windows, shooting us as they tracked our car, I casually mentioned to my ride, "Don't look over now on your side of the car, but there is a film crew shooting this whole thing." "Okay," he said with a shrug, completely unimpressed, and then drove for ten more minutes before dropping me off at the beach. Even when the crew jumped from their vehicle to film my exit, he never ruined their final shot by looking into the camera lens. What a pro.

One time my hitchhiking date was Patricia Hearst. As we walked toward Route 6 from Provincetown, we quickly got a ride, but I don't think the driver recognized us until we got in, me in the front, her in the back. He kept doing double takes looking over at me and finally said, "Are you John Waters?" and I said yes, and at the same time he looked in the rearview mirror I said, "And that is Patty Hearst." He looked totally shocked but I could tell he realized it *was* her. "He made me do it," Patty deadpanned, and I was so proud of her improvisational skills. We were now a hitchhiking comedy duo.

Coming back to Provincetown that day with Patty was harder because we had to hitchhike right on Route 6, a highway with cars whizzing by, which made it seem more like real hitchhiking. It took some time for us to get a ride and I could tell Patty was starting to get nervous, especially when we were finally picked up but asked to "switch cars" by the driver, who hooked us up with another ride from a friend in North Truro, the next town before Provincetown. Later, her husband, Bernie, whom I love but realize is the head of security for Hearst Corporation, was a little perturbed when she told him of our day's adventure. "Oh, come on, John," he said with impatience, "hasn't she had *enough* trouble?!" I guess he was right. But have I?

Is there such a thing as "unfamous"? If so, that is what I want to be on this trip, yet go right back to "famous" if need be. I'm recognized in public about 80 percent of the time across this country, but during the other 20 percent when I'm not, I get pissed when I realize how shabbily other people must be treated every day. When store clerks or airline reps *do* suddenly recognize me and get nice after being grumpy when they didn't know who I was, I get testy right back.

How will my so-called fame, or sudden lack of it, affect my life as a bicoastal tramp? Can slumming on the road or begging rides on interstate entrance ramps live up to my fantasy of being a David-Niven-from-the-gutter glamorous vagabond? Who could recognize me driving by at 70 mph, anyway? And even if they did, who would think, "Oh, that's John Waters, the filmmaker, alongside the road in the middle of Utah"? Once I climb in, will they believe it's me even if they know who I am, or think I'm just a John Waters impersonator? Which I am in a way every day . . . only older.

I will definitely carry a cardboard sign. That Depression-era gimmick has worked well for me in the past. Not SAN FRANCISCO OR BUST but just I-70 WEST with SAN FRANCISCO on the other side, a double feature of hitchhiking pleas. Plus a backup sign that a friend actually saw a hitchhiker carrying in one of those pot-harvesting Northern California towns—I'M NOT PSYCHO. Now there's a psychological profile that can stand alone. Of course, a scary driver might see that visual, chuckle to himself, and think, well, I am! and pull over, but I will maintain my belief in the basic goodness of people.

I'm not going to set up ridiculous rules for myself in the hitchhiking adventure. I mean, I'll have money, carry credit cards and a cell phone, and plan to stay in motels if no one is kind enough to invite me to their family's home for a sleepover. No tourist sites, though, or visiting friends. This is an irrational vacation, not a tour. Some friends tell me that off the interstate on the secondary roads I'll have a better chance of being picked up because those drivers are "hiding something," but am I anxious to get a ride with a drug dealer or a mule who is carrying kilos of heroin hidden in the chassis of the car? If I get stuck in the middle of the night, I'll do anything I have to do to survive—even call a limousine, if necessary. One thing I know, I won't take a ride on a motorcycle.

I imagine hitchhiker manners are a gray area. What if they're bad drivers? Do I offer to take over if they are falling asleep at the wheel and refuse to pull over for a nap? Suppose they won't let me? "Hey, wake up!" will get old quickly, and how many times can you grab the steering wheel in the nick of time after they nod off and begin to drift into the breakdown lane at full speed toward a family gathered around their vehicle while changing a flat? Oh God, suppose I have to help change a flat?! I have no clue how to do that. If I had to change a flat tire or die, I'd be dead.

And what about sleeping myself while someone else drives? That somehow seems rude to me. Don't people pick up hitchhikers to have someone to talk to? Letch after? Vent to? Besides, if I fell asleep, they could easily turn off the main road, go to a secret satanic location, and cut off my head and put it on a stick.

How do you say no if a car stops to pick you up on a lonely highway, you run a quarter of a mile to get in, and you see a gang of six tough black guys inside? See? I'm already racially profiling and I feel guilty. They could be normal college students, couldn't they, or 1960s freedom fighters lost in some mysterious *Twilight Zone* time warp? One of my favorite hip-hop groups? Even fans who recognize me from my old Court TV show, *'Til Death Do Us Part*? But if they're not and I smell trouble, what do I say? "I'm doing a reality show and there's a satellite camera filming us right now"? Maybe they'd believe it! I guess what I'd really do is just chirp, "Hey, homey, thanks for stopping," before yelling "SHOTGUN" and pushing the front-seat passenger over to the middle without showing fear.

Suppose it all goes wrong? Nobody picks me up. I'm robbed. Beaten. I will already have half the book advance, so I can't quit. Should I put my hitchhiking dough in a special CD account I can't touch before I leave, just in case I chicken out? Would I have the nerve to call my editor, Jonathan Galassi, and tell him of my cowardice, my literary spinelessness? Just imagining the humiliation of my Pope of Trash crown being so besmirched is enough to give me shingles, whatever they are.

Or could I just make up the whole book and say it was true? How would anybody know? It took years for scholars to figure out that John Steinbeck's supposedly nonfiction *Travels with Charley:*

In Search of America, a well-reviewed bestseller published in 1962 (and still in print), was in fact total bullshit. Instead of driving cross-country in a pickup, staying in campgrounds, and chatting up the locals, as the author claimed, he actually had company with him, stayed in motels and luxury hotels, and made up the conversations. According to writer Bill Barich, quoted in a recent *New York Times* article, Steinbeck was "discouraged by everyone from making the trip." He was too old, "trying to recapture his youth, the spirit of knight-errant." Uh-oh. Could that be me?

Nah. I don't think I could lie. I'm not sure I'd want to be JT LeRoy at this stage of my life, and besides, being the centerpiece of a literary hoax is one of the few ways to be "bad" that is never funny. But why not take a chance and, before I go, think up the very best that could happen on this trip? Imagine the worst, too. Both as novellas. And then, after fantasizing on paper, go out in the world, do the real thing, and hopefully live to report the results. Fiction. Nonfiction. Then the truth. All scary. Go ahead, John, jump off the cliff.

THE BEST THAT COULD HAPPEN

A NOVELLA

GOOD RIDE NUMBER ONE

HARRIS

It's a beautiful Baltimore spring day—the perfect 68° morning. I decide to leave twenty-four hours earlier than everyone in my office thinks I will, so I can avoid all their nervous goodbyes. Susan, my longtime assistant who runs my filth empire with an iron fist, has always thought this adventure a ludicrous idea but knows I am just as stubborn as she can be, so she long ago gave up on talking me out of it. Trish, my other full-time assistant, who will actually be transcribing this book (I write by hand on legal pads before she puts it on the computer), is a little friendlier to the idea since she was briefly a teenage runaway. Jill, my art helper, seems all for the idea. My bookkeeper, Doralee, has given up being surprised by anything that goes on in our office but knows I will continue to get a receipt for every single penny I spend while hitching, since no one could argue this is not a business trip. Margarett, my housekeeper, laughed the hardest I've ever heard her (practically in my face) when I confessed my cross-country plans.

Just before I walk out the front door to leave, I look out back and see the fox that lives on my property happily roaming my wooded grounds and take this as a good-luck sign. I turn on the burglar alarm and leave feeling . . . well, adventurous. I walk up my small residential street and am relieved that none of my neighbors see me carrying a hitchhiking sign or question why I am on foot carrying an obvious travel bag. I get to the corner of Charles Street and stick out my thumb and hold up my I-70 WEST cardboard sign that Jill designed for me. "Make the letters not *too* arty and certainly not STOP ME BEFORE I KILL AGAIN scary," I had mentioned, and she has followed instructions well. I don't feel ridiculous, I feel kind of brave.

I can't believe it. The very first car that goes by stops, and I run to hop in. An art-school type dressed in brown jeans and an old Charles Theater T-shirt is behind the wheel of a car so nondescript that I have to ask him what kind it is. "A very used 1999 VW Passat sedan," he answers in the kindest voice imaginable. I feel safe immediately. He doesn't even bat an eye that I'm hitchhiking, even though he recognizes me. "Wow, John Waters. I'm a fan," he announces, low-key. He so respects my privacy he doesn't even ask where I'm headed but offers, "I'm going as far as West Virginia if that's a help." "It sure is," I say, relieved I can avoid the tricky cloverleaf where I-70 West meets the Baltimore Beltway and there's nowhere to stand to bum a ride.

"Did you see Gaspar Noé's *Enter the Void*?" he asks with the excitement of a real film fanatic. "Of course—the best movie about taking drugs *ever*!" I answer, so happy he wants to discuss other extreme pictures and not my own. "I like the director's-cut version best," my driver continues, "it's more endless, just like an LSD trip." "I know Gaspar," I offer, "and you'd be surprised after seeing his films, but he's really a sweet guy." "I love fucked-up movies," my fellow film buff enthuses as he turns up the radio, and what's playing? "Hitch Hike" by Marvin Gaye. Unbelievable!

Is it me, or do I smell ganja? I'm a little out of practice as a pothead. I used to smoke grass every day of my life around 1964 to 1972, but now only rarely because it just makes me worry about mundane things. But sometimes, in the summer in Province-town on a Friday night when I have nothing to do the next day, I'll smoke a little weed and get "launched," as my young friend and part-time pot smoker Frankie calls it when I start ranting and laughing while stoned. And of course I'm a good host—I have a small stash of pot in all my places of residence in case guests might want to smoke. Legal amounts. I hope.

"I'm Harris," he finally introduces himself, and I silently think, that's Divine's real first name, but keep it film-zealot friendly rather than Dreamland focused. Harris is a good-looking guy who seems laid-back, something I have never felt like in my en-tire life. I'm thrilled my first ride is so seemingly uncomplicated. "Are you a student at Maryland Institute?" I ask, thinking col-lege would be the perfect reason for him to be in Baltimore. "No, I'm in business for myself," he says with a sideways glance that invites all sorts of speculation as we merge onto the Baltimore Beltway headed in the right direction.

"Have you seen Armando Bó's films?" I ask, feeling as if con-tinuing our movie-hound conversation is definitely part of my "payment" as a rider. "I love his movies," Harris yells with enthu-siasm as we head west on I-70, already on the first leg of my journey to San Francisco. "Armando's been dead for many years now but he deserves to be honored more," I shout over the music, and my highway host agrees. "That Isabel Sarli was *so* hot! Those tits were real, you know!" he hollers in mammary mania about the director's onetime mistress and the star of all his films. "*And* she's still alive!" I shout. "Seventy-five years old! I talked to her on the phone just recently," I brag, and I can tell he's impressed. "You're kidding?" Harris marvels in wide-eyed amazement. "I really did," I answer, holding up my hand to silently swear to God. "A South American trash-film enthusiast hooked us up, and although her

English was a little rusty—but way better than my Spanish—I got to gush how much her films, like *Fury, Fever,* and *Fuego,* meant to both Divine and me."

"How come you aren't making a movie?" Harris suddenly asks with shy concern. I explain I had a development deal to make *Fruitcake,* a "terribly wonderful Christmas children's adventure," wrote the script, was about to make it, and then the recession happened, the independent film business as I knew it fell apart, and now all the distributors and film financiers want the budgets to be under $2 million, which I can't do anymore. "Well, I'll back it," he says nonchalantly. "What do you mean?" I sputter, not believing my ears. "You can keep a secret, right?" he whispers conspiratorially. "Sure," I mumble, and I can, especially if it's a good one. "I'm a pot dealer . . . don't worry, there's none in the car, it's all on my West Virginia farm, but I've got plenty of cash. How much do you need?" "Five million, give or take," I confide with a chuckle, sure Harris is pulling my leg. "No problem," he says, beaming as if I had just asked him for spare change in Berkeley in the sixties. "But surely you're not serious?" I ask, thinking, how could this be possible? I've been trying to raise this budget unsuccessfully for five years. "It's no big deal," he says as we cross into West Virginia and I feel the thrill of illegal interstate financing. "Maybe we could form a limited partnership like I used to do in the old days," I offer. "Nah," he responds good-naturedly, "I'll just give you the cash and you pay me back if it ever breaks even." *Cash?!* I think in alarm. Five million dollars in cash?! "Good God, how will I ever explain this to the IRS?!" I ask Harris in bewildered excitement. "The Feds don't ask where you got it, do they?" he replies levelheadedly. "Just pay me back and I'll get the money laundered by a chain of nail salons I'm a silent partner in." "Okay," I say in shock, not wanting to blow the deal if he was possibly serious.

I'm so stunned by my new "business partner" that I don't

even notice we've exited the interstate and are now driving on a country road. "We're near," Harris explains as he goes around the block a few times and zigzags back and forth on even smaller rural routes. I guess he's making sure we're not being followed, but I keep my newly green-lit mouth shut.

Finally, we turn off on a beautiful dirt lane with a natural canopy of trees overhead and then veer off on an unmarked long driveway nestled in the hills of northern West Virginia and go about another half mile. Ahead of us is a lovingly restored but not overly yuppified 1850s farmhouse overlooking a pond with a waterfall gently cascading into it. Expansive trees and flowering plants surround the entire idyllic setting. His incredibly striking wife, barefoot already in May and dressed in a pair of fire-engine-red jeans and a long-sleeved black T-shirt, is watering the potted flowers on the outdoor patio.

"This is Laura," Harris introduces us, "and of course you know John Waters and his films." She smiles a warm welcome and I can't help but notice she smells like pot, too. "I'm going to give him five million dollars to make his new film," he casually mentions, and she doesn't look particularly surprised. "Oh, that's sweet," Laura says, hardly looking up from the pot of black tulips (my favorite kind) she's just placed artfully on an outdoor table. "We've been looking to invest in films for such a long time," she offers happily. I grin but remain silent in stupefaction. "I'll make us some lunch," offers Harris, before trotting off to the main farmhouse to prepare as Laura follows, eager to help.

I just sit there in amazement at my good fortune. This is my first ride and already I'm going to be back in the movie business. Harris and Laura soon return and we feast on delicious chicken salad made from free-range birds that Laura confides she strangled with her own hands just this morning. After a dessert of freshly picked blueberries, Harris carefully folds his cloth napkin ("From Martick's," he proudly announces, a recently closed restaurant much loved by downtown-Baltimore bohemians) and says, "Let's take a walk, John." I eagerly follow him to a remote point of his property, and Harris reveals that we are now going "to dig up the cash." I keep my mouth shut. "Oh, honey," he yells to Laura, "call up that FedEx place and make sure our buddy gets his lazy ass to work. Tell him we got a special shipment coming up."

Harris turns to me and asks gently, "Do you have a FedEx number? If not, we have a dummy one we can use." "We're going to FedEx the money?" I ask in awe, amazed that Harris plans on giving me the money *now*! "Sure," he replies, "you don't want to carry all that cash with you on your hitchhiking trip, do you?" "Well, no," I stammer, giving him the digits, which I know from memory. "Great," he says, jotting down the account information, "we'll FedEx it directly to your address." On cue, Laura walks like a gazelle down from the house, carrying a stack of flat FedEx boxes ready to be assembled. She has a lovely, serene smile on her lips. Maybe this is the first of their millions they're giving away. You can tell philanthropy brings her a new kind of delight.

Harris grabs a shovel from behind the naturally distressed original barn door and leads me to an even more distant part of his farmland that appears to be overgrown with vines. "Here," he announces as he pulls up several clods of phony earth covered in prop foliage and begins digging. Laura slips on a pair of rubber gloves. Harris hasn't even worked up a sweat before I hear the shovel clink on metal. "Bingo," purrs Laura as she gives me a friendly wink. "Pay dirt," jokes Harris as he begins to hoist up, with his thin but muscled arms, a small industrial safe with a combination lock. Laura hands me the first of the standard large FedEx boxes and gets out a pistol-grip tape dispenser. She quickly notices from my panicked expression that I have no idea how to assemble these boxes and gently takes the packaging back. "That's okay," she whispers gently, "you deserve to be directing, not doing manual labor." Laura snaps the carton together in one swift motion and seals it with tape like Quick Draw McGraw and hands me back the box with the skill of a next-day-delivery artisan. Harris drops the safe to the ground and Laura swiftly dials the combination and I avert my eyes, hoping to not look greedy or, worse yet, sneaky. Harris moves to another spot of earth about thirty feet away, rips up more fake turf, and starts digging again. I hear him whistling "There's No Business Like Show Business" with surprising skill.

"Here you go," Laura says softly to me as she opens the safe door and hands me the first bundle of ten thousand $100 bills, which she assures me totals $1 million. It seems heavy to me but she scoffs mildly and says, "It only weighs about twenty-five pounds. I've had to carry $3 million strapped inside baggy winter clothes at customs, and believe me, that's a backbreaker, but I never complain. Helping keep Americans high is never easy or without toil."

"Here's more cash!" Harris cheerfully announces as he manually raises a duplicate safe from another "grave" in the ground and spins the combination lock like a safecracker supreme. "This ought to pay for a lot of music rights," he chuckles happily to me, holding up the next million dollars in bills. "Won't Johnny Knoxville like getting paid in cash?" Laura asks with a kindness so rare in show business today. "He sure will," I agree, impressed that she is so well-read on my career that she knows whom I want to star in my next film. How we'll handle Johnny's agent in an all-cash deal is something I'll figure out later.

It takes about an hour more, but finally Harris and Laura have dug up three other little safes and unloaded all the do-re-mi into nine large FedEx boxes. I gather this is not putting much of a dent in their nontraditional banking practices. "We trust you," says Harris warmly as he seals the last box. "Yes, we do," adds Laura, with a criminal-capitalist inner peace I'll never forget.

"This is our small way of thanking you for all your films," she adds, "and we know *Fruitcake* will be a hit." "But don't change a thing in the script if you don't want to," Harris pipes in jovially. "We don't care if the film makes us our money back or not." "Come on," announces Laura with excitement, "it's time to get you up to the FedEx place. You've got a hitchhiking trip to go on." "And may all your rides be as prosperous as this first one," adds Harris with financial affection and artistic respect.

I embrace my new non-note-giving movie producers, and Harris and I load all the boxes into the trunk of his vehicle. We get in and wave goodbye to Laura, who is already back to potting her perennials like a serenely demented garden-club enthusiast. Just as we pull off, a black butterfly lands on her shoulder in a Douglas Sirk way, and she returns the farewell gesture with a smile that would put Julia Roberts out of business.

"Did you see *Zoo*?" Harris suddenly asks once we are on the road, eager to get back to cult-film talk. "Sure," I answer with pride, "that arty true-crime doc about the man who dies after getting fucked by a horse in Seattle. I toured presenting that film—even showed it at the Sydney Opera House." "That's the one," Harris agrees. "I felt for those guys who were involved," he reasons; "it was a sad story but told in a dignified way. Did you believe that animal-rescue worker who when interviewed on film after the zoo guys had left the ranch said she 'saw a small pony come up and give a bigger horse a blow job'? That was bullshit," Harris answers without missing a beat, knowing exactly the scene I was talking about. "I like animals," he continues, "but if that horse had a hard-on and did mount the guy, you can't call the sex act 'nonconsensual,' can you? If an animal gets it up, isn't he willing?"

Before we can finish this debate we pull up to the FedEx drop-off store, amazingly subtitled on the sign out front GOING POSTAL. Harris informs me that this is the only "corrupt" FedEx office in the country and he is their only customer. That he does so much business here keeps it open and off the map of corporate concern.

The clerk inside looks as if he just escaped from a Whole Foods employee jail. His hair is shaved into the FedEx logo, he wears a large nose ring, and "UPS" is tattooed onto his forehead. His onetime DHL delivery uniform has been sewn together with a regular USPS outfit to create the postmodern attire of a mentally unstable but proud letter carrier. His name patch reads RE-TURN TO SENDER. He and Harris are obviously buddies and greet each other with the hipster fist bump. No questions are asked as I fill out all the second-day-delivery forms, hoping to not seem too eager on the other end. "Done deal," announces Harris as he pulls out a giant doobie and hands it to Return to Sender. I guess it's some kind of tip.

"Thank you, Harris," I say sincerely outside as we get back into his totally unremarkable car. "Don't thank me," he modestly responds as he pulls out into traffic, always careful to obey the posted speed limit, "thank the pot smokers all over the Delmarva area. *They're* the real ones backing your new movie." With that, he pulls over to an entrance ramp to I-70W and bids me adios. "Here's my contact info," he says, handing me a business card printed on the old kind of "flash paper" that bookies and numbers-racket hoods used to use. I read the PO box number in Triadelphia, West Virginia, and Harris tells me to "read it again and don't forget it." I do. Suddenly with a flash of light the business card ignites, turns to ash, and disappears. "Happy trails," Harris says as I open the door to get out (suddenly a working film director again) and stick out my thumb. Harris accelerates and, looking at me in his rearview mirror, waves one last time just as he sees me getting immediately picked up by my next ride. And it's only 2:30 p.m.

GOOD RIDE NUMBER TWO

KAY-KAY

Imagine my surprise opening the passenger-side front door and seeing a steering wheel above the shotgun seat. Are we in London? I momentarily wonder in confusion. "I don't know how far I'm going, but get in," begs a nice middle-aged lady in the driver's seat, who wears a modest gray bouffant hairdo that must need weekly maintenance in a beauty parlor. Dressed in pastel suburban-style separates, she could be anybody's mom. I notice the small logo of the AOG DRIVING SCHOOL on the exterior of the front door and figure, what better hands in which to be driven?

I jump in and see the TOTAL FLEET SERVICES brand name displayed on the dashboard of this older (almost vintage) vehicle and realize a second brake is between my feet. "My name's Kay-Kay," she says nervously as I fasten my seat belt and feel immediate unease as she pulls out too fast and without warning into the slow lane and almost cuts off another car merging from the entrance ramp. This woman teaches people to drive?! I panic as I hear the blare of other drivers' horns. "I'm John," I say politely, and before I can even be glad she has no idea who I am, I involuntarily slam on my brake, as she obviously doesn't see the other car ahead of us slowing down, despite the thoughtful motorist's pumping of the brake light to alert us. "Sorry, I guess I'm just a backseat driver," I mumble with some concern. "That's okay," she assures me as she swerves around another car in the slow lane without even putting on her turn signal, "I need all the help I can get."

As the harrowing ride continues, I take more and more control over the wheel and she seems to be relieved. "I'm not really a driving instructor," she finally volunteers after another close call when I could mercifully swerve from my side without having to reach across and grab her wheel. "But why do you have this car?" I ask in bewilderment. "It's a long story but there's nothing else I could do," she gasps, looking suddenly as if she is going to cry.

Before I can quiz her further I hear a muffled banging coming from the rear of the car, which gives me newfound concern. "It's the brake pads," she volunteers without conviction. "We'll be okay." Hearing a thumping noise that causes further concern, I tell her, "We need to pull over. Something must be hanging off the car." "Don't stop!" she snaps with sudden seriousness as she instead turns on the radio at high volume. "Transfusion," a longtime favorite of mine by Nervous Norvus, comes on, and this fifties novelty song with the ghoulish lyrics mixed in with the sound of a horrible car crash, gives me the courage to defy her. "Why not!?" I cry over the music as I start to steer us toward the exit for the upcoming family rest area, and she, for the first time, steers her wheel in the opposite direction. I put on the brakes to slow down for a construction site ahead, but she floors the accelerator, hits the cones, and sends the panicked construction workers scattering for safety.

"Please, mister," she suddenly pleads, changing her tack, "don't pull over. I have to get to my sister's and she lives near Columbus, Ohio." "We'll get you there," I assure her, trying to distract her by hastily assuming the role of instructor and reaching over to turn on the windshield wipers and defroster to show her how they work. But Kay-Kay won't give up the battle. Our car is swerving dangerously back and forth on the highway, driven by different wills. The noise from the rear end of the car seems to be getting worse, too. Is it just my ears playing a trick on me or did I just hear someone yell "Help!"?

Finally giving up, she turns down the radio, takes her hands completely off the wheel, and lets me steer the car to a parking space in the next roadside travel plaza. "It's not my fault," she says to me with a newfound sorrow. *"What's* not your fault?" I demand about the same time I hear a man's voice yell, "You dumb bitch! Let me out!" "Fuck you, asshole!" she suddenly snarls, turning toward the back of the car with a ferocious anger that seems completely out of character. "Women drivers!" a gruff voice yells back, and I realize, good Lord, somebody's in the trunk! Drama! Just what I'd been hoping for—how perfect for my book!

"I'm a single lady," she suddenly sobs to me, back in character, as I turn off the ignition to listen, not sure what else I *can* do. "All I wanted was to learn to drive," she continues in agitation, "but no, this . . . this chauvinist pig starts quizzing me about my opinion on abortion . . . in the *first lesson!*" "Abortion makes you the mother of a dead baby!" the voice in the trunk butts in. "I asked God and she's pro-choice!" yells back my apparently militant feminist driving partner with an anger I would never have expected. "Look, I agree with you," I try to explain to Kay-Kay, hoping to calm her down. "I like kids," I continue, "but my abortion politics are simple. If you can't love your child, don't have it, because it will grow up and kill me." She nods her head in relieved agreement. "But still, you can't keep this guy in the trunk," I try to reason. "Who's that faggot?!" yells our hostage with a rudeness that instantly pushes me over the edge. "You filthy impregnator!" I shout back, suddenly as combative as Kay-Kay. "How dare you tell a woman what to do with her body?" "That's right, you fallopian-tube fascist!" Kay-Kay joins in with such rage that the veins in her forehead pop out and her hairdo partially collapses.

"Cocksucker! Whore!" yells our fanatical pro-lifer, banging on the inside of the trunk lid so loudly that a family exiting their car nearby looks over in suspicion. "I wish I was a girl so I could get an abortion!" I yell in ridiculous reactionary rhetoric as the mom, dad, and kids quickly hightail it to the food area, convinced I'm just a crazy person with Tourette's syndrome.

"All I wanted to do was to learn to parallel park," Kay-Kay begins wailing to me, "but no! He has to start in on my sexual politics. I've never even *had* an abortion, but even if I had, it's private! I shouldn't have to discuss my reproductive organs with a driving instructor, should I?" Before I can answer, she spins in her seat like Linda Blair's head in *The Exorcist* and begins addressing her captive. "Should I, *you asshole horndog?*" she screams with a venomous hatred of all things sexually unfair, before adding the final insult: "With humans, it's abortion, but with chickens, it's an omelet! What do you have to say about that, you yellow-bellied *coward?*" Kay-Kay's radical sloganizing does the trick. *"Coward? Coward?"* he bellows back. "You call someone who bombed Planned Parenthood a coward?! I'm an Army of God warrior! I am the sperm guardian of the universe!"

Suddenly he's quiet. He knows this time his big mouth has done him in. Kay-Kay blinks in sudden recognition and whispers victoriously to me, "AOG Driving School? Oh my God, it's a front for Army of God, the Christian terrorist group." Then she adds, loud enough for him to hear, "He ain't calling the police on anyone." I see a Trailways bus with a posted destination of Dayton, Ohio, pull up and let out some passengers for a pit stop and I think fast. "Okay, Kay-Kay, we're going to get you out of this car and I'm going to get you on that bus. Dayton's past Columbus—you'll get to your sister's. Give me the keys." She hands them over without a peep, and I'm relieved to see there's a trunk-release button. Kay-Kay breathes a little bit easier now that her driving lesson from hell has finally ended.

We both get out and slam the car doors shut. Suddenly we hear a less militant voice from the trunk. "Okay, look, I didn't mean that," he snivels. "Let's just try to end this misunderstanding without problems. Let me out and we'll all go our separate ways. Let's agree to disagree. I could be wrong . . . I apologize . . . you're not *that* bad behind the wheel, Miss Kay-Kay. With a few more lessons, you're going to be a legally licensed driver!"

Kay-Kay laughs out loud for the first time, and I see that she really is a moderate person who was baited into a political fervor she never knew lurked inside her. She now seems proud of herself; strong, ready to move on and let her abortion-rights road rage simmer down. I take her hand and lead her toward the bus. The driver, surely against company policy, is not guarding the front door but has instead joined some of his more out-of-shape passengers in a cigarette break while others remain in their seats dozing and the rest line up for artery-clogging Cinnabon treats inside the pavilion. Since he has to pass through Dayton, I have no trouble distracting the driver with phony questions about the best route there, and Kay-Kay sneaks aboard his bus with ease.

I aim the trunk release at the driving instructor's car and the trunk opens, almost as if it were surprising the other cars parked nearby. Slowly the pro-lifer sits up inside and peers out wearily. Realizing the authorities are not there to grab him, he immediately reverts to his fanaticism, grabs a handful of "Equal Rights for Unborn Women" flyers, jumps out, and begins aggressively approaching unsuspecting families who have stopped to stretch their limbs or take a whiz inside. "Get away," snaps a woman with two howling children and a lughead husband who makes no move to help her. Undeterred, our driving instructor approaches another harried family who look the worse for wear as they return to their car after visiting the snack bar. "Why is Mommy crying?" the young boy asks his dad, all sugared up and bewildered with concern. "Because you're an asshole," barks back the father with exasperated logic. Suddenly our clueless agitator butts in, chanting, "Birth control is for wimps!" before thrusting a flyer into the humiliated kid's hands with a complete lack of human understanding. "Eat me!" yells the son with a sudden untapped rage before kicking the pro-lifer as hard as he can in the balls.

The whole family, suddenly united in the face of unwanted intrusion, screams in derisive laughter as Mr. Big Mouth limps away holding his sperm-filled, baby-making family jewels. I look over at Kay-Kay. She has seen what I just saw. I could never make this shit up, and I think for the first time she realizes that she has somehow helped me. I smile at her in mutual creative respect and she waves goodbye, happy to have been a positive inspiration to someone. Her bus pulls off toward Columbus and real life with her sister, where our little adventure will never be mentioned.

I walk out to the exit ramp and decide to try a second version of my hitchhike sign: MIDLIFE CRISIS. I stick out my thumb, confident that roadside reality will bring me more perfect material.

GOOD RIDE NUMBER THREE

LUCAS

I'm thrilled the first few cars don't pick me up so I have time to gather my thoughts. The passing drivers are nice, making hand gestures explaining they are only going a short way or more elaborate ones that I can only assume mean they're turning off in a direction other than west. My luck not only continues, it does a backflip and lands perfectly beside me like a hitchhiking guardian angel. A beat-up beige 1965 Ford F-500 flatbed truck screeches to a halt right in the middle of the ramp without the slightest concern for the impatient drivers behind, who must be pissed at having to stop. But they don't have the courage to honk their horns. Because on the flatbed truck is a Ford Vic 1970s station wagon that has been customized for a demolition derby. WHIPLASH is spray-painted by hand in huge, scary letters on both sides with the car's local sponsor, THUMPER BUMPER, which I guess may be an auto repair shop, and ASSCAR (God only knows what that means) is scrawled on the hood. TETANUS TATTOO PARLOR completes the advertising on the tailgate. Painted in black on the driver's side is his entry number, 422. Good God, April 22, that's my birthday!

I peer inside the truck just to scope out the driver. I'm thrilled to be getting another ride so quickly, but still, first impressions count and I want to be as safe as I can be on this intrinsically *unsafe* trip. "Wham, bam, thank you, ma'am," shouts the driver. "I'm Lucas. Hop in!" "Thanks," I say, climbing inside, thrilled to hear that roughneck highway song "Looking at the World Through a Windshield," by Del Reeves, playing on the radio. "Jesus Christ, you were on *The Simpsons*!" he yells over the unmuffled sound of his truck's engine, pulling off and entering I-70 West. "Yes, that's me, John Waters," I admit modestly. "'Homer's Phobia'!" he correctly yells out my episode's title with a roar of laughter. I notice his two gold front teeth, so rare yet appealing in a white guy. His tight blue denim jeans splattered with grease, scruffy white(!) motorcycle boots, and a raggedy thrift-shop fifties sport shirt patterned with cartoon car-crash graphics only add to his renegade debonair charm.

Feeling comfortable with my new ride, I break my rule and mention I'm also a film director, and he asks, "Which ones?" as he guns ahead down the highway, passing cars right and left but driving safely. *"Hairspray,"* I mention, but he gives me a blank shrug. *"Pink Flamingos,"* I try, and get the same vacant expression . . . *"Cry-Baby? Serial Mom?"* I offer, but no luck. "Nah," he answers without embarrassment, "I only like cartoons."

I switch the subject to Lucas's life and tell him what a fan of demolition derbies I am. How I long ago covered one on-air as a pundit for that radio show *All Things Considered* and how I had recently attended another derby outside Baltimore and how surprised I had been at one of the side events before the race began. A used car in good condition sat in a fenced-in area as customers lined up and paid admission to enter (mostly dads and their younger male children). Each was handed a sledgehammer and the clock would start ticking and the father-son team had three minutes to beat the car and cause as much damage as possible.

"Great work, son!" a dad would congratulate Junior after he managed to smash the windshield. "Rip it up, Pop," a kid would yelp as his father knocked off a rearview mirror with one easy swipe. There were no prizes, only quality wrecking time with your family, and this seemed to be reward enough. By the time the derby had begun, the crumpled, ruined auto lay there, abandoned and dead. I wondered whose responsibility it was to haul away the carcass. Is there such a thing as "postproduction" at a demolition derby?

"It's fucking Maniac Night," Lucas explains, "and tonight I'm gonna win! We're gonna tear 'em up!" he hollers humorously, meaning him and his car. I want to go, too. Almost magically, as if he could read my mind like Kreskin, he smiles that sexy gold-toothed smile and leers in a friendly growl with a faint Southern accent, "Wanna ride in the car with me?!" "Sure," I stammer, wishing I were wearing those slip-on "fronts" I had made for my teeth in Baltimore with *JW* in fake jewels. "But are you allowed to have passengers?" I ask. "Hell, no," he replies, "but since when have I done what is allowed?" "But it will be late night if I stay for the race and then I'll have to hitchhike in the dark and I'll be nervous," I admit with shame. "Stay with me, Snake," he hisses with a male friendliness that is confusing in its undefined sexual connotations. "I'm custom-fit, hammered, and bent just like your boy Homer!" I gulp. "You're gonna be my good-luck charm," he announces with a flirtatious grin.

I am swooning with excitement when we finally get to Marengo, Indiana, having so much fun riding with Lucas that I barely notice it's already night. We've come a long way as we pull up at the Crawford County 4-H Fairgrounds. "Maniac Night" sounds even better when you read it off a weatherworn wooden marquee. Especially with $1,200 PRIZE added below. Lucas knows everybody! There's Anteater and Doo-Doo, two scary grease monkeys who obviously idolize my new best friend, and they help him get Whiplash off the flatbed truck and up near to the pit gate. I see a lot of other junker cars with souped-up names such as Ratrod, Gunthunt, Hatchet-Head, and Head-On Hard-On (which, it was explained, will be disqualified because of its un-family-friendly name). There's even one named Whitney Houston. I don't know about Lucas, but I've got a winning feeling building inside me.

As our heat approaches, Lucas sneaks me in under a fence and I climb in through our car's front passenger-side window because the doors are now welded shut. He hands me goggles, a helmet with WHIPLASH hand-stenciled on the front just like his, and a crumpled jumpsuit to put on over my usual low-key Comme des Garçons outfit that I have chosen to wear for the trip. "Material's fireproof," he explains, and since the family business my dad started is fire protection, I feel relieved as I struggle to suit up. As he slips into his own matching outfit, he catches me peeking at his naturally toned chest and winks. "Watch," he says as he pours lighter fluid all over his jumpsuit. "Go ahead," he orders me as he hands me a box of kitchen matches from under his seat, "set me on fire." I hesitate, then strike one and toss it on him. His outfit immediately goes up in flames, but he just laughs, feeling no pain. He waits a full fifteen seconds before he smothers out the blaze. Lucas is my action hero.

There is no glass in Whiplash. The windshield and the rear and side windows have been removed. Most of the interior has been dismantled, and the gas tank is now in the back where the seats once were. As I reach for the safety belt, Lucas snarls from behind the wheel, "Seat belts optional," and looks down to his crotch and points to the seat-belt buckle that once was on his driver's side but has now been redesigned into his belt for fashion. Being the wimp I evidently am, I slip on both the helmet *and* the seat belt that is, thank God, still attached on the passenger side.

I look over the dirt oval track with all the junkers' taillights facing each other and see Ratrod, a seventies Dodge Charger with its disgusting slob of a driver inside taking a big gulp of whiskey from a bottle, which I'm sure is against the rules. He glances at me and then catches Lucas's eyes, too, and begins making mock kissing noises with his brittle, chapped lips. I avert my eyes as Lucas snorts in derision, grabs his own dick, and squeezes it in the excitement of possible revenge. "That sandbaggy asshole," he growls, "always holding back, lurking around the side of the ring, too cowardly to strike first." I smell gasoline fumes and am in seventh heaven.

"Will death strike tonight?" the track announcer yells over the loudspeaker system that booms out to the entire fairgrounds. As the crowd cheers and the drivers rev their engines, the countdown begins. "Ten, nine, eight, seven . . ." he screams. There's nowhere to hold on to inside this car, so I just look over to Lucas with trust. He grabs his dick again and whispers over the din of fifty idling hot rods, "Wrecking cars gives me a hard-on." I smile back, not letting him know how excited I am. "Three, two, one," and we're off . . . backward, of course! Total chaos! Some car named Grenade Banger rams into my side door, but the seat belt keeps me safe. Every time I peek up and look out, another car is about to smash into us. Lucas is biding his time, though, and every time we are hit, he growls sexually in demolition lust. "We're tearing it up, John," he yells over the sound of crashing metal. As he floors it in reverse, I look back and see asshole Ratrod right in our line of attack. BANG! I am amazed to see Lucas's cock growing bigger underneath the flame-retardant material of his jumpsuit. WHAM goes another hit as we smash into another car (Gunthunt) in reverse, then back into another (Hatchet-Head) with such force that the fillings in my teeth tingle. "Dirtbags!" yells Lucas in full attack mode as he backtracks into two other cars (we're going too fast for me to see their names) with such ferocity that both are instantly put out of business. He is in an erotic frenzy. Lucas leers at me as he revs his engine, surveying the four or five rust buckets still left running. "My dick is so hard. Wanna see it?" "Sure," I yell in surprise over the sound of his peeling out backward and the impact of collision. The thrill of victory is pulsating in my pants, too. Encouraged, Lucas unbuttons his jumpsuit and, while zigzagging again backward, whips out (with some difficulty) an amazing cock that no gay man would ever refuse. "Beautiful," I say as he reverse-accelerates again with a vengeance. The car he hits this time (Nitro Ned) explodes with a hiss and then bursts into flames.

"Jerk me off," Lucas orders with beautiful, polite authority, and what else can I do but follow his orders? "Two vehicles left," Lucas pants as he scans the pit, "so make it quick." I take direction and don't stop even when I feel the hostile crash of Ratrod's vehicle into the back of our car. Lucas is so cool he doesn't even lose his hard-on. The crowd cheers. I sneak a look over and consider a blow job, but even I know giving head in the middle of a demolition derby is risky, and besides, I don't know Lucas that well yet. I see our enemy getting ready to strike. "Okay," Lucas moans sexually like the gearhead gladiator he is, "let's blast off!" He grabs my hand, spits into it, and thrusts it back on his cock with a wet splat. Could this be love? "Okay, John, we're gonna bust a nut," he announces, flooring the accelerator and speeding backward so suddenly that I get a whiplash, but I don't care. By now, I'm so worked up that I feel that I actually *am* his car. Just as he crashes into Ratrod for the final "kill," Lucas shoots a giant load through our nonexistent windshield into the sky with amazing projection, where it showers down beautifully like elegant fireworks. The crowd goes nuts. Lucas looks over to me in demolition tenderness and gives me the biggest, lewdest grin I've ever seen in my life.

That night we celebrate victory together. He lives alone. Imagine my thrill and amazement when we pull up to his trailer and I see it is the exact same model as the one Divine's character,

Babs, lived in, in *Pink Flamingos*, only painted silver and black. I know he never saw the movie, so I don't bring it up. Lucas counts his winnings with me beside him on his bed in what would have been Divine's bedroom. I refuse the cash he offers to share with me and tell him how much I appreciated such a romantic night. He blushes and then sheepishly asks, "Wanna watch some porn?" "Sure," I say, curious to see his cinematic fantasy tastes. Fumbling under the bed, Lucas takes out a DVD with a homemade label, inserts the disc, and pushes play. But instead of regular porn, I see a compilation reel of demolition derby accidents much like the cumshot reel would be if it were normal gay smut.

"I usually only get horny when I'm racing," Lucas whispers with lust, "but tonight I'd like to return the favor, especially for someone who has brought me such good luck." "Okay," I say in excitement as he eases over and unbuckles my belt. "Check out this next heat," he says with touching sexual vulnerability as he lowers my pants. "BAM!" I cry as I watch in amazement vintage amateur 8mm film transferred to digital of three derby cars backing into each other at the exact same time and flipping over in unison. "Show me more," I whisper as he begins stroking. "You ain't seen nothin' yet!" he purrs back with a newfound sexual gusto. Lucas, more and more aroused, fast-forwards to another notorious demolition disaster. "Okay, John, here you go," he moans as I see a 1975 Cadillac Coupe de Ville get broadsided in reverse by a ratty but rare 1970 Monte Carlo Chevrolet. The driver of the Caddy goes berserk, forgets all the rules of the race, and accelerates *forward* toward the attacker and smashes head-on into the Chevy. Both vehicles explode in flames on-screen, and in one escalating movement of Lucas's wrist we become one; sexually united in affection, deviant excitement, and demolition lust. We fall asleep instantly.

GOOD RIDE NUMBER FOUR

OFFICER LADDIE

The next morning Lucas makes me a delicious homemade breakfast of corned beef hash with a poached egg on top before giving me a ride to the entrance ramp of Route 70 headed west. Always a sweetheart, he bashfully presents me with a belt buckle with the word *W-H-I-P—L-A-S-H* split into two levels of letters. Lucas can see how much I love his gift just by the way I hold it in my hands. I give him my best mustachioed sneer, jump out, and simply say, "Thank you." Maybe being a human four-leaf clover for a crazily rugged but tenderhearted and slightly deviant demolition derby driver only comes once in a lifetime. "Give my love to the Simpsons," he shouts good-naturedly, then peels out in his truck perfectly so the gravel shoots up all around me but not *on* me.

Uh-oh. Here come the cops. When the officer steps out from his vehicle, he looks mean. "What do you think you're doing?" he snarls in an unwelcoming way. "I'm hitchhiking to San Francisco," I explain politely, "and I know it's illegal to do that *on* the interstate so I'm hoping to get a ride here on the ramp." "ID!" he snaps without comment on my legal position. He looks at my license. "You homeless?" he demands without the slightest bit of sympathy. "No . . . I'm a film director," I announce haughtily as I start to take out my Directors Guild of America card. "Freeze!" he yells as he pulls out his gun and aims it right at my head. "You've got to be kidding," I say with alarm but still try to keep my cool. "I wasn't reaching for a weapon," I cry, "I just wanted you to look at my directorial credits."

Suddenly another cop car comes speeding up with the light flashing. Officer Fuckhead seems relieved. This cop, also overweight but kind of goofy-looking, jumps out with a cheerier expression on his face. "Okay, Officer Bradford, what's the problem here?" he demands. "We got a vagrant with an attitude problem," the first cop snorts. I don't say a word. The second cop lowers the first cop's hand with the gun away from my head and I let out a sigh of relief. "I'll take over here. This man is famous!" "Thank you," I mumble, not believing my ears. "Fine with me," grunts the first cop as he heads back to his police car, "but I never heard of him."

"Thank you, Officer . . . ?" I murmur in relief as the asshole cop pulls away, turns on his siren, and begins chasing a car that might have been doing five miles over the speed limit on this road where not one car has passed us by. "It's Laddie," he answers. "Where you headed?" "San Francisco," I say optimistically. "Great town. My kind of place!" he announces with a whistle before jovially telling me, "I'll give you a ride to Terre Haute, right before you cross into Illinois, and that way no Indiana cops will give you any shit." I eagerly agree. As we pull off, he suddenly says with a knowing wink, "I loved you in *Fargo!*" Oh, no, not again! I think. Another fan who thinks I'm Steve Buscemi. "No, I always get that," I protest. "I'm not Steve Buscemi." "Oh, yes you are!" he yells with a startling conviction. "I'm really not," I argue. "I love him and we've met many times but—" "Come on," Officer Laddie interrupts, "let's do lines from *Con Air.*" Okay,

I remind myself, I said before I left I hoped people didn't recognize me, so why not play along? "But I forget them," I beg off. "Loved your work," spouts Officer Laddie, suddenly doing a perfect imitation of John Malkovich in the film. "Really, I can't remember the dialogue," I stall, then suddenly have an idea: "I'm not really Steve Buscemi! I'm Don Knotts!"

Thinking my obvious pulling of his leg will end this charade, I'm astonished when it doesn't. He believes me! "You know Andy Griffith!?" he asks in wide-eyed wonder as we speed along I-70 West, obviously not knowing that both of these actors are dead. What the hell? He's giving me a long ride; why not go along with it? "I sure do!" I say with Knottist nervous pride.

"You like poppers?" Officer Laddie suddenly asks with a mischievous grin. "Well . . . sometimes," I stammer, shocked again by the unpredictable behavior of the overweight Indiana police officer. "Me, too! Not for sex, though," he explains as he reaches under his seat and pulls out a bottle of Liquid Gold. "Wow, I haven't seen that brand for a while," I admit. "I got 'em all—collector's items," he brags like a true connoisseur. "Jolt! Ram! Blue Boy! Even foreign ones like France 5 or English Jungle!" he shouts, fumbling in the glove compartment to pull out different brands. I stare back in awed appreciation. He snickers. "What I *really* like poppers for," he whispers conspiratorially, "is *driving*!"

"Here, Don Knotts," he offers, handing me a bottle of Rush. "Call me Barney, please," I answer, keeping up the charade. "Hold the top while I get a good snort?" Officer Laddie asks in proper popper etiquette. I unscrew the cap and hand him back the opened bottle and pinch his one nostril and then the other as he takes a big whiff in each and drives with one hand. He hands the bottle back to me and I pretend to take a bigger sniff than I really do as Officer Laddie turns bright red in popper dizziness and turns on the radio. "The Giggler" by Pat and the Wildcats comes on—that great obscure, astonishing garage-rock instrumental with the maniacally cheerful chuckling vocal added for novelty appeal. Amazing. I thought I was the only one who knew that 45 rpm, but I guess I was wrong. Officer Laddie lets out a howl of laughter and shouts to the world, "Aunt Bee, look at us now! POPPERMANIA!" He turns on the siren full blast and accelerates. I'm popper high, too, so I don't care. Under the influence, he still seems to be driving safely to me.

Officer Laddie begins mock-disco-dancing in his seat and waves to passengers in other cars, who oddly enough seem delighted, give him the thumbs-up, and start mock-dancing right back at him. I start laughing uncontrollably when I look out into the countryside zipping by my window and see cows looking up at the sudden noise of our siren. "Cows don't get high," I blurt out stupidly to Officer Laddie as the muscles in our bodies relax and our heart rates increase and the blood pounds through our veins in hilarity and chemical excitement. "They sure don't," screams Officer Laddie over the music before we both break into uncontrollable laughter in our joint amyl nitrite bond of lunacy.

As the popper high quickly vanishes, Officer Laddie pulls over on the side of the highway and we look out to an incredible vista, a scenic overlook of majestic America. He reaches into the backseat and grabs a box of donuts. "Hungry?" he offers, taking a coconut-topped Texas-style one for himself. Realizing it's almost lunchtime and I can't demand healthy food on the road, I eagerly grab a chocolate-frosted cruller. "Beautiful, isn't it?" he says, and I assume he means the donut. "Yes," I agree, but then I see way in the distance a moving mass of dark clouds and suddenly realize he means the storm. "Is that a tornado?" I ask with sudden alarm. "It sure is," he says, smiling; "maybe we can get a show!" Since I'm not from this part of the country, I'm not sure how scared I should feel. "Are we safe?" I ask as I hear the faint wailing of the tornado-warning siren in the distance and see the now clearly formed tornado funnel zigzagging across the landscape. "Nobody's ever really safe except in Mayberry, are they?" he asks with a grin. "But Don Knotts is deceased," I argue, "and so is Andy Griffith," figuring now is not the time for games. "Nonsense," Office Laddie responds, "I saw both of them on TV just this morning."

When the tornado suddenly switches course and seems headed straight for us, I panic, but Officer Laddie just yells out, "Dorothy!" in tribute to Auntie Em's great line in *The Wizard of Oz* without ever considering the possibility I might not know the reference. With an abruptness that takes my breath away, the dark funnel turns white when the clouds part for a second and the sunlight peeks back in, lighting up the tornado and forcing a rainbow to appear at the same time the twister is churning through the farmland, miraculously missing houses yet gobbling up nature itself with a ravenous appetite. "See?" Officer Laddie yells over the roar of the tornado. "We're over the rainbow on *both* sides of Oz!" Awestruck at the incredibly magnificent once-in-a-lifetime view of a tornado *and* a rainbow, I hold on to Officer Laddie as branches and limbs from trees become missiles hurled toward us. We duck each one just in time as the tornado veers slightly to the left and just misses sucking us up inside.

In the sudden calm and eerie silence following the storm, I can't think of anything to say but "I'm really John Waters. I made the first *Hairspray* movie." Officer Laddie looks at me with sudden recognition. "Oh my God. Of course you are," he says with happiness, "and you're not going to believe this, but I'm playing Edna in our church group's production of *Hairspray*." Good God, I think, the miracle of *Hairspray* never ends. "Come on," he begs, grabbing both of my hands with enthusiasm, "let's do 'Timeless' together. You know the words!" And even though I have to think for a moment, he's right, I do, even though I didn't write them for the Broadway musical version; Scott Wittman and Marc Shaiman did. I croon the lyrics as Wilbur and Officer Laddie, playing Edna with the perfect lack of condescension, warbles back. We harmonize together while cars whiz by, honking their horns in applause as we shuffle along the side of the highway in perfect vaudevillian happiness with the ravaged, torn-up countryside behind us making the perfect backdrop for our shared musical madness.

GOOD RIDE NUMBER FIVE

YETTA

Officer Laddie has to get back to work, so we do our curtain calls to the applause of honking horns from oncoming traffic and then, like everybody else in showbiz, go our separate ways. I'll always remember this lovely man and what a help he was on my cross-country trip; however, I have no time for elaborate goodbyes, it's time to get another ride.

But I'm in the middle of nowhere—the border between Indiana and Illinois. I see poking up the road, at a ridiculously slow speed, a beat-up station wagon whose driver is putting on signal lights to turn onto Route 70W, so I excitedly stick out my thumb. I see what appears to be, from my quick glimpse, a very old lady behind the wheel. She pulls over on the entrance ramp and I'm not sure if it's because she wants to give me a lift or her car has died. I run up to the door and peek inside. "Hi," says the overweight lady with snow-white hair pulled up in some kind of goofy Pebbles Flintstone topknot. She is wearing a floral muumuu getup, jeweled plastic slip-on sandals *with* black seamed hose that have seen better days. Her face, although deeply wrinkled, is somehow familiar, but that seems impossible. I hop in and notice that even though she wears no makeup except for a touch of red lipstick that seemed applied by a blind person, she is featuring false eyelashes—the kind you buy in a joke store.

"Loco Moto," that great honky-tonk hillbilly instrumental by Cornbread and Jerry, with the organ mimicking an approaching train whistle, is playing on the radio, which I think must be another good sign. "I'm only going to Hermann, Missouri," she says with a chatty voice that also rings a bell. "Thanks for the lift," I say as she pulls out at a ridiculously slow speed and merges into the interstate without showing any concern at the drivers who slam on their brakes behind her in the slow lane and then lean on their horn before angrily speeding around her. "Green tree. Pretty lady. Car. Car. Truck," she recites, naming out loud almost everything she sees. "Don't mind me, I'm a gabberbox," she chuckles. "A gabberbox?" I ask, confused at her term. "You know, hon, I talk a lot," she explains before breaking into a laugh that is eerily familiar. "Oh, you mean a *chatterbox*," I say, and she just continues laughing, but then pops a giant cough drop in her mouth, one with a strong cherry odor. "I talk mental," she announces with pride. "Are you from Baltimore?" I ask, hearing her use of the working-class white expression *hon*, which is still heard in certain blue-collar neighborhoods in Baltimore. "No, no," she answers without any apparent geographical pride, "I'm from San Francisco, California." The off-kilter lilt to her voice is familiar and I rack my brain: *Who* does she remind me of? "Do you miss the Bay Area?" I ask, wondering if she could have even read my San Francisco sign from the distance of her moving car. I try not to stare at this batty old broad but somehow I *know* this woman. "No, I'm real happy in Hermann, Missouri! I've got a secondhand convenience store called Yetta's." "You mean overstocked items?" I ask politely, trying to imagine what on earth a secondhand convenience store could be. "No, goofy," she says in a nasal, singsong voice like some kind of dotty comedienne, "it's just used products, like a thrift store. I get outdated prescription drugs, half-used deodorant sticks, recalled over-the-counter cold medicine . . . they still work! Sometimes it's a bunch of bullshit when they say there's some sort of health scare. I try 'em first, and if I'm okay, so are my customers!" "Is that legal!?" I blurt, imagining a store straight out of one of my old movies. "I don't know, John," she giggles, "but the local police are nice. They buy stuff, too!"

"John!?" I ask in shock. This woman recognizes me? It can't be! "How do you know my name?" I wonder out loud. Suddenly she looks nervous. "Well . . . you don't recognize me?" I stare at her quizzically and she smiles sweetly and then says the one word that explains it all. "Eggs!" she cries in the most identifiable voice in the world. "EDITH!?" I scream so loud, she jumps. "Yes, honey, it's me . . . ," she shyly admits. "You're alive!?" I shout, completely losing my cool at seeing the onetime star of many of my early movies. "Well, you don't believe in ghosts, do you?" she chuckles with that famous off-kilter delivery. "But, Edith," I stutter, "I thought you died in California." "I didn't really die. I just needed to get away, John," she confesses timidly. "I wanted to retire from show business. Let my fans remember me when I was beautiful." "Beautiful?" I think with ironic amazement before correcting myself—yes, she was beautiful and still is. "But your teeth," I blurt, "who fixed your snaggletooth smile?" "I saved up money from the store and got them. You like 'em? Look, they come out," she explains as she lowers her jaw and removes the bottom row. "No, no! It's okay," I beg, "put them back in!

"How did you know I was here, Edith?" I marvel. "Officer Laddie and I are friends," she explained, "we sometimes sing show tunes together just for fun. He buys used shampoo from me, too. He called me and told me he left you off hitchhiking and I couldn't believe it. I just had to see you one last time." "But why didn't you ever call me, Edith?" I cry. "All those years! I dreamed you were alive, I really did!" "I just was afraid you'd want me back in movies," she says quickly. "It was too hard for me to memorize those lines." "But you were a star, Edith!" I shout for the world to hear. "Well, not as big as Divine was," she humbly argues, "and he deserved to have all the fame." "But you and Divine were great together in *Polyester*," I gush, and for once she is silent. "That was then, John," she finally says. "I'm happy now, too."

I start crying. I can't believe Edith Massey is alive. "How old are you now, Edith?" I ask in amazement. "Ninety-four years old and still kickin'," she answers with a coquettish giggle. "But how did you fake your death? I thought you were cremated," I pry. "Weren't your ashes illegally scattered by your friends in Los Angeles at the same cemetery garden where Marilyn Monroe's were?" "Well, silly, you never *saw* my dead body, did you?" she asks with girlish mischief. No, I think, picturing Divine's Alfred Hitchcockian belly peeking up as he lay in his coffin at the funeral home. "I never saw David Lochary's body, either!" I suddenly blurt to Edith. "Is he still alive?" "I don't think so, John," she politely reasons, "but I don't keep up with the Dreamlanders, so I wouldn't know." "But who helped you?" I grill her, amazed that she had pulled off her fake death with such aplomb. "Gene did," she admits, mentioning her last roommate, who had called me from the hospital in Los Angeles where Edith supposedly only had a few days left to live. "But I talked to the doctors," I remembered. "That was Gene's friend," Edith confesses with a titter. "But I still talk to Gene," I wail, amazed that he's kept this secret for so long. "It was my secret, John," Edith explains with a sudden seriousness. "He kept it and I hope you will, too. But I missed you, John, I really did."

I sob out loud. "Pull over, Edith, please! Let me give you a hug! I can't believe you're alive!!" Edith's eyes get a little misty, too. "Okay," she says as she veers over in front of another car, which swerves away in the nick of time. "But remember, I work. I gotta open my store at noon." On the side of the highway, Edith and I embrace. "Would you ever be in another movie?" I ask with excitement. "No, honey," she answers kindly. "I liked being in the underground movies. I'd be too nervous to act with real movie stars. Besides, our old movies are still playing, aren't they?" "Yes, Edith, but the fans and the press would go nuts to see you again!" I try to convince her. "No, John," she says with finality, "who'd take care of Lovey?" *"Your cat is still alive?!"* I yell in shock. "Well, not the Lovey you remember," she patiently explains. "She died in my arms, but I have had six more Loveys since and I love them all just the same." With that, Edith pulls back into traffic and for once it is a smooth merge. "Wanna see my store?" she asks, pulling me shockingly right back into the present.

Yetta's is located outside St. Louis in the tiny town of Hermann. "Why did you pick here?" I ask as we pull into the "free parking" lot behind her storefront shop, located between a church and a sausage factory. "Well, Gene and I ran out of gas, so I decided to stay," Edith tells me happily. "I was ready to work in the sausage factory. I *love* sausage, but Gene wanted me to be my own boss. He had some money, and he stayed with me for a few weeks and helped me open the store." "But no one recognizes you?" I quiz her as we get out of the car and she opens the back of her wagon and I help her carry in a big, damaged carton of Sure deodorant. "Just once," she admits as we struggle toward the shop. "A punk-rock girl asked me if I was 'the Egg Lady,' and I just said, 'What do you mean?' and she let it go. I changed my name to Yetta just because I always thought it was a pretty name. Remember you named one of my eggs Little Yetta?" "I do remember, Edith," I say with astonishment and sentimental nostalgia at hearing her say this name from the outtake bonus feature from the *Pink Flamingos* twenty-fifth anniversary DVD. "You need some used cosmetics, John?" she asks as she fumbles for her keys. "I got Maybelline eyeliner pencils and they're only about half sharpened down. No tops, but you can use tinfoil for a cap."

Yetta's is a jerry-rigged showcase of damaged products: toiletries out of their boxes and thrown into a 25¢ bin, makeup jars half-filled, shampoo tubes squeezed almost empty, loose Band-Aids without the paper wrappers, outdated sunblock, and a "pharmacy" section that is incredibly startling. Inside display cases with cracked, broken glass that must have been retrieved from a dump are prescription bottles with all the original patients' and doctors' names blacked out with a felt-tip pen. "You need a sleeping aid?" asks Edith, with the kindness of Marcus Welby, M.D. "We got all kinds—Ambien, Halcion, even some Percocets." "No, Edith, I can sleep fine," I answer, picking up a Viagra pill out of a "2 for $1" bin and then putting it back, remembering I was hitchhiking and loose pills without a doctor's note might be trouble down the road. "Don't you have trouble with junkies?" I ask. "I don't know what they do with the pills, John," she says with a shrug. "I'm not nosy. They're always nice to me so I don't say nothin'."

A male customer I didn't even see come in approaches the old-fashioned, taped-together register with a half-broken toenail clipper that seems to have been rusted from some kind of flood. "They still work?" he asks Edith as he takes out a tattered plastic change purse. "We don't promise nothin' here at Yetta's," Edith announces, ringing up his 15¢ purchase, "that's why we're cheap." "I'll take these," I say, plopping down on her counter a few items I've picked out. "Okay, John," says Edith . . . I mean Yetta . . . as she jots down all of my purchases on one of those little receipt books with the carbon paper between each page. "Two eyeliner pencils, ten cents; Halo shampoo—bottle *almost* full, ninety cents; recalled Excedrin, one dollar—it don't have nothing wrong with it, John, I tried it!" She adds it all up, "carrying the one" out loud, and announces the total. "Two dollars, but you can have it all for a dollar ninety," she bargains. "No, Yetta," I protest, "two dollars is fine."

I look around the store and see all the customers are gone. "Edith, I love you!" I whisper. "I love you, too, John," she says as she takes my hand to lead me to the front door. Before I can leave, a twig-headed white boy with tweaker eyes enters and asks urgently, "Got any bottled water?" "Just Delta water," Edith proudly volunteers, "over there on the left. That's a collector's item. Delta Air Lines don't make their own water anymore." "Thanks," says the raver type, anticipating the strengthened high the water will make on the already-digested Ecstasy in his system, "I'll take four bottles!" As Edith rings up his sale, he sees my hitchhiking sign and says, "I'm going to just outside Topeka. Want a lift?" "Sure thing!" I yell as I kiss Edith goodbye. She looks into my eyes and coos, "Babs, where do eggs come from?" I don't miss a beat, go right into the dialogue from one of the most famous *Pink Flamingos* scenes and answer quietly with full intimacy in Divine's voice, "From little chickens, Mama. They lay them and we eat them. There will always be chickens . . ." "Eggs! Eggs, eggs," she whispers back so only I can hear before going out of character and mouthing silently, "Don't be strangers," her signature sign-off line I remember so well from our shared past.

GOOD RIDE NUMBER SIX

CRAWFORD

My luck never seems to run out on this trip. I don't even have to stick out my thumb and already I've got a good ride with a Pierre Clémenti look-alike with dreadlocks. I wonder if black people are mean to this guy, thinking all white boys with this hairdo are rich "trustafarians" who are stealing their culture? I can't help but imagine what *my* hair would look like in dreadlocks! Ha! His name is Crawford and he definitely has a bohemian charm despite the dark circles under his eyes that usually come along with most freegan-type anarchists who love MDMA-type drugs but are too cool for "cuddle puddles," glow sticks, outdated happy-face tattoos, or baby pacifiers and now drift from one illegal dance party to another being cooler than Coolio. Everybody makes fun of hipsters these days but I still love them.

"You do molly?" he asks as he guzzles that Delta water down to bump up his drug high, like an alcoholic with a fresh pint of hooch. "No, I think my drug days are pretty much behind me," I confess, trying not to be so square that he throws me out. "I mean, I can't think of a new drug that sounds appealing. Roofies?" I joke. "I'm afraid I'd stay home and date-rape myself all night long." "Salvia?" he offers, and I'm proud I know what it is—the still-legal plant that Miley Cyrus got high on in that video that went viral. "No," I back off, "I hear it causes hysterical laughter in some people, which sounds great—if I still made movies." (Hey, you do! Remember that $5 million is waiting for you in Baltimore.) "I'd put it in popcorn, though, whenever the studio forced me to have test screenings," I add. "Cool, man," Crawford vaguely answers before chugging down another bottle of Delta water. "But then I read that salvia can also cause 'extreme bouts of mysticism,'" I continue. "No thanks! Everybody has their limits." "Ever try helium?" he blurts as he grabs a partially deflated HAPPY MOTHER'S DAY Mylar balloon from the backseat, unties it, and takes a big huff. "Yowee!" he yells in a gas-induced high-pitched squeaky voice. "How about meow meow?" he quizzes me in the exact Alvin-the-Chipmunk tone that always makes me horny even though both Alvin and this guy are probably straight. "I read some kid took meow meow and ripped his balls off," I say, laughing nervously. "Yeah?" answers Crawford, not realizing how much he was paying tribute to David Seville's little creatures with that accelerated voice. "Then what? Don't tease me with narrative, bro."

I can't believe my ears but I think I hear in low volume on the radio the Chipmunks themselves singing their first great hit, "Witch Doctor," and turn up the volume full blast. Crawford sings along, cranking the volume even higher before grabbing back the balloon and inhaling. "Hold it in as long as you can," he orders me in a vibrating voice, and we both do so, exhale, and scream out the chorus in a frantic, sped-up Chipmunk voice that salutes our alarming cross-generational musical tastes.

Time flies when you're doing helium and I've almost forgotten I'm hitchhiking. Crawford is a great driver when he's this light-headed, or maybe I'm just so dizzy that I don't notice his speeding. I finally feel "bad" in my old age, suddenly one with youth. A real filth elder at last.

The sun is going down as we pull up to a junkyard outside Topeka, Kansas. A graffiti-like announcement, CONTAMINATION GENERATION, is scrawled over the old JUGHEAD'S AUTO PARTS sign, and lots of kids seem to be pouring inside. Crawford gets out and is instantly mobbed by punkish girls with pinned eyes, all of whom seem to be happily hallucinating. He's some sort of star and I didn't even realize it. Nobody recognizes me except one overweight girl, who says, "You look like John Waters. Bet everybody tells you that." I answer, "They do," and she leaves it at that.

We walk by "security," although the need for a guard when the event is free is beyond me. This guy seems to be the last of the auto-part *Dawn of the Dead* gearhead scavengers who were left behind after the junkyard closed down. There's nothing left of value to secure. Every working car part has long been picked clean. The air bags are defused, the trunks emptied, tires stripped. The carcasses of these damaged vehicles are piled three and four stories high.

But there's life, all right. A freakazoid fashion show is taking place atop a three-tier pile of Vandura 2500s. Fat Bettie Page–type squatter girls proudly model *Road Warrior*–meets–*One Million Years B.C.* couture as radical crusties cheer them on. Different bands are playing on stages made from wrecked Ram 3500 vans or crumpled school buses that look as if they were hit by a train. Yobjob, a British trance band, grinds out the static sound of repeated beats, while tripped-out pirate kids whirl in otherworldly abandonment. A noise band called the Fire Starters plays their greatest hits—each one sounds exactly the same and none lasts longer than five seconds, while young, tattooed, branded freaks, some with artificial limbs due to motorcycle accidents, pogo dance in mock nostalgia.

Crawford hurries through the adoring crowd as fans hand him all sorts of new drugs I've never even heard of. Suddenly there is a loud roar in the distance that sounds as if a million chain saws have been turned on. A huge forklift carrying a smashed Cadillac with Crawford's band's name, THE VON BRUSSELS, tagged across the windshield rumbles through the parting crowd. Marshmellow, a fiercely sexy slum goddess with more piercings than I've ever seen (including Ubangi lip plates and hanging earlobes) and a neck tattooed with terrorist-group logos, plays a guitar made of animal umbilical cords, strengthened with, I bet, freshly sniffed glue. Otis, a cute, nonracist skinhead-type guy I would really go for (if he wasn't once a woman and *had* had bottom surgery), is blasting a boom box playing a synthetic symphony of terrifying animal mating calls that sound like human cries of distress. The forklift drops their Cadillac stage atop a larger, burned-out bread truck that is roasting on a huge bonfire in the middle of the junkyard. Crawford is hoisted up by a crane to the stage and embraces the two others in a hotbed of sexual unity. I realize that not only are they a band, they are a revolutionary threesome, and it is a lovely sight to behold.

Crawford is the lead "singer," if you can even begin to call his tortured screams mixed in with mock opera arias "singing." Suddenly the entire junkyard is his stage. The other bands give up, knowing they can't compete. Women and men begin taking off their clothes and dancing tribally with a fury that would make any adult nervous. It's like Mortville-à-go-go.

As the bonfire begins to rage below them, Crawford gives the signal, and both Marshmellow and Otis stage-dive off the forklifts and land on separate OverBuilt Model 10 car crushers. The crowd is going wild, watching the fire lick its way up, knowing Crawford is timing the musical finale to the tweak of the audience's drug trips. I watch the hypnotic orgy of deafening sounds reach its *Boléro*-type finale as Crawford's vocal cords are pushed to such a limit of howling, screeching volume that both his eardrums pop and blood shoots from his throat just as he jumps off his

bread-truck-roof stage as it bursts into flames and lands in Marshmellow's car-flattening platform. Taking his plasmatic cue, Otis
ignites the ferocious engine of his machinery and begins crushing
automobile cadavers as Marshmellow does the same, and Crawford
breaks into spasmodic Saint Vitus' dance moves and joins them
in shrieking a warlike, speaking-in-tongues gibberish that only
the Devil himself could ever translate. I get the vapors and collapse.

The next morning I awaken, neatly tucked in a bed made out
of an old ambulance stretcher nestled inside a onetime-fancy Pace
Arrow movie-star trailer, the kind Melanie Griffith and Stephen
Dorff both had on *Cecil B. DeMented*'s set. Like every vehicle at
Jughead's Auto Parts, there's been a tragedy inside, but enough
time has passed to mute the original horror of the event. Only
three walls are left standing, and one is crumpled. Obviously
there has been a hideous accident. Maybe a 10K light crashed
down from a crane on set? Or on the way to a location a Teamster
driving the honeywagon truck fell asleep at the wheel and rear-
ended the movie-star trailers? There's been a fire, too. You can see
multiple flame marks near the kitchen area. Maybe freebasing? I
see a burned-out tiny piece of a movie call-sheet clinging to the
springs under where a couch once was and pick it off carefully.
"Day 8. *Drive Angry*," it reads. God, I saw that movie.

I look out the front window and all is silent. It's like a happy
Jonestown. All the tripper kids are sleeping, passed out next to
each other, smiles on the zonked-out faces, some holding hands,
all lying in rows. I half crawl back to the bedroom area and see
Crawford, Marshmellow, and Otis asleep, all their limbs tangled
around each other in love and support. I have such faith in young
people. I don't wake them. I let them dream in peace.

GOOD RIDE NUMBER SEVEN

READY WHIP

It's another beautiful fucking morning in America. For once I
have to walk a bit but I don't mind, it gives me time to reflect on
what a good idea this whole hitchhiking thing has been. Still
reveling in my newfound bliss, I hear a car screech around the
corner and come speeding up the little street toward me. Whoa!
Somebody's in a hurry! Usually I am uptight about anybody driving too fast when I'm in the car, but my rides have been so lovely,
I throw caution to the wind and stick out my I'M NOT PSYCHO
sign to see how it works. The car's driver hits the brakes, does a
donut wheel, and flips open the passenger's-side door from his
side. "Where you going?" I ask, a little put off to see an Italian-
looking guy about forty years old with long hair and some kind
of orange jumpsuit hugging his wiry body. His arms are covered
in rudely altered religious tattoos (Little Lulu and Richie Rich
replace Jesus' disciples at the Last Supper) and he has a dollar
sign inked on each hand. "Hell," he answers with a winning
snarl, "get in!" I do.

As he floors it, I hear a police siren in the distance and panic
a little when my driver accelerates even faster and goes right past

the I-70 entrance ramp even though I tell him that's the way I'm headed. "We're goin' the back roads," he announces, leaving no room for debate. The hair on my neck stands up when I suddenly realize his orange jumpsuit is actually a Kansas Federal Prison uniform. Even I have heard of Leavenworth, whose name is stitched across the front. "I'm Ready Whip," he says, "and I'll take you as far as Hays, Kansas, *if* we get that far!" I hear more sirens in the distance, and Ready Whip turns off on another little country road and takes an even more out-of-the-way detour. "Are you in trouble, Mr. Ready Whip?" I ask, trying to be nonchalant, as some poor squirrel, used to slower traffic, unsuccessfully tries to cross the road and is flattened by our late-seventies Ford Galaxie. "Cut the 'Mr.,'" he orders with a sexy command, "just call me Ready Whip, 'cause my dick's ready and I'm always ready to whip it out." "I see," I say with open-minded astonishment. "But first I need some new clothes," he announces as he pulls into a tiny little town that doesn't *have* a name. Before I can begin to imagine shopping with my new host, he slams on the brakes when he sees a pitiful Laundromat that doesn't look as if it's been remodeled since the fifties. "Go in there and steal me some underpants." "WHAT?!" I say in alarm. "You heard me, Mr. John Waters, I know who you are. I seen you on TV in the joint—on *Danielle Steele's Family Album*. What a piece of shit." Before I can defend one of my most obscure acting credits, he barks, "Hurry up—I need jeans, too, thirty-four-inch waist, medium T-shirts, and socks for an eleven-and-a-half-inch foot." Shocked and feeling like Caril Ann Fugate taking orders from Charles Starkweather in that real-life fifties crime spree, I do what I'm told. The police sirens in the distance seem to have quieted, so why not?

Inside the Laundromat, there are only two customers, a pregnant teenage girl with her whining baby and a farmer who is asleep on a broken-down plastic chair that for some reason is chained to a radiator. I case the joint, realizing how completely out of place I look. "Forget your laundry, dumbbell?" the probably unwed mother cracks. "No, I just need to buy soap, if it's any business of yours," I snap, feeling a little of Ready Whip's anger almost by osmosis. "Machine's broke," she mutters as she opens the dryer door, puts her baby inside, and rocks it back and forth without shame until the infant gurgles happily. "You gotta dollar?" she suddenly demands. "My clothes are in the washer but I don't got dryer money. Two dollars a load?! Do these fuckers think I'm made of money?" Seeing the only spinning dryer full of clothes, I think fast. "I'll give you ten dollars if you keep your mouth shut," I offer. "Mister, I don't go on 'dates,'" she responds with, in my opinion, uncalled-for haughtiness. "I don't want that, sugar," I answer, trying to be friendly in a film-noir kind of way, "I got a date of my own and he's waiting outside." She watches in silence as I fling open the dryer door and start rooting through the farmer's still-damp laundry. He still doesn't move. Maybe he's dead. "Give me twenty," she suddenly demands as she spins her baby around one full turn in the dryer without letting it fall out. I give her the money. She takes her child out of the dryer and unwraps a Zero candy bar from her purse and lets the kid nibble the white chocolate. "Knock yourself out, soap bubble," she hisses as she puts the bill in her pocket and burps the baby, a little *too* hard if you ask me. I grab the only pair of jeans inside that aren't overalls (the most hideous outfit a man can ever wear), all the socks, a few pairs of boxer shorts, and one still-wet T-shirt and rush out the door.

"What were you doin', ironing?" Ready Whip impatiently cracks as I jump in his car with his motor running. "So?" I ask him, holding up the wet Hanes T-shirt for his approval as he speeds away. "Beats this piece of shit," he answers as he starts to unbutton his jumpsuit while continuing to drive. "It's a thirty-three waist," I read from the worn Levi's label on the back of the jeans. "It'll fit," he grunts as he suddenly steers the car over to the side of the road, gets out, kicks off his prison sneakers (the kind with the Velcro straps so you can't use the shoelaces to strangle yourself), pulls off his filthy socks, and begins to strip out of his jail uniform. He seems completely unperturbed that he is now totally nude by the side of the road. "Memorize this dick, John," he demands, and even though I'm completely startled by his sudden sexual frankness, I do. Fantasies are like extra cash, they need to be banked for later use. I chuckle to myself, remembering Quentin Tarantino's hilarious line onstage when I interviewed him for the Provincetown Film Festival. "What was the best thing about your success?" I had asked, and he answered, "Pussy . . . no, the *memory* of pussy." Now I know what he meant. Cars continue to whiz by, drivers shouting catcalls to Ready Whip, but I just watch him nude the way a cultist would a beloved midnight movie while trucks honk their horns in one long chorus of indignation. He turns to me full frontally and makes his dick jump without touching it. I'm not sure what I'm supposed to do, so I applaud. "One day I'm gonna tell my children that John Waters looked at my dick . . . ," he growls, stuffing his still fully erect penis back into the freshly stolen jeans of the farmer, "but right now we got business still to do." What could *that* mean, I think in sudden nervousness. "Down, boy," he orders his cock as he struggles to zip up, just as if he were a ventriloquist talking to his dummy. He wriggles his torso into the now almost dry T-shirt and I can tell he's turned on by my lustful eyes as he climbs back inside the car.

"Now, put on them socks," he demands with a strange affection as he sticks out one foot toward me and wriggles his toes. I shove on the sock with care and tenderness and an unhealthy desire to please. "That tickles, bitch," he says with a giggle, and I debate if I should be offended, but when his big toe pops out of the hole in the sock the farmer never thought to mend, I decide to just go with the flow. "Size eleven and a half," he brags, "don't touch, just look . . . go ahead, take a cell phone picture of them if you want." I fumble for my BlackBerry.

But before any red-hot photo session can take place we hear a new police siren wailing in the distance. Only this time it sounds like more than one. Ready Whip jams those puppies back into his prison shoes and we're outta here. "Fuck those pigs!" he yells in a rage I haven't heard since the sixties. "I got a bank job to do, porkers!" he shouts as we zoom down the country lane. So *that's* what he does for a living, I think, impressed before suddenly realizing I should be frightened. "You're not gonna rob a bank now, are you?" I sputter. "I'm not, *we* are," he answers with confidence. "No, look," I beg, "my friend Patty Hearst got in a lot of trouble for helping to rob a bank and it wasn't even her fault. I mean—am I a hostage?" "Hell no, dude, I just want you to watch," he says, laughing. "Watch what?" I ask in confusion. "Me and my dick . . . being *bad*," he whispers with a narcissistic, exhibitionist wink as we pull into a small gravel parking lot outside a tiny brick building. SUNFLOWER BANK, HAYS, KANSAS reads the low-tech sign. "Open them peepers, Mr. Creeper, and watch my cock," he purrs, "'cause ol' Ready Whip luvs doin' a bank job!"

He grabs a can of Mountain Dew from under the seat, puts a brown paper bag over it, and aims it toward the bank. "Armed and dangerous," he cracks, with one final adjustment to his crotch, which already seems to be anticipating the crime scene and its erotic possibilities. "Wait forty-five seconds, then follow me in and act surprised," he directs as he opens the car door and gets out, carrying the paper bag with the "gun" concealed inside.

I do as my director tells me, timing the forty-five seconds exactly on my watch, excitedly imagining the triumphant entrance of Ready Whip's penis inside the bank. I get out, pretend to be an extra in a movie, and casually stroll across the parking lot and enter.

I see Ready Whip approaching the teller, a black woman in

her twenties dressed in an atrocious maxiskirt, sensible shoes, and a hairdo no one would ever copy. A goofy-looking man in the little office on the side, who may be the boss, is explaining to an angry lady farmer why there is a fee for a cash deposit to her savings account. Ready Whip aims his Mountain Dew gun at the clerk and shouts, "This is a holdup!" and grabs her around the neck. I may be the only one that notices the groin bulging in Ready Whip's jeans. She starts screaming, the manager just stands there with openmouthed shock, the farmer-lady customer laughs out loud and mutters, "Serves you right," and the rent-a-cop puts his hands in the air and starts crying. "Hey, you," Ready Whip growls to me with convincing menace and a slight thrusting of his groin that I can't imagine anyone else notices, "get your skinny ass over here and hand over your wallet." I play my part convincingly and beg him not to kill me, and he grabs me with his free hand and puts it around my neck, still allowing me a partial view down to his now blatantly hard cock. Maybe it's my paranoia, but I think the girl hostage sees it, too! She hands over the bags of money to Ready Whip and the manager tells her, "Continue doing as you are told. Nobody needs to get hurt." "Please don't shoot me," the guard begs, "I got tickets to see Drake tonight in Wichita." "Call the cops and I pull the trigger," Ready Whip threatens as we make our getaway, both the girl teller and me still strangled by his arms around our necks. Ready Whip zigzags us both across the parking lot to the car, waving his gun as a few pedestrians dive behind parked cars. He throws us both in the front seat, gets behind the wheel, and we make a break for it at a sudden high speed. I wonder why Ready Whip doesn't point the gun at the girl anymore. Stranger, she seems to calm down immediately, even when he gives me my wallet back. "You looked hot in there, Ready Whip," she suddenly coos as Ready Whip once again adjusts his erect package inside his pants. She pulls off her wig to reveal a partially shaved head with the words READY WHIP trimmed in her hair in some sort of modified Mohawk. She snaps off her rigged breakaway maxiskirt and blouse and I see that every inch of her ebony body that was covered by her disguise is filled with white tattoos. She is wearing a corset and a push-up black bra with a black net see-through minidress. "Polk-A-Dotty, meet John Waters," says Ready Whip as he whips out his dick and displays it proudly. Polk-A-Dotty!? *That* was the name of the very first hand puppet I owned as a child, I silently marvel, all the while hypnotized by Ready Whip's crotch presentation. "Where the hell did you two meet?" she wonders, watching the penis performance herself with voyeuristic zeal before tearing her eyes away to count the stolen money from the bags. "Six thousand dollars," she purrs between quick looks back to Ready Whip's own personal Bethlehem Steel. "He's been watching it, too," our cock conductor gently murmurs, "just like you do, Polk-A-Dotty." "For seven straight years!" Polk-A-Dotty brags to me proudly as Ready Whip throbs his cock to the left, then to the right, then straight up and down. It's like the exhibitionist Olympics. "Look but never ever touch," he whispers to us both as he floors the accelerator, and Polk-A-Dotty and I turn to each other in acceptance, happy to share.

But even at this high speed, nosy authorities try to ruin our newly formed mutual admiration society. We hear the sound of helicopters above and then the faint sound of police sirens in the distance. "Fuck," yells Ready Whip, "I was just about to come." To drown out the sounds of the cops, he turns on the radio and, wouldn't you know it, "Chain Gang" by Bobby Scott booms through the car's shitty sound system. "This is the Kansas State Police," we hear amplified from an overhead police loudspeaker. "Ready Whip, you are surrounded. Pull over your vehicle. Drop your weapon and release the hostages." "WATCH MY DICK ONE LAST TIME!!" Ready Whip orders as he swerves off the road onto an even narrower path, and we do, God, we do, but the sound of crashing branches on the hood and crunching foliage under the car distracts me for one second and I look up and see a big tree ahead, right in our speeding path. "Look out, look out!" I scream in my best Shangri-Las "Leader of the Pack" vocal imitation, but it's too late. We collide with nature and Ready Whip's head goes through the windshield, but amazingly, our air bags, unlike his, go off and save our lives. We look over and are relieved to see that Ready Whip had climaxed the instant he died, a happy ending indeed. "Run!" Polk-A-Dotty suddenly screams, and I see the Kansas police charging toward us. We take off holding hands, joined together in a mournful voyeuristic afterglow few could understand.

GOOD RIDE NUMBER EIGHT

BUSTER

We're in some kind of abandoned state park. I pull Polk-A-Dotty down an overgrown walking trail and we keep running, past broken-down and rusted playground equipment, boarded-up restroom facilities, rotted picnic tables, even an abandoned baseball diamond that has been completely scorched by some sort of brush fire. We cross a slimy, polluted creek under a bridge that has partially collapsed. We hear police dogs approaching, not far in the distance.

Remembering a famous case in Baltimore where the fugitive Joseph Palczynski escaped by simply hiding in a tree because police tracking dogs aren't trained to smell "up" and the cops never thought to look to the sky, I motion for Polk-A-Dotty to follow me up a large evergreen. She has already changed into a pair of heels, but this girl is no fashion amateur—not only can she run in spikes, she can climb a tree wearing them, too! We freeze on two separate branches as the cops and their snarling bloodhounds run right past us. Hearing the chopper landing at Ready Whip's death scene, we make a break for it.

As soon as we turn a corner in the shitty little spoiled-nature path, we see a miracle. A motley caravan of broken-down wagons, trailers, and flatbed trucks pulling vintage amusement-park rides that anybody could tell has seen better days is taking the most obscure route away from the interstate to avoid detection. THE HIPSTER CARNIVAL, reads the hand-painted logo on the first truck in line, with the added come-on below: WE'RE ON THE RUN LOOKIN' FOR FUN! Polk-A-Dotty takes over, realizing she's more of a hot-number hitchhiker than I'll ever be, and sticks out her thumb. I hide in the bushes.

The caravan slows down and Buster, the ringleader owner, eyes her suspiciously. "Lookin' for work?" bellows the fifty-year-old Robert-Mitchum-meets-Richard-Tyson-from-*Two-Moon-Junction* look-alike. "What've you got to offer?" she answers back sassily, and the other Hipster Carnival workers, a peculiar collection of freakish yet bohemian drifters, peer out from their trailers. "Looking for a girl I can throw knives at for my act," Buster gruffly answers, before adding with pride, "I don't drug-test my employees, neither." The roughneck carnies cheer and laugh in support. "What happened to the other girl?" Polk-A-Dotty asks with flippant sauciness. "I missed," Buster explains with a hint of sadness. "Is she going to be all right?" Polk-A-Dotty quickly asks. "Nope," answers Buster without any further explanation. "Okay, I'll take the job on one condition," she barters. "What's that?" Buster answers, amazed at her nerve. "My friend John Waters can come with us."

I step out of the bushes, and after a moment of complete silence, I am astonished that not only Buster but the entire crew of this decrepit little carnival burst into applause. I feel even more glad to be famous here than I do in New York City when garbagemen yell out my name and give me the thumbs-up. So crossed-over. Accepted.

"I love the chicken-fucking scene in *Pink Flamingos*," Buster announces with genuine respect. "Those fucking things hurt,"

Macaroni, "The World's Thinnest Model," mimics Cookie Mueller's line correctly, with a slight lisp, from her trailer before blowing me a kiss with her bony hands. "John Waters, I'm putting you in the freak show," proclaims Buster with leadership, as Orca, "The Meanest Fat Lady," shrieks out Divine's line "Filth is my politics! Filth is my life!" with a gusto that takes even me back. "As what?" I stammer to Buster, happy to have yet another career. "One look at you and I know," he says like a wizard: "SEE A MAN WITH NO TATTOOS!" "Oh my God, he can see through clothes!" Polk-A-Dotty murmurs in awe, and while I won't go that far, I have to admit he's right. I'm tattoo free. We leap on board, thrilled to be rescued. Something putrid this way comes.

After several hours of traveling (highlighted by hearing the catchy country-bumpkin tune "Travelin' Boogie" by Zeb Turner *twice* on the radio), giving "patch" money to local cops on the way (including the stupid fuzz taking away Ready Whip's body), we stop outside of Last Chance, Colorado, at the parking lot of an abandoned small strip mall. A video shop's smashed windows have been boarded up and defaced with graffiti paying respect to forgotten horror sexploitation films, *Olga's House of Shame*, *I Dismember Mama*, even the porno parody *I Spit on Your Snatch*. A Pic-N-Pay discount store has obviously had a fire—it's in such bad shape even homeless people would shun it. A Beverage Barn liquor store seems deserted and long ago looted. Colorado noxious weeds have taken over the parking lot, giving us the perfect setting in a low-life natural landscape.

I'm shown into my new trailer, which I'll be sharing with Pimple Face, a nice enough guy who obviously doesn't let his oozing zits, boils, and abscesses bother him. He seems to be in a great mood as he describes how he quit school and devoted his life to eating potato chips. I also meet Borehead the Clown, but it's hard to have a real conversation with him because he's had that "trephination" operation where a hole is drilled in your head and you are then high forever and can never come down. He talks complete nonsense but everybody here pretends to understand.

Polk-A-Dotty checks in on me and confides she already made out with Buster "and that motherfucker can kiss!" I'm so happy she's graduated to a man who wants to be touched. Maybe my good influence has been a help in the next chapter of her neurotic happiness. I curl up in an out-of-commission old Tilt-A-Whirl car seat that someone has thoughtfully made up for me as a bed inside a trailer and slowly drift off.

I wake up the next morning to the sound of hammering, buzz saws, and generator noise and peek out. Good Lord, the Hipster Carnival is almost completely set up. I step outside in the sparkling-clear day and see a small crowd of cool people who obviously know about the secret carnival and have followed online where it will open up next. I see Pimple Face unchaining the ramshackle front gate and letting customers inside. I'm amazed that he's *not* in the freak show, he's just a roustabout.

I start to mosey through the crowd but Polk-A-Dotty rushes out, dressed in a sexy little magician's assistant outfit, and turns me right around and shoves me back in the trailer. "Oh, no, you don't, Mr. John Waters, you're a sideshow attraction now, nobody gets to see you for free." Before I can even argue that *nobody* in Last Chance, Colorado, will know who I am, she whips out a white ski mask with a caricature of my face and my mustache drawn in black and pulls it down over my head. "There you go. Nobody will think it's the real you!" I look out through the eyeholes and feel exactly the way Michael Jackson's son Blanket must have felt when he was young.

"I go on in fifteen minutes! I'm so excited!" she gushes as she grabs my hand and starts dragging me through the oh-so-groovy crowd, many of whom seem to be getting high. "Even as a screwed-up little girl, I wanted to be a human target," she confesses as we pass the "joints," different games of chance. I see the Meat Wheel, where you spin and, if you're lucky, win a pork butt or some veal cutlets. At the Mystic Coin Toss, happy customers are rewarded with vintage no-longer-available cigarettes, unfiltered Kools, L&Ms, even Montclairs.

"Shirleen, this is John Waters," Polk-A-Dotty introduces me to a blowsy but tough-looking middle-aged white lady who only has one arm but seems to be able to serve the black cotton candy at her booth *and* make change easily with the added help of her mouth. "She's in the sideshow, too," Polk-A-Dotty proudly announces before whispering so Shirleen can't hear, "Look at her eyes." "Nice to meet you," Shirleen says, giggling, ignoring my mask and offering me some of her goth spun-sugar treat. As I decline politely, I notice some movement in her eyelashes. "Crabs," whispers Polk-A-Dotty. I try not to let my pupils bulge in surprise, but Polk-A-Dotty's right, Shirleen has crab lice in her eyelashes *and* eyebrows! Every once in a while she'll absentmindedly pick one of the little parasites off, examine it briefly, then crush it with her fingers. "Also known as Lady Vermin," she announces, sticking out her hand to shake. "Proud to be working with you!"

PUKE-A-WORLD, reads the giant banner hanging over the midway rides. "Come on, let's go on one," Polk-A-Dotty begs with childish excitement as I see three dented Drunk Driver Dodgem cars giving sparks off the tin ceiling as they circulate around a pile of old rubber tires. Big cans of Colt 45 are being given out to the boisterous, already inebriated drivers waiting in the line. "Eight, four, two, seven," they count backward incorrectly, while others purposely walk wobbly-legged in a supposed straight line. "I've got the whirlies!" yells a new ticket buyer as he jumps in the Dodgem car and promptly passes out at the wheel.

"I can't go on rides that go around in circles, I get sick," I beg off to Polk-A-Dotty. "But that's just the point, you're supposed to puke on these rides!" she argues, pointing to an old, rusted Round Up, the caged ride where you don't even get strapped in the spinning wheel as it raises its axis because the centrifugal force keeps you in. I look up and see an entire metalhead family puke at the exact same time and scream in delight when the vomit flies back in their faces.

"Buster tells me his rides are the best because they really *are* scary," Polk-A-Dotty confides, impressed. "Most are either defective or have had maintenance issues. Many have never been serviced because he gets them for free from third-world countries. Isn't that fantabulous?" Before I can answer we're in front of the Caterpillar, a favorite ride in my youth that you *never* see anymore. "Awww," sighs Polk-A-Dotty in hard-boiled nostalgia as she watches, with me, the continuous string of cars revolving and undulating in a wavelike circular track at a growing speed. At maximum velocity, a green canopy rises and encloses the riders with a caterpillar-like covering, hiding them from the nosy crowd. "Watch!" Polk-A-Dotty waves, with a look in her eyes I'm beginning to know means there's a shock about to happen. As the canopy retreats we see that all the riders have begun to have sex undercover and with erotic lateral force. Some are masturbating, others are in threesomes, one couple even manages to do it doggie-style without being thrown from the car. I'm having so much fun I debate just staying here forever.

"I'll go in here!" I shout, seeing the Liberal Horror House, one of those rides that takes place completely inside a bunch of connected trailers. Little cars go through on tracks, and various scary objects pop out to give the rider a fright. "The best one in the country," I confide, "is the Haunted House located in Ocean City, Maryland. It's worth a visit to this town just to go on it. I've also loved forever a 1962 Diane Arbus photograph called *House of Horrors, Coney Island*, which shows the inside of the ride with some of the lights turned on and the ominous track for the car visible. Can anything be as scary as these two things?" I ask Polk-A-Dotty with giddy excitement.

"We'll see," she says as we spot Chilidog, a ride jockey whose specialty Polk-A-Dotty has already heard used to be picking up wallets that fell out of riders' pockets when they went upside down on rides and then denying he had found any such things. But that was *before* he worked at the Hipster Carnival, and now he couldn't be more helpful as he buckles us in the vintage little car and sends us on our way, zipping off and banging through a door with a photo of Richard Nixon on it. Inside it is pitch-black, and even Polk-A-Dotty screams when a Barbara Bush skeleton drops down in front of us and shakes like a goblin. Jerking along around sharp corners, suddenly the car breaks down and we hear a witchlike voice scream, "You're out of gas, just like the rest of the world!" We pull away with a sudden jerk just before the car behind almost crashes into us. It's hot as hell in here, I think before we see a globe of the world drop down and burst into flame to tell us in a leftist way that global warming is still an issue— even here, when everybody is high, drunk, and happy.

As we ride around another corner and into the next section of the Horror House, a naked man wearing an oversize strap-on penis is lit up. Without warning a huge load of fake sperm is shot right at us while the words s-a-f-e s-e-x blink on and off in scary Halloween-style letters. Suddenly hipster interns jump out in disguise as minimum-wage, uneducated workers and steal our wallets at gunpoint, emphasizing how many small circuses and carnivals are not unionized.

As we screech out in our car and exit into the blinding daylight, trying to wipe away the fake semen that *must* have stained our outfits, we are relieved to see the frightening load was created in disappearing white ink. Chilidog returns our wallets, in newfound honesty, as Polk-A-Dotty excitedly tells me Buster pays a good salary to his workers, not in filthy lucre but with high-grade herb.

"Time for work," announces Polk-A-Dotty, and I see the Freak Show tent in the distance and gulp. I'm at ease playing myself, but appearing onstage as a performer without writing my own script is terrifying to me. "But, Polk-A-Dotty," I beg as she drags me over to the back of the tent to enter, "I don't know what I'm supposed to do!" "Just take off your shirt and pants and show the audience you don't have tattoos!" *"What!?"* I cry. "I'm not getting naked in front of a crowd!" "Why not?" she pooh-poohs. "The audience won't be criticizing your body—they will just be amazed to see you don't have tattoos in this day and age. You'll be a triumph."

"Five-minute warning," Buster whispers to me with professional stage management the instant we enter through the tent's back flap. I take off my "disguise" mask as Polk-A-Dotty gives Buster the deepest soul kiss I have ever seen in my life, sucking his entire mouth into hers. Gasping for air, Buster returns the favor, twisting his long tongue around hers like a lasso and then deep-throating it down to her tonsils with expert sword-swallowing, gagless oscillation.

Onstage is Clementine, "The Girl with the World's Largest Feet." This boast seems to *not* be exaggeration. "Bigger than Clarabell's," she brags to the crowd, who stare back in awe. She must wear a size twenty! Her toes are longer than my hands. Her ankle's the size of my waist. She wears a bracelet on her big toe. "Huger than Mr. Natural's," she roars. These hipsters get the R. Crumb reference and applaud wildly. "Sexier than Olive Oyl's," she shouts, trimming her toenails with a pair of regular-size scissors. Surprising even me, Clementine flops back in a chair and holds her enormous monster-size dogs in the air for the world to see. "Even bigger than Shaquille O'Neal's," she screams, and I seem to be the only one in the tent who doesn't get it. "He's a famous basketball player," Polk-A-Dotty whispers in explanation. "I'm sorry," I mumble, "I don't follow sports."

Buster, dressed dashingly in his black leather knife-wielding costume, goes onstage as Clementine grabs up the large-size bills, some still stained with cocaine traces, that the crowd has thrown to her for tips. "And now, ladies and gentlemen . . . ," Buster begins as I am grabbed backstage by Hal and Clara, the freak-show performers who have been on earlier, wowing the audience with their "Human Pretzel" contortion act that ends with both auto-fellatio and auto-cunnilingus. "No," I protest as Hal gently unbuttons my shirt and then Clara, with the help of Polk-A-Dotty, yanks off my pants. "I can't be naked! I'm in my mid-sixties!" I argue violently as they make me step out of my shoes and socks. All I have on is my boxer shorts. "You have to at least flash," Polk-A-Dotty argues. "Just let them see your cock and ass are tattoo free for a second!" "You look great," Hal says with encouragement. "Fashion free at last," Clara says, beaming with respect.

"All the way from Baltimore, Maryland," I hear Buster announce, "making his first appearance with the Hipster Carnival, not as a film director, not as a smart-ass talk show guest or an overexposed documentary talking head but as the *freak* he really is! More shocking than Octopus Man, more horrifying than the World's Biggest Rat! Here he is! You won't believe your eyes! John Waters! The Man with No Tattoos!!"

Polk-A-Dotty whispers, "Break a leg," and shoves me onstage. I've gone on so many times that I almost start doing my stand-up routine, but I get a bigger reaction from this audience than I've ever received at a college. They gasp! They shriek! They look down at their overinked limbs and recoil. They look back at my skin, not judging me physically, just filled with admiration at my nonconformist courage of never getting a tattoo. Filled with the excited liberation of nudity, I drop trou and reveal the truth. I really *am* tattoo free. The house goes crazy. I am showered in money, poppers, joints, even blocks of gold hash.

I pull my boxer shorts back up and Buster rushes onstage and holds one of my arms in the air as if I were Rocky Balboa, and I forget I even *am* John Waters. I bow deeply, then run backstage and get dressed back up like myself to the congratulations and embraces of all my fellow freak-show brothers and sisters. But now it's Polk-A-Dotty's big moment and I want to be here for her just the way she was for me. Buster, still onstage, pulls back a red silk curtain to reveal a large circular wooden board with leather restraints for arms and legs. "Ladies and gentlemen, I'd like to introduce my newest assistant," he announces proudly, "and let's hope her career turns out better than the last girl's. Her name is Polk-A-Dotty, and *I* am her knife master!"

Polk-A-Dotty slinks onstage to cheers, dressed in a one-piece gold bathing suit, throws off her cape, and is courageously strapped to the wheel by Hal and Clara. Buster takes aim. I hold my breath along with the crowd, and he spin-throws the sharp blade, which whacks in between Polk-A-Dotty's legs with precision. She moans in newfound pleasure. Without hesitation, Buster quickly throws two more knives, hitting perfectly under her arms, and then even quicker three more that outline her head, just missing by fractions of an inch, producing the perfect soundtrack for the finale of this exciting, dangerous act. I am so happy for Polk-A-Dotty, she is such a star, and she has finally found a danger-top who can make her feel even more glamorous than an exhibitionist bank robber could. Buster unleashes Polk-A-Dotty from the wheel and together they take their well-deserved bows. Macaroni hugs me backstage with her skinny little arms and I hug her back but accidentally crack two of her vertebrae. "Don't worry," she whispers, "that happens all the time."

After many curtain calls, Buster calms the crowd down. "I have one last surprise," he announces, and Polk-A-Dotty looks offstage at me and gives me a wink. "John Waters will now take the place on the wheel for the most dangerous stunt of all." The spectators scream their approval as I stand there, paralyzed, not believing my ears. Polk-A-Dotty rushes to me, grabs my hand, and drags me back onstage. "Do you trust me, John?" Buster asks, and all the freaks in the Hipster Carnival wait for my answer with loving patience. Polk-A-Dotty gives me a lunatic grin of sisterhood as I melt, swallow hard, and then answer, "I trust you, Buster." The relieved and loyal cries of acceptance from my new family of fucked-up Cirque du Soleil rejects give me a strange courage I've never had the nerve to imagine.

Polk-A-Dotty herself straps me on the wooden wheel, and Hal and Clara give me a spin and I try to pretend I'm a ballet dancer, focusing on one spot so I don't get dizzy. Then the crowd shouts out new excitement, but I can't see why they are cheering. As I spin faster and faster, I concentrate on Buster's image each time I'm right side up. Holy mother of God! Buster's now got a large hatchet in each hand. HATCHET THROWING?! Is this the Rapture or is it not? Suddenly I feel and hear the loudest whack right by the right side of my head and then in a split second another one to the left. I am momentarily deafened, but as the spinning begins to slow down just a bit and my vision and hearing gradually return, I hear the audience cheering anew and then see Buster putting on a blindfold. Good God, did I want *THIS* much of an adventure? He throws the hatchet between my legs with such force that the wheel splits in two but my strapped-on body holds it together. The crowd goes absolutely bananas. I feel like the Chicken Lady character in the pit at the end of *Freaks*, but this time I've given the Tod Browning–directed movie classic a tribute happy ending it so well deserves. At last I am one with show business.

GOOD RIDE NUMBER NINE

BERNICE

Last Chance, Colorado, may have been the *first* chance I've had to be happy naked in public, but the carnival must move on and so must I. Before the whole troupe wakes up I sneak a note inside Polk-A-Dotty and Buster's trailer thanking them for introducing me to a new kind of living theater, the closest I'll ever get to Artaud's Theatre of Cruelty . . . only nice. You can never have too many careers, I've always said, and now I write them, "If the book doesn't turn out or *Fruitcake* underperforms, I'll be back to 'spin for my supper.'"

The sun is coming up and there's no such thing as rush-hour traffic in this part of the country but, yet again (!), the very first car that approaches pulls over. The problem is, *how* do I get in? The entire vehicle, a beat-up yellow eighties Chevy Citation, is completely filled with books—every kind imaginable—hardcovers, trade paperbacks, but especially mass-market editions, some missing their covers. The passenger seat is piled so high I can't even see who's behind the wheel. Slowly, like a jigsaw puzzle being assembled in reverse, I see a face as she throws the books in the back, under the seats, even in her lap. "Sorry," the rather haggard-looking woman in her late sixties, with the weakest chin I've ever seen in my life, mutters, "I like to read."

"I can see that," I answer good-naturedly as I jump in, pick books off my seat, and then pile them back in my lap. "I like to read, too," I say, taking a gander at the eye-popping cover art of the vintage sex paperback *Teen Girls Who Are Assaulted by Animals*. "This one is amazing," I say, wondering what the editorial meeting at the publisher's could have been like to green-light this title. Here's a niche audience I hadn't imagined. "*All* books are amazing," she corrects me with a passion. "Are you a librarian?" I ask cheerfully, knowing, after being the keynote speaker for several of their conferences, how wild librarians can be. "Not officially . . . ," she answers with practiced bravery. "I was . . . ," she confides, "and then something happened and I wasn't." Oh. "I'm John," I introduce myself, trying to change the subject away from her obviously painful past. "They call me Bernice," she answers without fanfare, "*and* I read your last book. I loved the chapter 'Bookworm,' but you're too 'literarily correct' for my tastes."

Before I can stick up for my published reading recommendations, she suddenly brakes for a car that swerves around some tire rubble on the highway, and a huge pile of cheap paperbacks stacked pack-rat style in the backseat collapses on top of me. I pick off *Saddle Shoe Sex Kitten*, *Some Like It Hard*, and *Freakout on Sunset Strip*, with the amazing politically incorrect subtitle *Fags, Freaks and the Famous Turn the Street into a Hippy Hell*.

"They're not for me," she explains as she pulls off I-70 onto a rural road; "they're for my book club readers." Before I can protest that I can't go off the interstate, she tells me, "Don't worry, I'll take you back to the highway." We cut back into an even less traveled country road, turn the corner, and see a *Tobacco Road*–style hut constructed entirely out of paperback books missing their front covers. The owner has shellacked the books to make them semi-weatherproof, but the elements have not been kind—the volumes, soaked through many times from rain, are swollen, tattered, and can't offer much in the way of protection. "Publishers don't want cheap paperbacks returned when they don't sell," Bernice explains. "The newsstand managers are supposed to rip off the covers and turn those in and they get their refund. The retail outlets are expected to then just throw away the books, but I rescue them from this biblioclasm and redistribute the volumes to alternative readers at the lowest end of the used-book market. I know it's hard to imagine, but a few very dedicated collectors only *want* books with torn-off covers. It's these specialized readers I serve. I am not alone. Flea-market vendors, paper-recycling workers, relatives of deceased dirty-book collectors, we are united in a mission to do what libraries cannot: bring the customer the lowest of the low in literature.

"Ah, there's Cash," she says as a skinny, grubby fortyish-year-old white guy with a potbelly and a Prince Valiant haircut comes out of his self-styled reading room. I quickly realize by "Cash" she means her customer's name, not actual money. Her books are, of course, free. "Cash is a very specific customer," she explains. "His books must be soft-core and pre-porn, with a missing cover done by a collectible artist. He then actually reads these smutty volumes, writes endless critiques of the writer's style, which he never allows anyone else to read, and then uses the 'read' book as a building block for another room in his shantytown abode."

"Hi, Bernice," shouts Cash in some sort of regional accent too obscure for me to identify. "Hello, sir," she says with a literary grin, "this is my friend John." Cash completely ignores me, so Bernice just goes into her routine. "I got some good ones for you today," she promises as Cash's eyes light up and he licks his lips in anticipation. "Here you go," she teases, "*She'll Get Hers* by John Plunkett." "With a missing cover by Rafael de Soto," Cash yells back with postmodern literary enthusiasm. "I remember that one,

Cash," Bernice reminisces like the specialist she is; "that was great pulp art but it's gone now!" "Who wants to go to an art gallery?! I want to read!" yells Cash as he grabs the volume and hugs it to his chest in literary fetishism. "How about this one?" tempts Bernice, holding up a yellowing paperback with both the front and the back binding ripped off. "Remember the pulp jacket with the sexy lady on the couch clutching the pillow like her lover?" she quizzes. "*Restless* by Greg Hamilton," Cash shouts back like he's on a quiz show, "with cover art by Paul Rader. And I'm *glad* the cover is gone. I *read* these books, Bernice, I don't look at them! I read every word until I understand perfectly what the author was saying just to me; the last reader these volumes will ever have." Bernice hands him the damaged volume and he grabs it with a scary gratitude. "See you next Thursday, Cash," Bernice promises, and with that, we're back in the car and off to the next outsider reader.

"I'm no judge of what people read as long as they *read*," explains Bernice once we're on the road. "Are all your books dirty ones?" I ask with great curatorial respect. "No," she answers proudly, "I've got true crime, too. A lot of libraries won't carry the really gruesome ones. Just like bookstores, they discriminate— putting the true crime sections way in the back of the store. Hidden. Near the gay section." Before I can agree she gives me a sudden look of traumatic desperation that stops me in my tracks. "Believe me," she whispers sadly as we suddenly pull into the driveway of a suburban ranch house, "I *know* about censorship."

Out comes Mrs. Adderly, a most unlikely matronly true crime reader still dressed in her housecoat. "Hi, Bernice. I'm glad you're here. I got in a fight down at the library just yesterday. They take my taxes, why can't I have a say in what books the library buys?" "Hi, I'm John," I butt in. "I thought the library *had* to get you a book if you ask for it." "Oh, they *say* they do," Mrs. Adderly answers without missing a beat, "but they lie! I happen to be obsessed with 'womb raiders.' Are you familiar with that genre?" she asks me point-blank. "You mean women who tell their husbands they're pregnant when they're not and then follow real pregnant ones, kill them, cut out their babies and take them home claiming they've just given birth?" I reply. "That's the ones," acknowledges Bernice, impressed I'm so well-informed in this specialized field. "Well, I read *Lullaby and Goodnight* by D. T. Hughes," Mrs. Adderly continues, "but there's another one I want. *Hush Little Baby*, by Jim Carrier, where the 'raider' cuts out the baby with the mother's car keys and the baby actually lives! Well, this literary snob of a librarian says to me when I ask if she has the book, 'There's no need to know about somebody *that* ugly.'" "Yes, there is!" I yell in outrage, completely agreeing with Mrs. Adderly's anger. "The public needs to know," I rant, "that when you're pregnant, strangers are following your every step, ready to jump out and cut out your baby with your car keys! Womb raiders are everywhere." "Exactly!" agrees Mrs. Adderly, thrilled to have someone else in her corner. Bernice gets a sly grin on her face and whips out a mint-condition bound galley of this very title and hands it over. "Oh, Bernice," Mrs. Adderly gushes, "you know how to make a true crime buff happy. Thank you from the bottom of my black little heart."

We're off. I'm impressed. Bernice turns on the radio and we hear that delightful little country song "Swingin' Down the Lane" by Jerry Wallace and merrily sing along, harmonizing over the instrumental bridge between verses. I continue picking through the books on the floor by my feet and laugh at *One Hole Town*, a hilariously titled soft-core vintage gay stroke book. "You want that one?" she asks with generosity. "Sure," I say, mentally adding this rare title to my collection of cheesy gay-sex paperbacks. "It would go right along with my 'chicken' volumes," I tell her. "You mean titles with the word *chicken* in them?" she asks immediately, understanding my oddball bibliophile specialty. "Yes,

I've got *Uncle's Little Chicken*, *Trickin' the Chicken*, *Chicken for the Hardhat*, even *Chain Gang Chicken*." "I know them well," she announces with bibliographical respect.

"And you, Bernice," I gently pry, "what kind of terrible books do you collect?" She freezes, suddenly protective of her most private scholarly taste, but then seems eager to have someone in whom she can confide. "The novelization of porn parody movies," she admits with great pride. "It's a small genre, but one that is growing in importance," she explains with deep knowledge of her field. "I tried to introduce these specialized volumes to the general public when I was head librarian in my hometown of Eagle. But Colorado is such a backward state! Trouble started as soon as I displayed *Splendor in the Ass* and *Homo Alone* with the covers out instead of spine in. Busybody little prudes noticed and made a big deal out of it, but I stood strong against censorship. Porn parody titles need to be discovered *and* celebrated. I was vilified in both the local and the national press, but I didn't care! I fought back! I passed out valuable, extremely rare copies of *Clitty Clitty Bang Bang* to any high school reader in the library who asked for it. Satire needs to be taught! These youngsters loved *Clitty* but I was fired! I called the Kids' Right to Read and the National Coalition Against Censorship organizations, but they wouldn't help me. I became a scapegoat for the humor-impaired."

Before I can offer my unbridled support, she pulls her car over to the I-70W entrance ramp and we are buried in sliding paperback books. With great concern and kindness she asks gently, "Do you have the *Twelve Inches* series?" "Yes," I murmur in excitement, trying to stack Bernice's volumes back up in some kind of order. "I've got *Twelve Inches*, *Twelve Inches with a Vengeance*, *Twelve Inches Around the World*." "But do you have *Twelve Inches in Peril*?" she demands with excitement, whipping the title out from inside her glove compartment and holding it up like the Holy Grail. "No!" I shout with rabid delight, quivering in reverse literary excitement. We look at each other in our love of disreputable books and she hands it over, completing my collection. "Thank you, Bernice," I say in heartfelt appreciation, caressing this title like a sexual partner. "You must go now, John," she says with sudden concern. "I can't be exposed. My readers will continue to hide me. They know. They know I'm the best damn alternative librarian in the country." "You should be proud, Bernice," I say as I get out, bow in respect, and blow her a kiss goodbye. "Run," she says with urgency; "run to read!" But where do you run to in Parachute, Colorado?

GOOD RIDE NUMBER TEN

GUMDROP

Up the hill, that's where. And lo and behold, here comes a truck.
Please, dear God, let him stop. Even though I don't really believe in God (or at least any of the ones I've heard about), my
prayers are answered. I run up to the idling Kenworth eighteen-
wheeler, lugging my bag, and climb up into the cab. Behind the
wheel is Gumdrop, a cross-country trucker driving for Farley's
& Sathers, a large candy company. He started his route in the
Midwest and he's on his way to a candy wholesaler in L.A.
A little too far south for my journey but a good ride to Utah,
where I'll jump out and head north to Reno and then down on
into San Francisco. Imagine my delight when Gumdrop starts
talking about candy! Mexican Hats, Red Hot Dollars, Dots; he
likes the same treats as I do! He's cute, too, but I don't get any
sexual vibes, he's just sweet . . . like Swedish Fish.

"How about Jujyfruits?" he asks with a wink and a smile showing a chipped but beauteous front tooth. "You're kidding," I answer, "they're my favorite candy of all!" "Filling-rippers," he yells
enthusiastically, agreeing with my candy-connoisseur opinion.
"My dentist warns me off Jujyfruits, but I say fuck him," I brag.

"I love those chewy little pellets." "But not Jujubes, right?" he asks with sudden concern. "No, they're too hard," I answer. "That's because they use potato starch instead of cornstarch as their primary thickener," he explains, "and Jujubes are cured longer, making them tough, hard as nails . . . inedible, if you ask me." "I agree," I answer in breathless candy brotherhood. "Nothing resists a bite more perfectly than a fresh Jujyfruit."

"Guess what," Gumdrop says, leering. "I got a whole truckload full of them!" "Jujyfruits?" I ask in a sugar frenzy. "Yessiree," he boasts, "they make them in Creston, Iowa, and that's where I'm coming from. You should see the plant! Huge tubs of Jujyfruits! Thousands and thousands of those sweet little nuggets popping out of the sugar machines every minute. They don't make the small boxes anymore, damn them, but I got twenty thousand movie-theater-sized boxes in the back of this truck . . . and"—he pauses with drama—"can you keep a secret?" "Sure!" I pant, just imagining the orgy of flavor in the rear. "I got mint ones," he whispers conspiratorially, "the flavor those confectionary fascists discontinued in 1999." "Good heavens," I moan, "I haven't had a mint Jujyfruits since then! I thought they were totally unavailable!" "They *are*," he answers with penny-candy vigor, "unless you're in the distinguished company of yours truly. I didn't get the name Gumdrop for being a candy dabbler. I've been saving 'em." "Look," he whispers with pride as he pulls out a small trash bag filled with mint-flavored forbidden treats. "Can I have one?" I ask, shaking in candy awe. "You sure can, John," he answers, and my mouth is watering so much I don't even realize he has recognized me. "Here . . . ," he offers, picking a few mint-green Jujyfruits from the bag. I nibble some out of his callused hands the way a horse would go for a lump of sugar and he doesn't seem to mind. I savor the tangy flavor that may once have been the most unpopular shade, but what does the public know? I've been thinking outside the Jujyfruits box for years and I'm honored to report that this discredited chewy little fella retains its original flavor with gusto.

"Look, I gotta be honest," Gumdrop announces as we finally turn back onto Route 70 West. "I loved *Pink Flamingos* but I hated that *Hairspray* shit." "You hated *my Hairspray*?" I ask, nibbling our highly collectible treats on my own. "The one with Divine and Ricki Lake?" "Yeah," he says with a shrug, "I like crazy shit, man. Ever been to a pirate truck stop?" he asks with newfound friendliness. "I don't think so," I respond, already intrigued. "What are they?" "The illegal ones with strippers and gambling," he explains with obvious excitement, "and free liquor!" "Sounds good to me," I cheer. "I hate that NATSO organization," he seethes, "all these goddamn safety rules, weight restrictions. I don't want no 'truck plaza,' I want a fucking truck *stop*! No fenced parking lot! No security cameras. Just some kick-ass trucker fun!"

"Let's go!" I scream, realizing we've been on the road for hours, it's getting dark, and I'll need a place to sleep. "I know a great one and it's just outside Fillmore, Utah," he enthuses. "It's not on any Triple A map. It is an outlaw truck stop, all right— the Gas and Go-Go!" "Yay!" I yell, probably too enthusiastically. "I'll pay for the rooms." "Now, John," he suddenly counsels, "I gotta get one thing straight. I'm not a fag. Nothin' against 'em, but a hairy ass crack just don't do it for me." "That's okay," I mumble, oddly touched by his total unawareness of politically correct gayspeak. "Not everybody is queer. It's no big deal." "But I'll watch over you," he offers almost tenderly. "I'll make sure nobody fucks with you. Deal?" "Deal," I say as we pull into the scary-looking Gas and Go-Go truck stop parking lot.

Lot lizards patrol the corridors between trucks and I can see full-tilt female-male blow jobs going on right out in the open. Truckers are walking around openly guzzling from liquor bottles and laughing and slapping each other on the back in off-work revelry. I get out of the truck and I see Gumdrop swallow, without water, two pills that look like black beauties. "God, do they still make them?!" I ask. "Want one?" Gumdrop offers kindly, but I decline, trying to imagine flying on speed at my age. Gumdrop high-fives a few other drivers he obviously knows and leads me toward the truck stop's "Party Palace," which has all the windows blacked out and just one small lightbulb illuminating the entrance. Frightening hookers approach us but Gumdrop barks, "No oral!" and they back off in respect.

"Don't worry, they got fags here, too," Gumdrop tries to comfort me, but I'm not concerned, I'm having a great time already. I'm introduced to a big hog of a bouncer named Joe-Eddy. "I loved the rosary job in *Multiple Maniacs*," he says gruffly as he rubber-stamps my hand with a gearstick penis logo. "Thank you," I answer as he hands me two "free speed VIP" tickets. "Fuck your brains out," he welcomes Gumdrop, who just chuckles and asks, "Is Fumbelina working tonight?" "She sure is," Joe-Eddy responds lecherously. "I love that bitch," Gumdrop explains as we enter the dark, hot truck stop nightclub that has been off the beaten path for so long that it is now completely claimed by law-breaking truckers lucky enough to know this place still exists. Everybody inside seems to be high on crank. Big-time. They're drinking, too, and truckers clap wildly as the strippers slide up and down poles made out of truck tailpipes. One girl slaps her ass with an oil dipstick as she dances to "Hot Wheels," an amazing Johnny Cash soundalike tune with the lyrics about taking pills to stay awake while driving long-distance on the highway. I love this song! When I hear the trucker-horn sound effects mixed in with the chorus, I know I'm in the right place. Maybe I can use this song in my next movie soundtrack!

Gumdrop leads me to a bar and orders me a free vodka without even asking what I drink. He just knows. He gets gin for himself and guzzles it down in one gulp and burps out the sound of a busted truck muffler with amazing realism. He drags me

through the partying drivers, many of whom are dancing reck-
lessly with other scary women. I see a red-hot dancer who looks
like a gal in a Russ Meyer movie undulating with precision in
a bikini top and a micro-miniskirt. Gumdrop races ahead and
stuffs a $20 bill down her cleavage. On cue, she retrieves the bill
from between her giant tits, pretends to drop it, spreads her legs
in a practiced stance, and bends over to pick it up. She is, of
course, wearing no underpants. Knowing the routine, Gumdrop
leans his head over between her legs and looks up to Cupid's cave.
Fumbelina purrs, "Smile, you're on *Candid Camera*" and "takes a
picture" with the expert muscle control that can only come from
years of training. I have never seen a man look happier than
Gumdrop does at that moment. He fumbles for another double
sawbuck and in between her knockers it goes. Once again, she
pretends to be all thumbs as she retrieves it and "drops" the twenty
and slowly . . . very slowly bends over to pick it up. "Take two,"
Fumbelina chuckles as Gumdrop takes his place below and says,
"Say cheese," through a shit-eating grin. Again she snaps his
"photo" with vaginal precision. I can see Gumdrop's eyes beaming in gratitude. "Fumbelina, this is John Waters," he says politely, poking me in the side to let me know I, too, should give
her a twenty. "Nice to meetcha," she says as I slide a bill inside
her supervixen breasts, and Gumdrop slaps me on the back in
approval. Fumbelina "fumbles" the bill, drops it in choreographed
clumsiness, bends over to pick it up. I hesitate, knowing what is
expected of me. "Don't worry, I'll retouch the picture," she says
with a giggle, and I take my place between her legs looking up
into her natural lens. "Hold still for focus," she orders, and I do.
Click! Yikes, a snatchshot! I feel like Lee Miller as she modeled
for Man Ray's first solarized photography, the "rayograph."

"See over there?" asks Gumdrop, pointing to a curtain in the
back. "Yeah," I say, noticing a few truckers sneaking behind it
every once in a while. "Take a look, John. You'll be okay. I'm

gonna let you explore a little on your own. There's a bunch of you cocksuckers back there," he explains in the nicest, most unjudgmental voice imaginable. I laugh out loud at his clueless homophobic words that belie his gay-friendly attitude. He just doesn't know. I'm not offended; actually, it's kind of sweet. I realize Gumdrop would like a little more quality time with Fumbelina, so I decide to be brave. "Okay," I reply, still sounding a little worried. "I got your back," he says assuredly. I look around at all the tough guys ear-banging each other in amphetamine delirium, laughing at nothing and celebrating the very act of not thinking, and feel safe here in this paradise of trucker sexuality. Who needs intellectuals when you're having fun?

I head toward the mysterious curtain, hesitate, pull it back, and go inside the hidden annex. It's little but, oh, brother, I'm in fag heaven, as Gumdrop might innocently say. Queer-bait go-go boys are everywhere, and the truckers in this audience are just as wild and hopped-up on speed and hooch as their straight brothers out front. Every time a new dancer is announced they shout "Whip it out!" or "Get it! Get it!" just like characters in my old films might. "Basket" seems to be a real favorite. He's got a huge, tattooed cock that he stirs drinks with when he kneels down on the bar. And then there's Chicken Little, who's just my type, a baby-faced ruffian who, much to my initial astonishment, "coldshakes" Viagra onstage and then shoots up just as Gerard Malanga did with heroin in 1966 as the Velvet Underground played in Andy Warhol's *Exploding Plastic Inevitable*. Some of the truckers are jerking off in the friendliest way possible. Chicken Little's dick gets harder on the Viagra, and he circulates the room slapping customers in the face with it as they roll up bills tightly and insert them up his ass. Wow! This is my kind of club! But since I've already had two peculiar sexual encounters today, I decline Chicken Little's face-slapping (whap! whap! whap!) "helicoptering" offer when he gets to me.

I'm startled to feel Gumdrop's arm around my shoulder. "Shoot your shot?" he asks, unembarrassed and possibly totally unaware that this was the name of one of Divine's early techno record hits. "No, but that's okay," I respond in our newfound kinship of roadside honesty. "I did," says Gumdrop with a twinkle in his eyes before adding with a knowing laugh, "Come on, my diet pill is wearing off." "Hey, that's a line from *Hairspray*," I respond; "I thought you didn't like that movie?" "Well," he chuckles, leading me to the exit, "I liked that *line*."

We head back toward his truck and I ask if there are rooms we could rent so we can get a good night's sleep. "Nah," he says, "you don't want to get in any bed in this place. Besides, I'm gonna take another upper." "But I've got to get some shut-eye," I beg, "I have to catch a new ride tomorrow." "I told you I'd watch over you, John," he says with unaffected kindness as he pops two more pep pills and swallows them down dry-mouthed. "You get your forty winks"—he motions to the cab of his truck as he climbs up— "I'll just watch." "Watch what?" I ask, confused, but flattered at his nocturnal offer. "I'll just watch you sleep all night and make sure nobody harms you," he says tenderly. "Will you let me do that, John?" "Yes," I answer, completely touched by his unsexual kindness, "I certainly will."

GOOD RIDE NUMBER ELEVEN

SPACE CADET

When I awake after one of the most peaceful night's sleeps in my life, Gumdrop is in the exact same position, sitting in the chair, watching over me in bed. He looks a little tired but still wired, and he could use a shave. Otherwise, he's still my nocturnal protector. I get up quickly and gather my few things. I know Gumdrop's got a shitload of Jujyfruits to deliver and he has to head south. No way I'll risk hitchhiking on I-70 through Utah where there's not even a rest area for hundreds of miles. It's time for us to part.

He gives me a lift to a local porn wholesale-outlet warehouse and drops me off, assuring me this is a "destination location" that many interstate truckers visit. I know I'll never see Gumdrop again, but we do have our Jujyfruits memories and that's all I can ask for, traveling these lonely highways. You only get a *real* fairy godfather for a few hours in life, I'm afraid.

He's off and I'm all by myself, the way everybody *really* is no matter where you are. There's not a car in sight on the road, so I just stand there feeling the power of being alone and hopeful. I see a desert-rat-type guy in his late forties coming out of the porno outlet empty-handed. Who would come all this way to an X-rated warehouse and not find a thing? This big guy, who looks part cowboy, part mental case, gets in a broken-down early-eighties AMC Eagle and peels out toward me. Will my amazing luck continue? Of course it does. He stops and I get in.

Up close, he looks like a real space cadet. I introduce myself and, no internal debate here, my rider has no idea of who I am. I tell him where I'm going. "Headed that way," he mutters, "right to the middle of nowhere." I'm not sure if seeing him come out of a porn outlet is a thing I should quiz him about, but I do. "You like adult movies?" I ask with as much nonchalance as I can muster. "Never look at that shit," he says without rancor; "I just sell my old tapes when I need the money." "Your tapes?" I ask with newfound interest. "Yeah . . . I used to do that shit for a few years . . . way back . . . *before* I had my encounter." "Uh . . . what kind of films?" I gently pry. "Gay porn," he answers unembarrassedly. "I ain't queer but I could get my dick hard no matter who was sucking it." He chuckles with nostalgia. "What was your porn name?" I ask, trying to look into his ravaged face to remember a possible stud from yesteryear smut. "John," he says shyly, and then it hits me like a ton of bricks. "Johnny Davenport?!" I shriek. "Shhhh," he scolds, suddenly paranoid, "they'll hear you." "*Who* will hear us?" I ask, confused, as I look out to the empty landscape surrounding us. "Them people," he answers vaguely before correcting himself; "well, not 'people' exactly, but just . . . them."

"God, you were my favorite porn star," I gush with shocked enthusiasm, remembering the weird sexiness this muscular Eddie Haskell look-alike stud muffin with the curly hair and the humongous cock brought to the screen. "That was all bullshit," he mumbles, dismissing my praise without an ounce of vanity. "I especially loved you in *Powertool*," I continue, not being able to control myself, "when you did that great jailhouse face-fuck scene as Jeff Stryker watched, jerking off from another cell." "Yes, Jeff was all right," Johnny admits with only a slight tinge of nostalgia for the bad ol' days. "I know Jeff Stryker!" I tell him. "I saw his show, *Jeff Stryker Does Hard Time*, in New York. He was so amazing. Especially after the final curtain. As the ticket buyers left the theater, Jeff stood at the exit door wearing an open bathrobe showing his fully erect penis, and each theatergoer could pose for a photograph with Jeff *and* his dick." Johnny doesn't look impressed. "I have his contact information—want it?" I excitedly offer, imagining the prospect of these two retired sex machines hooking up again. "No!" he spits out with sudden anger. "I don't care about those fuckers and I told you to keep your voice down. There's things you don't know—they're listening," he whispers with an insane urgency.

But I'm too worked up to stop. "Johnny Davenport," I say again, pinching myself that I'm actually in the car with him. "You were so good in *The Young and the Hung, Part Two*! I loved you in *Full Grown Full Blown*, too!" "You think I know what those pieces of shit were called?" he asks with contempt. "I just needed cash." "But you won the 1987 X-Rated Critics Award for Newcomer of the Year," I argue, trying to give him a little self-worth and letting him know he still has fans out there and they've been searching for him for years. "Yeah, yeah, yeah," he grumbles, "I've heard all those lies, that I'm a mountain man living in Albuquerque with a wife and kids . . . it's all hogwash. Now shut up about that crap!"

Suddenly I'm silent. I look at my watch but it's stopped. Johnny gets a strange look in his eyes and a tiny grin appears on his weather-beaten lips. This guy has been in the sun too much in his later life. He's still strangely handsome, but scaly, almost like a butch Gila monster who's obviously got a screw loose. "They heard you," he announces with clarity, then slowly pulls the car over to the side of the road. It is eerily quiet but suddenly the radio comes on all by itself. "Flying Saucer Rock and Roll," by the all-time favorite rockabilly singer, Billy Lee Riley, blares out, but Johnny barely reacts and certainly doesn't see the humor in this novelty song. My eardrums start popping as if I were on an airplane and I feel the car begin to vibrate even though we're not moving. "Ever fuck a spaceman?" Johnny asked with a sudden horny gaze. It's the last thing I remember.

Suddenly we're on board a spaceship that is so cheesily decorated it could be a set from that Zsa Zsa Gabor movie *Queen of Outer Space.* There are aliens, too. Stupid-looking ones. Nude. Green, of course, sporting soft bodies, Margaret Keane eyes but weirder—almost like the "cunt eyes" Crackers rants about in *Pink Flamingos*—a line that I still can't believe I actually wrote. They've got no hair (although a few seem to be wearing bad wigs) and have fingernails that curl around like claws. They've got big dicks, too. But no balls. I'm afraid to look and see if they have assholes. There doesn't seem to be a female in sight.

Johnny suddenly seems relaxed. At home. Even when they all whip out from some fifties sci-fi microwave-type appliance what appear to be liver dinners and start eating with disgusting table manners. "Okay," Johnny warns me, "they're getting ready." "Ready for *what*?" I ask with sudden nervousness. "For sex," Johnny announces with full acceptance. "What do you mean, 'sex'?!" I shout with growing apprehension. "Look, I'm no bottom in real life," Johnny explains, "but with these little fellas . . ." He lowers his pants and turns his butt to the space creatures. "It's magic," he says to me in an almost spiritual way. A horny little alien heads toward me and starts making weird little froglike croaks. Good God, I think, I'm too old to get fucked! "Is this safe?" I yell to Johnny in a panic. "Do they use rubbers?" But it's too late. Johnny is being slowly penetrated by one of these ghastly creatures, but he shows no pain. In fact, his face reflects a delighted contentment I've rarely seen in a man his age.

I feel a clawlike tentacle unbuttoning my belt from behind, and a wave of body odor like I've never smelled before overwhelms my senses. I refuse to look into the face of space rape, so I close my eyes. The rubbery appendage turns me around and begins to unzip my zipper. What the hell, I think; you've never been fucked by an extraterrestrial, go for it. But can you "top from the bottom" with a little green man? "Please, no fingering," I beg, remembering the Fu Manchu–type nails I saw earlier on these creatures. My limits are respected. But then something . . . some rodlike growth with a fiery magnetic field and a friendly elasticity rubs up on me. I pass out.

I awake in Johnny Davenport's car. I remember little. Good God, what time is it? I wonder, seeing the sun coming up and looking at my watch in confusion. "It's the next day?!" I scream in horror, trying to recall the vanished hours. I feel confused, scared, but Johnny seems calm, content. "Don't worry," he advises with experience, "you'll feel it soon." "Feel *what* soon?" I shout in panic as vague memories of some kind of sexual rear entry stir in my mind. "I'm not pregnant, am I?" I cry out in paranoia, unsure of the scientific realities of post–alien sodomy. "No," Johnny answers with patience, understanding my bewilderment, "but doesn't your asshole feel different?" "Different?" I consider, not really allowing my anus to have mood swings. "Well . . . no," I answer, embarrassed. "But wait," I admit as I feel a little tingling out back in my most private area. "You have a magic asshole now, John. So do I," he announces gently, like some sort of holy man. Before I can scoff I feel a pleasant turbulence in the air beneath my balls. "The magic only lasts for four hours or so, but listen . . ." Johnny farts eerily and poetically, and it's the exact opposite of a fart joke. A masculine aroma of courage and spice fills the air. I think of that porn movie with my favorite title of all, *My Ass Is Haunted*, and wonder if the director also was back-door probed by a spaceman. "Use the anal magic wisely," Johnny explains like some sort of Glinda, the Good Witch of the North. "'Wisely'?" I repeat, not sure how to interpret this specialized advice. "Watch," says Johnny as he lifts his leg and points one of his still round and sexy ass cheeks toward my forehead. Suddenly I feel hair grow. I grab the rearview mirror and look in amazement at my receding hairline filling in with follicles. "It works," Johnny boasts as he spins around in his seat and gets in a semicrawl position with his concealed magic anus aimed at the top of my head. My gray hair turns chestnut brown. "See?" he boasts as I notice a subtle vibration in the rear of his pants. "Go ahead, try yours," he gently suggests, so I give in and concentrate. Slowly but steadily my asshole propels me out of my seat with a supernatural power that allows me to hover in the air inside the car. "Oh God," I whisper to Johnny in a trembling but awed voice, "what can I try it out on?" "There!" my new guru says as he points to unidentifiable roadkill outside the car. The handle of the door pops open without my touching it, and I space-glide out of the car and through the air with a miraculous grace and land right next to the carcass of the unfortunate animal. I hear majestic music that I soon realize is coming from my asshole and quickly learn I can control the volume through breathing. "You got it!" encourages Johnny as he rises in the air of the front seat propelled by his own magic asshole, which joins in with my symphony of unearthly anal notes so that our assholes build to a melodious crescendo. The roadkill's eyes pop open and the bloodied animal shouts, "Anarchy rules!" just as the fox did in the funniest scene in Lars von Trier's *Antichrist*. Johnny smiles at me as the resurrected critter runs back into the desert. I get back in the car, and without discussing it he pulls off and we give our assholes a rest from their bewitched duties. I meditate on my newfound anal inner peace as Johnny drives away, staring straight ahead on the highway, knowing that he is only a "bottom" when alien-abducted, still a real "top" in human life. He lets me out at Exit 62 on 80 West, Lakeside, Utah, where he lives. I don't worry I won't be able to get a ride here in the middle of nowhere. I've got a magic asshole and a new head of hair. For three more hours, at least.

GOOD RIDE NUMBER TWELVE

A STAR

Such bliss. Such power. Such anal reinvention. And lo and behold, I see a limo approaching on the lonely highway. A beat-up one, but still . . . a real limo. I don't even wonder if it will pull over. My magic asshole is already twitching in excitement. Not only does the vehicle stop, inside is Connie Francis. You heard me, Connie Francis.

I can't believe my eyes. I recognize her immediately, sitting in the backseat, wearing more makeup than Divine ever did, but without the joy. Spackle. Thick Pan-Cake makeup that seems to be put on with a trowel. She's had work, too. Permanently "surprised." With those telltale puppet lines all plastic surgery victims have extending from the corner of the pulled mouth out across their cheeks. She looks sedated, almost as if you waved your hands across her eyes, she wouldn't blink. She's "even." Ever so even.

I have been obsessed by Connie Francis's late career for years and know she still occasionally performs, even doing four-and-a-half-hour "greatest hits" concerts. God, if you can imagine the beauty and the horror of these shows, you will understand why I continue to be her devoted fan. Except for her chauffeur, who I soon realize is not a real driver but her manager, she's alone. A legend so oblivious to real life she may not realize the music business has completely changed since she first became a star. A famous singer who's sold more records than the Beatles but has had to compete with her own horrific personal life: A onetime accordion-playing child star with demon-father issues. A love affair with Bobby Darin she never got over. Four failed marriages. Being raped at a Howard Johnson's by a still un-known and uncaught assailant. Commitment to seventeen hos-pitals for mental illness. Who's sorry now? I am, goddammit, for all the hell Connie Francis has had to endure.

But she doesn't seem fazed today. No, she speaks in a mono-tone but answers all my questions with the most minimalist responses possible. "Yes," she is Connie Francis. Silence. She's going to Reno for a one-night concert at the Nugget, which is "really fifteen minutes outside of Reno in Sparks, Nevada," as her manager corrects her. "No," she's "not hot," she blankly an-swers after I ask, noticing the fur coat she is wearing with the pelts hanging off the hem. "Wow! Very *Hills Have Eyes*," I joke, hoping humor might lighten Connie up a bit. "Is that a musical?" she asks without showing the slightest real interest.

"John is a movie director," explains her manager, Wilson, who has now introduced himself; "he made *Hairspray*." She looks at me blankly, and at first I wonder if the reason she doesn't recog-nize me is my thick, luxuriant hair, but "No," she says slowly, "I don't watch movies." "Yes, you do, Connie," coaches her man-ager as if he's feeding her lines in an interview; "we saw *Hairspray* on a plane from London that one time." "What plane?" she asks, momentarily confused before giving up and mumbling, "All mov-ies are the same, aren't they?"

Connie never once asks me why I'm hitchhiking and neither

does Wilson, but after riding in silence for quite a while she says in a flat voice, "I like your hair." No one has ever said that to me in my life. "Thank you, yours is pretty cool, too," I offer, noticing the teased and dyed do that obviously requires frequent touch-ups. "My hair sometimes hurts," she answers vaguely before whipping out her makeup bag and slathering on more liquid foundation.

Suddenly we get a flat tire. I can't believe it. "Shit!" yells Wilson as we pull over to the side of the road with the sound of flapping rubber and the rim hitting the highway causing a sudden racket. He gets out. I don't know what to do. Connie has not shown one sign that she realizes what has happened. She stares straight ahead without blinking.

I hear Wilson open the trunk and curse some more, so I get out for moral support. "Cheap-ass rental company! Just a donut wheel and no jack," he gripes. "Do you have Triple-A?" I ask. "Yeah," he deadpans, "*if* we had cell phone service out here." My asshole makes a sudden hoodoo secret signal to me, and only then do I realize I should ask my magic helper for assistance. I can feel the gentle whirring at the end of my digestive system, eager to be of service. I check my watch. I only have twenty minutes of anal power left. I act fast. I aim my magic anus at the flat, and the tire inflates at such a speed lavender smoke flies out like some cheap special effect. Wilson looks at me in fear. "It's okay," I attempt to explain, "my asshole is magic." I hear Connie Francis laugh out loud. Wilson stares with openmouthed amazement.

Suddenly I hear Connie singing from the backseat, "Stupid Cupid". Wilson glances at me in gratitude and runs to get behind the wheel. I hop in the backseat but Connie doesn't even look over as he pulls out. She is suddenly animated, almost deliriously cheerful as she keeps on singing lyrics from hit to hit.

"Where The Boys Are," she wails, sometimes a little off-key, but who cares? Connie Francis is giving me a concert in the backseat of a limo. Talk about a good ride!

"We'll stay all night and sing 'em all!" Wilson shouts in encouragement, using an old *Judy at Carnegie Hall* line as he speeds down the highway. We're both thrilled to see Miss Francis so energetic. She immediately goes into a bellowing version of "Everybody's Somebody's Fool" and I throw caution to the wind and join in with her on the refrain. Wilson turns on the radio and lo and behold, my all-time favorite Connie Francis hit, "V-A-C-A-T-I-O-N," is playing. All of us shout out the letters and even my rectum sings along.

It's almost as if Connie Francis can hear my wazoo because she looks over at me for the first time and makes real eye contact, winks, and goes into a yodeling version of one of the cuts from *Connie Francis Sings Jewish Favorites*, an album I own and have forever fetishized. Suddenly I can hear my own asshole going a cappella the way the vocalizing anus did with "Surfin' Bird" by the Trashmen in *Pink Flamingos*, only now it's cuing Connie to go into "Lipstick on Your Collar" and she does! My asshole is doing a duet with Connie Francis! I can see Wilson is watching us in the rearview mirror, happy to see his client so inspired, happy to be in show business.

I check my watch. Oh, fuck. Like Cinderella at the ball, my booty bewitching time is about to expire. I shake my thick hair like a young Ringo Starr, and Connie goes off the charts and into a whole new realm of music. Suddenly channeling Ol' Dirty Bastard's scary voice and skyrocketing to a new level of coolness, Connie raps an all-new ghetto version of the once-tepid theme song to *Follow the Boys*, a movie she starred in but has always disparaged. I watch her in awe as I feel the hair on my head thinning while my asshole lets out a final whistle of disappearing jubilation. Connie slumps back in her seat. Wilson stares straight ahead, afraid to look back at his rhyming chanteuse. "You're staying with us," Connie mutters with a glary-eyed expression. I do.

GOOD RIDE NUMBER THIRTEEN

DELMONT

The Nugget was fine. They got me a separate room and I ordered room service and took a long hot bath. I adjusted to my old receding hairline once again staring back at me in the mirror under all that intense hotel bathroom lighting. My asshole seemed unfazed to be returning to its everyday functions, too. I was okay.

I didn't go to Connie's concert, but why would I? I'd had my own private one yesterday. I heard it went well, though; she performed for *seven* hours and sang all her hits, every single one of them, in five different languages, and dared anyone to leave before she finished. Sounds like a triumph to me.

I let Connie and Wilson sleep. I know she must be exhausted after the big day we had together. I slip a farewell note to each of them under their doors and walk out into the blinding sun of Sparks, Nevada. Since I don't want to run up my host's bill any more by raiding the minibar for hitchhiking water supplies, I walk to the nearest gas station, about ten minutes away: the longest I walked during this entire hitchhiking trip.

All that complimentary tea I drank in the hotel room this morning makes me have to pee again, so I ask for the men's room key—something that always makes me feel like more of a "porcelain pervert" than I actually am. I'm relieved to see the bathroom is a single, has a lock, and that no "payday" is awaiting me in the toilet. And good, there's graffiti, too. I stand and pee and read a few of them: "I'm so horny I could fuck the crack of dawn." "Here I sit brokenhearted, tried to shit but only farted." How original! Can't anybody come up with something new? Wait a minute, what's this little one, written between the tiles in tiny letters? "For a good time, call Delmont 775-208-0823." What the hell. I do. "Hey," answers Delmont in a vaguely friendly way after picking up the phone on the second ring. "Uh . . . hi," I stutter, suddenly realizing this Delmont is a real person. "I'm calling about your . . . ad. I was hitchhiking through town and—" "Finally," sighs Delmont, cutting me off midsentence. "It's about time! I've had that little notice up for two years and no one has *ever* called me. I've been sitting here waiting!" "Well, maybe you weren't home when they called," I offer up weakly, embarrassed that I am the only one desperate enough to give him a try. "True," he says with a self-deprecating chuckle, "I'm on the road a lot, but I have an answering machine and I always check it. Nobody ever left me a message."

Suddenly all business, he quizzes me. "So how old are you?" "Sixty-six," I answer, expecting to hear a click and a dial tone. "Cool!" he says with a suddenly sexy voice. "I like old guys." "You do?" I ask in surprise. "Yeah. Go ahead and ask me what turns me on," he replies. But before I can do so, he boasts, "I'll tell you. I like crow's-feet, some wrinkles, receding hairlines." "So how old are *you*?" I ask, dreading the answer. "Twenty-eight," he says proudly. Jesus Christ, I could be his *grandfather*, I think. Does anybody have "grandfather issues"? If this is a type, it's new to me. There's not even gay slang for this kink. I've heard of Daddyhunt.com, but Granddaddyhunt.com? Come on! "I live with my dad *and* my grandfather," he volunteers, instantly blowing my sexually neurotic suspicions, "and I love them both, but I have to travel for work." "What kind of work do you do?" I pry, feeling like a contestant on a salacious dating reality TV show. "I sell knives door-to-door," he answers as if that is the most normal job in the world. "What kind of knives?" I stammer, flashing back to spinning on that wheel in Buster's carnival. "You know, butcher knives, carving knives, cleavers. Everybody has knives," he boasts like the great salesman he is. "Hey, look," he suddenly cuts to the chase, "you all talk or do you want to hook up?" "Uh . . . sure," I gulp, amazed I'm going this far. "You still in the filling station?" he asks. "Yes, I'm in the bathroom," I admit as I hear another customer politely rapping on the door to see if the men's room is in use. "I'll pick you up," he announces, seemingly in a rush. "I've got a '75 Chevy Chevelle, puke green. Just stand out front—I'll be there in ten minutes." Click.

"Christ, now what have I gotten myself into?" I mutter as I exit the bathroom, avoiding eye contact with the middle-aged preppy guy who lets me pass, probably worried just as I was that an unflushed turd awaits him in the toilet on the other side of the door. I stand out front, but it sure doesn't take him ten minutes. Delmont pulls up almost immediately. He is incredibly handsome but, I can tell, doesn't realize it himself. Gap between his two front teeth. Skinny. Long hair—the kind that even looks good dirty. Black Levi's, Beatle boots, motorcycle belt turned sideways so the belt buckle is forty-five degrees to the left, and a commie-style blue work shirt—the kind I haven't seen since the hippie days. "Get your ass in here," he says with a smile that makes me believe he doesn't recognize me as that other John Waters person.

"Damn, you look good!" he says with a happy leer and, as far as I can tell, no irony. "I'm John. John Waters," I offer. "And I'm Delmont Perkins," he says before leaning over and completely unnerving me by kissing me on the mouth. For a long time. We pull off; I am rattled but he seems happy. "So where you hitching to?" he asks as if he doesn't have a care in the world. "San Francisco," I say, realizing I'm still about three or four hours away. "I'll take you," he says without giving it another thought. "You're kidding!" I blurt, not believing my good luck. "Sure I will, as long as you don't mind me selling some cutlery on the way—I can live anywhere as long as I got my knives," he answers with confidence. "Fine with me," I say, remembering fondly to myself that little-known horror movie *Door-to-Door Maniac*, starring Johnny Cash.

Delmont pulls over at the first rest area we see and I think he needs to use the restroom, but no. He immediately opens the trunk and pulls out a custom-made briefcase and approaches a frazzled-looking woman getting out of her car in the parking lot. "Excuse me, ma'am," he says with an easygoing charm that is already winning my heart, "you need any kitchen knives?" She freezes for a second, but his sexy smile inspires trust. "What kind you got?" she answers, much to my amazement. Just like the Egg Man in *Pink Flamingos*, Delmont opens his display kit and shows off a whole range of "the world's finest cutlery," encased dramatically in red velvet. "Who says you can't have a love affair with a knife?" he asks, pulling out a "trimmer" and flicking the jagged edge with his finger, drawing a tiny drop of blood. "Cuts through a tomato like butter," he announces like the connoisseur he is, and lo and behold, she buys it. I'm impressed!

"See?" he says as he jumps back in the front seat and leans over and gives me another kiss, this one longer and deeper. "Damn! I love kissing you," he says, and grins as we pull off and I try to believe my romantic luck. "Kissing is what makes you a good queer," Delmont announces as if he's discussing a scientific experiment. We don't drive for long. He pulls over his Chevy to the side of the road and switches on the radio. Wouldn't you know it? "Hitchhiker" by Bobby Curtola is playing. I've only heard the song once or twice in the past, but suddenly the lyric about a hitchhiker on the road to love takes on new meaning. We make out for about twenty minutes.

I look up and see a fucking cop approaching the driver's side of the car. I didn't even notice the police car pull over! Who would, necking with such a cool guy as Delmont? "Jesus, the cops," I mutter in panic, but Delmont just smiles in confidence. "Don't worry," he whispers, "watch me. I'm gonna sell him a knife."

"License and registration," the cop barks as he looks down into the car. I pray he doesn't notice our obvious arousal. "Sure," says Delmont. "Hey, Officer, you interested in bringing home your little woman a nice present tonight?" "What d'you mean, boy?" the cop snarls while checking the valid ID, thinking at first Delmont is trying to bribe him. "It's just that I sell knives for a living and we're having a sale this week." "Yeah?" I hear the suddenly interested cop answer as Delmont starts to get out of the car to get his kit out of the trunk. "Stay in your vehicle!" the officer shouts, pulling his gun in a moment of panic. "Okay, okay," Delmont laughs, his hands in the air, "but I can't show you my wares without getting out the samples." "All right," I hear the cop mutter, calming down, "but never leave your vehicle when the police stop you without the officer's permission." "Yes, sir," agrees Delmont as he opens the trunk and starts his sales spiel. "We got twelve-inch, eight-inch, double-serrated—the kitchen knife of your wife's dreams," Delmont boasts as he opens up his kit, grabs a butcher knife from inside, and *whack! whack! whack!* dices an empty paper-towel roll like an onion on the floor of his car's trunk. "How much?" the cop asks, impressed, as he hands Delmont back his license and registration. "Two-for-one sale," Delmont hawks with pride as he sits back down in the car with the door open. "Butcher and paring knife," he offers, "one day only! Sale price $59.95." "You take credit cards?" our burly officer asks, giving me a disinterested once-over as he pulls out his wallet. "Sure do," says Delmont as he whips out a portable credit-card terminal and swipes the cop's MasterCard through without a hitch. "Drive safely, lover boys," the cop says with sudden goodwill before he strolls back to his vehicle, happily thinking of all the action he's got ahead of him once the wife gets a load of these brand-new classic kitchen knives.

"So what do you do?" Delmont asks nonchalantly as he pulls back on the road and turns on his homemade mix tape featuring "Bumming Around," by Jimmy Dean. "Not that I care," he adds over the perfect lyrics we could apply to our budding romance. "I'd like you even if you were unemployed," he chuckles before giving me a wink. "Uh . . . I've made movies," I finally admit with a tinge of dread. "Ahhhh . . . I hate movies," he reluctantly confesses while I sigh in relief. "Overpriced tickets, fake stories, and those movie stars—no one's that cute in real life." "Well, you are," I exclaim with honesty, then terror, realizing the most frightening thing of all: Delmont would be the perfect boyfriend.

"So can I live with you?" he asks with sudden ease and little fear of rejection. "Sure," I say, not believing I am agreeing to anything so preposterous. "I mean not all the time . . . ," he explains, "I gotta be on the road traveling and you'll be in Hollywood being Mr. Fancy Pants, I guess." "No!" I wail. "I don't live in L.A. I live in Baltimore and New York and San Francisco and Provincetown." "Can I 'Occupy Waters' then?" he asks, seemingly unimpressed. I'm not sure how to react. "I'll chip in," he offers; "knives don't pay as well as movies, but I'm no freeloader. I'll buy the food, pay all the gas and electric bills, and contribute more money at Christmas when knife sales go through the roof. Sound fair?" Well, how's that for a prenup? I think, amazed. "It's a deal," I say with the dreaded combination of affection and lust pounding through my veins.

Delmont pulls up to my apartment building in San Francisco, and the doorman comes out to help us unload our few belongings. He's not used to seeing me arrive with a boyfriend of any kind, but I introduce him fearlessly and Delmont shakes his hand. We glide through the lobby in confidence and board the elevator up to our crazy new life together.

Once inside my apartment, Delmont lets out a whistle of approval, looks out at the view of all San Francisco below from my living room window, kisses me again, and then takes off his clothes and hops in the shower. I take off my clothes, too, but give him his privacy. I hear the shower go off, but Delmont is still singing the Marvin Gaye version of "Hitch Hike" as he dries off. The first song I heard on this trip and now the last. Amazing! He steps out of the bathroom naked and sees me. "Mmmm . . . you look great," he whispers sexily in fully developed gerontophilia. "Come and get it." Oh my God, I'm in love.

THE WORST THAT COULD HAPPEN

ANOTHER NOVELLA

BAD RIDE NUMBER ONE

STEW

Of course, it could all go bad. Really bad. Rewind. Start over. Think negatively.

I walk out of my house before Susan and Trish come to work. Naturally, it starts to drizzle, but I've worked up the nerve to actually leave, so I can't chicken out just because it's raining. I feel like a complete fool and try to hide my homemade signs until I at least get to the corner where I plan to begin to hitchhike. Wouldn't you know it? Who's the first to drive by but the headmaster of the nearby private school with whom I am always battling (often in the press) because of their aggressive and, in my opinion, privileged expansion plans. "Where are you going?" he asks as he slows down and pretends to be neighborly. "Oh, just on vacation," I offer, thinking what a mistake that was for me to let him know I'll be out of town so now he can start their newest construction noise even earlier in the morning because he's certain I won't be around to hear *or* complain. "You're hitch-hiking!?" he hoots, forgetting his good manners. I just keep walking, but I hear his laughter as he pulls off in the comfort of his late-model car. What do I care? I'm on an adventure and he's going to work.

I stand at my corner and stick out my thumb. "Faggot!" someone yells, and I pretend that this isn't a bad sign. I wait a long time. No one picks me up—even when the cars are stopped at the red light. They plainly see me. The ones that do recognize me laugh in my face, and the ones that don't, lock their doors. One contemptuous man is staring at me from his vehicle in hatred and mouths "Fuck you" before peeling off. Another woman says right to my face, "I hate your movies," and then, when she pulls off, swerves over and tries to hit me. Another driver finally stops after passing me by and I run up to the car, carrying my bag, which seems already too heavy, but when I get to the passenger door, he gives me the finger and accelerates. It starts pouring. I take out my newly purchased poncho and put it on, but since it's orange, drivers assume I'm a construction worker doing road maintenance and angrily curse the imagined rush-hour delays. Hours pass; I can't believe no one is picking me up! It's still raining. Maybe I'll wait until tomorrow when the weather's better, I think. You coward, my inner devil's advocate argues back. Suddenly a bus swerves over to the slow lane to pass a car turning left and splashes a river of rainwater over my entire hitchhiking self. I am drenched. Fuck this, I think, and give up for the day. I walk the two blocks home with my tail between my legs.

All my staff bursts into hysterical laughter when they see me walk through the front door looking like a drowned rat. "Real funny!" I yell, pissed. "If I have to give back the book advance, how will I pay you?" I go upstairs, slam my bedroom door, and dry off. What a terrible idea I've come up with, and now I can't get out of it.

The next morning, I sneak out before dawn. At least it's not raining. It's unseasonably cold, but I can't expect our weather research across the nation to be perfect even if it was based on average temperatures for the second week of May. Once again I'm at the light. "You just want attention, don't you?" hisses a woman, who I can tell is debating going through the light just to avoid me. Trying to be friendly, I smile and say, "There's a gas crisis—I'm being green," but she pretends not to hear. "I'm sick of reading about you in the newspapers!" she snarls, and pulls off the second the light changes.

Finally, a car stops and I rush to get in. By now, I'd accept a ride from Freddy Krueger. But no, this guy is a different kind of horror. I can smell liquor immediately when I get in the car. Old sub wrappers are on the floor, mixed in with empty half-pint bottles of whiskey. The air conditioner is on so high that I can see my breath when I open my mouth to thank him for picking me up. He slurs his name, "Stew," when he introduces himself and pulls out in traffic without turning on his blinker once I tell him I'm headed to I-70 West. "There Stands the Glass" by Webb Pierce, one of the most god-awful country songs about liquor, comes on the radio, or at least I *think* it is on the radio until I see Stew is playing a homemade CD of this dreadful song over and over.

"Where are the seat belts?" I cry in nervousness after fumbling around both sides of the passenger seat. "I cut them out," he admits with a boozy laugh. "I hate those things. How am I supposed to mix drinks all strapped up?" I realize quickly that Ride Number One is not only an asshole but probably driving with a revoked license. "I've got eleven DUIs," he brags, "but fuck 'em." "Look ahead," I plead, realizing he's had his eyes off the road for quite some time. "Oh, don't you worry," he lectures, wagging his fingers as he careens onto the entrance ramp of the Baltimore Beltway, "I drive good when I'm drunk! Those Mothers Against Drunk Drivers bitches make *me* mad! M-A-D mad!" he adds, and bursts into plastered laughter at his bad joke.

It starts raining again. I'm immediately concerned that Stew makes no move to turn on the windshield wipers. He unscrews the cap of another half-pint of hooch and chugalugs it down. "Goddammit," he curses as he frantically tries to wipe away the condensation building on the inside of the windshield. "Can you see on your side?" he asks with anger. "No!" I scream. "Turn on the wipers!" "Ahhh, those pieces of shit don't work!" he snarls. "Well, stop then," I beg, "just pull over. Please! It's dangerous!" A truck passes, splattering even more water on the windshield, but Stew seems unperturbed. He takes out his cell phone and starts texting out loud, "O-F-F T-H-E W-A-G-O-N," as he drunkenly tries to type the letters on his keyboard before turning to me and hatefully admitting, "That's to my sponsor—that dumb turd—he thinks he's better than me." "You're gonna kill us!" I shout, lurching toward the dashboard controls, trying to figure out how to turn on the defroster. Stew throws down his phone in fury and starts flicking the switch to the wipers on and off, and for a few seconds they actually work. Just in time for me to see him mow down a small dog that is running across the highway. "Watch out!!" I scream, but it's too late. For such a small animal, I'm amazed at the loud thump it makes as it is crushed and sucked up under the axle of Stew's car. "Stop!" I yell in a panic. "Let me out, you're drunk."

Stew just laughs and holds out the bottle, offering me a slug. "No," I protest. "At least let me drive!" But before he can answer I see he has veered off Route 70 toward Cumberland. "Hey, I thought you were going to West Virginia," I scream in alarm. "I don't know where the hell I'm going," he mutters in alcoholic distress. I grab the wheel just in time and force him to swerve around a parked car he is headed straight for, pulled over on the side of the road. He slams on the brakes and my head hits the dashboard. Luckily the air bags don't go off. I guess they're broken, too.

Suddenly Stew pulls a handgun from under his seat and I freeze. But it's not me he's threatening; it's the "nosy bastard" authorities from his past that have tried to "interfere" with his "joy of drinking." "Goddamn judges," rages Stew in torment as he fires a round of bullets out the window. "Put the gun down, Stew," I say in the most evenhanded voice I can muster. "Fuck AA!" he shouts for the world to hear. "Bill W., I'll blow your brains out, too!" he threatens the long-dead founder of Alcoholics Anonymous. Before I can even attempt to pull the gun away, Stew gets a stunned look on his face and then projectile-vomits. I grab the wheel, he grabs it back. The stench of his puke covering his side of the windshield seems to give him no pause. Still retching as he drives and braking erratically, he slows down as he unsuccessfully attempts to wipe away his own bile with one of the many brown-paper bags that litter his car. I gotta get out of here. I open the door halfway and see the gravel beside the road whizzing by. I look back at Stew and he grabs my travel bag away from me and pukes again. I jump out anyway and land painfully on the side of the highway but manage to roll just as I've seen stuntmen do on movie sets.

Stew keeps going. My jacket is ripped and my pants are shredded on one knee, which I see is bleeding. I don't think I broke any bones, though. At least I'm alive. Off-route already. Now with no luggage. Still in fucking Maryland.

BAD RIDE NUMBER TWO

ADAM

I pull up my pant leg and see I'm really scraped up. I limp up the road and can feel the stinging on the side of my face from hitting the gravel. I see a car coming and I stick out my thumb, but even that hurts because my shoulder feels pulled from its socket. Where are my fans when I need them? A fairly new Nissan Sentra passes by and I glimpse the driver do a double take and then slam on the brakes. I hobble up to the vehicle like that character Chester in *Gunsmoke*. I look inside and see a harmless-enough-looking overweight nerdy kind of guy behind the wheel. A real *Confederacy of Dunces* type.

"Taffy Davenport!" he yells, and it only takes me a second to realize he's reciting dialogue from one of my movies. "Thanks for stopping," I say, jumping in and happily buckling my seat belt to the sound of "Hitchin' and Hikin'" by Johnny Sea, playing on his CD player. Great. A country song that laments a failed hitchhiking journey. Just what I *don't* feel like singing along with. "There's just two kinds of people, Miss Sandstone, my kind of people and assholes," he answers, mimicking Mink Stole's delivery from *Pink Flamingos*. "Can you just take me somewhere near

I-70 West?" I beg. "Oh, meeting someone? *Who?!*" he answers in a faux rage, repeating another line from my movie so obscure that even I can't place it at first. "Okay," I answer, realizing this fan won't quit, "just let me off somewhere going west." "Going to a gang bang or something?" he responds, this time channeling David Lochary. "No, just a road trip," I answer, refusing to play along with his little dialogue game. I mean, I'm flattered he knows the lines that well, but jeez, give it a break. "We were just wondering," he continues in character, "where you were planning to spread your VD today? That's all—hussy." He shrieks with laughter and I just sit there in stupefied silence. My cheek hurts. I pull his rearview mirror over and see the bruising already coloring one side of my face. "Beauty, beauty, look at you," he mumbles just as Paul Swift did, fumbling his lines in *Female Trouble*, "I wish to God I had it, too!" He sees me wince in pain at the cut on my leg and switches to a whole other monologue. "I love the taste of it!" he rants like Divine. "The taste of hot, freshly killed blood!" Suddenly he grabs back the mirror to his side of the car and takes an exit I'm sure I don't want. "Hey," I yell, "I told you I need to go west!" "You know I hate nature," he answers, again switching film references, this time to *Desperate Living*. "Look at those disgusting trees," he quotes Mink Stole's character, Peggy Gravel, "stealing my oxygen!" "Let me off," I shout in panic, but he just speeds up. "All natural forests should be turned into housing developments!" he screeches, still in Mink mode, as he swerves into a driveway of a suburban house and slams on the brakes. "I wish I could stuff my whole head in your mouth and let you suck out my eyeballs!" he growls in a piss-poor imitation of Turkey Joe's line in *Desperate Living*, dialogue that I *used* to be proud of and now curse the day I wrote it.

"*John Waters!*" screams a frightening-looking woman way too large and old to be wearing the tube top she's featuring—also too early in the season, in my humble fashion opinion. She comes charging down the front path. I freeze. My "biggest fan" leaps out of the car and falls to his knees in front of this lady, who seems used to this role-playing behavior. "Oh, Mother, it's me, Divine," he cries. "I was just humiliated in front of the media!" Wait, I think, that's not a line from any of my movies! But just before I can nail him on his mistake, I realize, yes, it is! It's from the sequel to *Pink Flamingos—Flamingos Forever,* which was never shot; only the script was published in book form. To be honest, I could have found him a funnier line, but this idiot isn't asking for direction.

"I knew you'd meet my son, Adam," Mom yells as she grabs me in a bear hug. So that's his name! Adam. Good. I'll remember it for the restraining order if I can ever break away from this insane woman, who is smashing her large breasts into my chest before planting a disgusting kiss on my lips. "Good morning, Francine, you've put on another twenty pounds," she screams to Adam, also channeling dialogue from my films, but moving on to one of my more mainstream efforts, *Polyester.* "My own mother's insane!" roars the son, reverting back to one of Mink Stole's shrill lines from *Female Trouble.*

"Adam's perfect for your movies," shouts the now belligerent stage mother. "Let him audition!" she begs, and I am at last relieved to see she is talking in a nondialogue way. "Send a résumé in to Pat Moran," I respond as always, "she casts all my movies. Don't call her—she hates that," I add, trying to protect her from nutcases just like these two. "Do 'Gator,'" orders the mom to her son, completely ignoring my professional advice. "Hey, Taffy, come suck your daddy's dick," he shrieks, obviously unembarrassed to repeat X-rated dialogue in front of his mother. "'Queen Carlotta,'" she orders with excitement, like some kind of agent from hell. "Seize him and fuck him," he shouts in Edith

Massey's nasal voice, without the slightest trace of tiring of this tedious routine.

"He'll blow you, too, if that's what you want," offers up Mom without batting an eye. "Right, Adam?" she asks her son with a grin before turning back to me and explaining, "He's got nothing against the casting couch if that's what it takes." "Whip it out and show it hard," he wails, continuing on as Queen Carlotta. "Come on, Daddy, fuck me! Don't bother with the head! The V of my crotch is what needs attention." I wrote this? I wonder in horror. Then I run.

Even that doesn't stop them. "Run, you bastard, run!" the mother screams, imitating another obscure line Divine used to threaten a mailman who just delivered her a gift-wrapped turd for her birthday in *Pink Flamingos*. "Pig fucker!" Adam bellows for the world to hear, obviously not caring that the neighbors would have no clue as to why he is shouting obscene dialogue to his mother on their front lawn. "Lick my royal hemorrhoids," I suddenly yell back, finally driven to such distraction that I am reduced to searching my own inventory of filthy soliloquies to communicate with these fanatical idiots.

But that only seems to enrage Adam and encourage him and his mom to get violent. "Get him, Bonkers!" I hear Adam yell, quoting the name of the dog that commits suicide in *Polyester*. But *this* Bonkers ain't depressed; he's insane like the rest of his household. He comes tearing out the front door, teeth bared, charging right toward me. Despite my injuries I run for my life, and that *really* hurts. "We will outfilth the asshole or assholes who sent this and then *they must die!*" screams Mom, sounding somehow even more formidable than Divine did in *Pink Flamingos*. "You have exactly fifteen seconds to get off my property, motherfucker, before I break your neck," wails the son in a desperate bid for faux Dreamland Studios stardom. I painfully climb up the chain-link fence of another house, dive over to safety just in time to escape the dog, which is nipping and snarling at my heels, and feel my BlackBerry fall out of my back pocket and land in enemy territory. The dog barks in a rage and suddenly squats down and takes a shit on my phone. Adam and his fucking mom shout their approval.

BAD RIDE NUMBER THREE

FAYE

Hey, what's this? A car stopping for me and I haven't even stuck out my thumb? Could my hitchhike luck suddenly be changing? "Need a lift?" says the hard-as-nails-looking lady behind the wheel. "Sure," I yelp as I leap in and give the finger to Adam and his asshole mother as they watch in the distance, hopefully pissed that I got a ride so quickly.

"I'm Faye," my new ride announces with an assertiveness that somehow is a little off-putting. "I'm John and I'm going all the way to San Francisco," I say, trying to be as friendly as possible without staring at the huge legs she is showing off in a miniskirt. The top of her body seems like another person's: flat chest, normal hips, and a hint of turkey neck. But those legs! God, R. Crumb would love her to wrap these gams around his neck in sexual dominance. "Why're you going there?" she asks in horror. "I have an apartment in San Francisco," I volunteer. "So then why are you hitchhiking, stupid? Why didn't you fly?!" I ignore the word *stupid* and pretend I'm having a conversation with a normal person. "I just wanted to see what America looked like on the ground," I converse in the friendliest tone I can. "I hate

San Francisco," she mutters, ignoring my response, "all those stupid hills! No, siree, I'm not going there! I got everything I need in Kentucky!" Sensing another argument, I don't quiz her about what those exact needs are.

"Ever fuck a junkie?" she suddenly asks in the most nonchalant way possible. "What?" I say, giving myself time to comprehend her intrusive question. "You heard me. Did you ever fuck a junkie?" "Well . . . not knowingly," I answer, trying to be truthful. "Why not? I love junkies," she says with sexual militancy. "Aren't you worried about hep C?" I stammer. "THAT PISSES ME OFF!" she yells. "Well, I'm just talking about how hepatitis is often spread through unclean needles," I mumble. "You just judged an entire cross section of a sexual minority," she challenges me with new hostility. "But I thought junkies couldn't get it up," I weakly argue. "Some people," she boasts, jabbing her thumb to her chest, "LIKE a limp dick!" "And you have the right to your desires," I timidly agree, praying she'll change the subject, but oh no, she's on a tear.

"Are you a fag?" she suddenly demands. "Well . . . yes . . . ," I admit. "That's what I thought!" she spits out with a condescending sneer. "It pisses me off," she continues ranting. "Fags can 'come out' but others can't be 'strung out'? Is that it? Something wrong with 'smack in the sack'? You people can bitch but we can't itch?" "Of course you can," I stutter before she cuts me off with "You homos should understand there's such a thing as a 'scag hag.'" "A scag hag!?" I repeat out loud, thankful, as always, to hear of a new sexual minority. "You heard me!" she rages. "Don't needle tracks make you whack?" she continues with sloganeering confrontation. "Not really," I admit in an understanding liberal voice. "Why not?" she challenges back. "Doesn't a stiff rod on the nod make you shoot your wad?" "No," I argue; "besides, junkies don't even *like* sex." "There you go," she screams, "penile profiling just like the rest of you bum bandits!" "Hey, wait a minute," I protest, finally hearing enough and deciding to give Faye a little of her own medicine. "I just was unaware there was 'hot muff for hard stuff,'" I say, hoping my new pro-scag-hag motto will lighten her mood. "That's a good one!" she laughs. I'm relieved. For a moment.

"Wanna see the pussy that's driven a thousand junkies crazy?" she suddenly asks with a newfound hostility. "Well, no, I don't," I answer truthfully. "It's nothing personal. You're a lovely woman," I lie, "and I'm very thankful you stopped to give me a lift, but it's a little late in my life for me to 'come in.'" I hope my little joke will take away the sting of my rejection, but it backfires. "You're prejudiced against me because junkies don't have the hots for *you!*" she challenges, inching up her skirt with an antagonistic exhibitionism and hitting play on her CD player. "Please cover up," I beg as I actually hear a cut from one of the world's worst gospel albums, *The Addicts Sing*, and see the freshly shaved V of her crotch. "I love women, it's just that I'm not sexually attracted to them," I explain over the tortured, clean-and-sober vocals of "You Are the Finger of God." "Oh, it's good enough for every junkie in the best recovery houses up and down the Eastern Seaboard, but it's not good enough for you?" she seethes. "Get it or get out!" I look out the window and see the sun is going down. It's night and there's not even a house in sight. I look back at her bald mons pubis. Sophie's choice. "I'll get out," I say with newfound clarity. *"Fine!"* she snarls, not even bothering to cover herself. "Faye's way or the highway!" she declares, screeching over to the side of the road and slamming on the brakes. "Beat it, Mary," she yells, and I do, happily. She peels out, spraying my already cut and bleeding body with gravel. I can still hear the Addicts' awful music blaring as her taillights fade in the distance.

It's suddenly dark. Cars fly by and the drivers don't even look over to consider picking me up. I'm not even back on Interstate 70 yet and I'm completely exhausted. Some of the scabs from my earlier injuries have now stuck painfully to the fabric of my jeans, and every movement prevents their fragile healing. The moon's not even out! It's already come to my worst nightmare; I have to sleep out in the open. With no clean clothes for tomorrow. No phone. Like a bum.

I climb down a slope into a sorry little cluster of trees. Scenic it's not. I'm lucky enough to discover a discarded take-out bag filled with the spoiled leftovers from a Chinese dinner. I realize I'm starving! I haven't eaten all day. I dig into the carton of soggy white rice and rip open the only plastic packet of soy sauce left and mix them together. Someone's picked a few red-hot Szechuan peppers out of their kung pao chicken and I gobble them down and try to ignore the burning in my throat. I blot my tongue with a stale fortune cookie and pretend I'm full.

It's suddenly freezing but I try to make do. I curl up in a ball and crumple up the carryout trash and use it as a pillow. Just as I'm about to doze off, I realize I have to take a shit. God, how I hate the human body. I so resent that I have to defecate daily. I didn't even get to think up this disgusting little act and now I have no choice. Just do it, I tell myself, praying there's enough foliage around to use as toilet paper. It's hard to shit outside. You have to remove both your jeans *and* your underpants. I begin. Suddenly I hear a rustling nearby and then an ungodly animal noise. I grope to find leaves but I can't, so in a panic I use a flattened rice container as toilet paper. Before I can be sure I'm clean, something lunges at me and I can feel sharp teeth biting into my ass. I scream, but of course there's no one around to hear me. I grab at the creature and still with no pants on roll around, battling for my life. For a split second, I see the face of a raccoon, and it's got some kind of hideous yellowish foam around its mouth. Adrenaline pumps through my system. I grab the wild animal and with both hands begin to strangle it. The raccoon struggles back, biting my hands, spewing rabid saliva all over my face, but once I get it by the throat and start squeezing, I can feel that victory could be mine. I choke even harder and finally the diseased creature lets out a terrible-sounding death rattle before going limp in my bloody hands. I struggle to put on my pants and run up to the highway and begin waving my hands to oncoming traffic much as Marilyn Burns did at the end of *The Texas Chainsaw Massacre*.

BAD RIDE NUMBER FOUR

PAULA

Finally my luck must be changing, because though it's the middle of the night, a car stops. I limp to the passenger side and look in, praying for a friendly face. I don't get one. I see a harsh-looking woman behind the wheel, wearing an expression of great hostility. "Get in," she says in a flat, emotionless tone. I look in the backseat and see one of the most frightening drag queens on earth—one that couldn't "pass" as a woman even to Stevie Wonder or the late Ray Charles. She has a large bouffant hairdo, stenciled eyebrows, and a face full of wrinkles. Her looks could stop a train. "I'm her mother," she says in a man's voice, not even trying to assume any kind of femininity. I shudder. "We're going to Indianapolis," the woman in the front barks in an impatient tone. I hesitate. "And we're in a hurry," adds the horror in back, looking as mean as can be. I look out at the road in the darkness and don't see a headlight anywhere in the distance in either direction. What the hell? I'm street-smart; I can talk my way out of anything.

I get in and put on my seat belt. For the first time I see the woman in front smile, but it's the smile of a snake. "I'm Paula," she says with a new glare of malice, "and *that* is my mother." "Nice to meet you," says the obvious man, holding out a long, veiny hand with chipped nails painted an especially hideous shade of purple to match the lipstick that has been applied with great care. "I see you got a cut there," Paula announces with little sympathy. "Yes, I had a very bad ride and then I was attacked by a wild animal," I try to explain. Both Paula and her "mother" break into hysterical laughter. Oh, great, a new set of loonies. I look straight ahead and we drive. Every once in a while Mom starts cackling and Paula loses it and joins in. "What's so funny?" I ask, unable to hide my discomfort.

"I guess I'm the one that should be asking that, aren't I?" Paula suddenly snaps with a new combativeness. "Hallelujah!" adds Mom. "What do you mean?" I stammer. "We know who you are, asshole," Paula snarls. "Yeah, Mr. *Shock Value*," snarls her supposed mother, mentioning the name of my first book. "How did you know I'd be here?" I wonder out loud. "One of your shit-head fans has been tweeting his butt off about you hitchhiking and how he spent quality time with you." "Facebook, too," pipes in the hag in the back. "You think other people's nightmares are funny, don't you?!" Paula growls accusingly. "Huh?" I ask, completely confused, but then add nervously, "No, I don't. I think I've tried to have compassion for both the crime victim *and* the criminal," I sputter, wondering which of the cases I've written about has so offended them. "It wasn't my fault," growls the cross-dressing man in the back, whose hostile face is made even more grotesque by the elaborate and out-of-fashion hairdo he's wearing. "I was addicted to speed," adds this monstrous mother, "and my children were just trying to help!" "Yet you think it's fucking funny," spits out Paula with a vengeance. "I went to jail and you had a party!" "A party? What party?" I panic, thinking how this deadly duo must have me mixed up with somebody else. "That little bitch thought she was better than us!" hisses Paula.

"When her own parents ran off with the carnival and dumped her with me!" adds the skinny battle-ax. "It was for her own goddamn good!" hisses Paula with a sadistic smile. "That's right," adds the gaunt drag monstrosity no politically correct pronoun would ever adequately describe, "to teach her a lesson!"

Suddenly these words hit me like a ton of bricks and I turn around in my seat. "Gertrude Baniszewski?" I scream in terror. The Indianapolis single mother who, with the help of her children and their neighborhood friends, tortured and finally murdered Sylvia Likens, a foster child they had taken in? "That's her," snaps Paula, "and I'm her daughter!" Oh God, Gertie's child, all grown up but still scary—the one that escaped from prison twice but still only served two years for her part in the grisly torture slaying. "But Gertie is dead," I cry, knowing the infamous Indianapolis killer died from lung cancer in 1990, having being paroled after serving fourteen years of a life sentence and then living quietly in Iowa under the name Nadine Van Fossan. "Do I look dead?" Gertie Jr. yells with a vengeance, and I see her coming at me with some sort of wire she wraps around my neck. Paula starts chanting evilly, "To teach her a lesson. To teach her a lesson," in obvious tribute to her mother's pitiful legal defense against the charges of this terrible crime, and as I fight, I feel a rag go over my nose with some sort of awful chemical smell. The last thing I remember hearing is both of these freaks chanting a new, terrifying premeditated cry of revenge: "To teach *him* a lesson! To teach *him* a lesson!"

I awake in a basement room. Oh God, *the basement*! The name of that amazing book by Kate Millett that was subtitled *Meditations on a Human Sacrifice*. The same room in the house where Gertie, her kids, and the neighborhood delinquents did their dirty deed in 1965. I'm tied to a table. As my field of vision comes into focus, I see Paula coming at me, holding a chipped dinner plate. "Want some crackers?" she growls, offering me some crushed-up Ritz crumbs. When I shake my head no, she goes into a mini-tirade. "See," she grunts, "that's what we offered Sylvia but she wouldn't eat either, and *we* were the children who were hungry!" "Taking in other people's ironing," I hear the faux Gertie mumble before seeing her out of the corner of my eye. "That's what I had to do to get money to feed that brat!" she seethes. "I had asthma, too!" Before I can answer, she burns me with a lit cigarette. I howl in pain. "Think it's funny now?" spits out Paula. "No," I yell, fearful of what's next. "Maybe I'll get a portrait painted of *you*!" Gertie snarls with an overwrought vengeance as she burns me again right where I'm already scraped. "I didn't mean it," I argue, knowing what she is referring to—the hideous oil painting I had done of Gertie's mug shot and later published in *Shock Value*. "Yes, you meant it!" seethes Paula as she approaches and pours scalding water on me just as they did to Sylvia. "Maybe we should bake a cake?" Paula sniggers as I scream in agony and remember the smart-ass refreshment I served at a book party I threw to privately celebrate Millett's shocking volume. The cake I had made by a bakery in Province-town with the terrible words in frosting on top that Gertie and gang carved into their victim's chest: I A-M A P-R-O-S-T-I-T-U-T-E A-N-D P-R-O-U-D O-F I-T. On the page, a sentence. On a chest, the most terrible novel ever written. "Let's put on *your* birthday message," growls the Gertie clone as she comes toward me with some sort of homemade tattoo gun made from a video gaming console with a large-size paper-clip needle attached. Paula rips open my shirt. "Please," I beg, "I was young. I didn't realize your circumstances. You were poor. You've served your time. It's all over now." "It's not over until Gertie has been avenged," this Halloween drag version of Indianapolis's scariest killer mother wails in my face as she brings the tattoo needle down on my skin. "I A-M . . . ," Paula begins spelling out their new terrible hate message, and I feel the agonizing pain of the unsafe ink pound-

ing into my skin with a vengeance. "A-N A-S-S-H-O-L-E,"
Gertie cackles with glee at her updated skin carving. Should I be
thankful that the word *asshole* has fewer letters than *prostitute*?
Through my screams at my punishment it's hard to feel grateful
for anything. ". . . A-N-D P-R-O-U-D . . . ," whispers Paula on
cue as Gertie inks away with practiced sadism before completing
the message they both are dying to see and say out loud: "O-F I-T."
Gertie hesitates, straightens her wig, and goes a step further
than the original. "To teach him a lesson," she mutters victoriously as she adds an exclamation point on my chest to this horrifying, infamous true-crime declaration. Paula lets out some
kind of war cry.

The pain is forcing me in and out of consciousness, and suddenly I realize they are taking me somewhere. I half walk, half
stumble up the stairs with my two captors hurrying me along,
paying no attention to my cries of alarm at the increased pain
and the liquid oozing out of my freak tattoo. I smell of burned
skin. At least I make it out of the basement alive, something
Sylvia Likens never did. It's light out. Christ, I've been impris-
oned overnight! They throw me in the back of the car and, without a word of where we are headed, peel out. "Torture" by the
Everly Brothers comes on some oldies station they are listening
to, and they shriek in harmony to the lyrics of emotional despair
but screech in laughter every time they get to the "Baby, you're
torturing me" chorus. Gertie *really* looks bad now, her five o'clock
shadow bursting through the Pan-Cake makeup like poison oak.
I can see that somehow she looks a little like Paula. Could it be
her brother?! Oh God, spare me that!

I have no idea where we are but I see signs that we are entering Indianapolis. Finally we pull up to a scruffy lot in a random
suburban neighborhood. I see a street sign reading "E. New York
Street" and my blood runs cold. That was the street Gertie's house
was on! I see a number: 3852. Oh my God, I remember now that

the murder house has been torn down, but this abandoned, trash-filled piece of earth must have been 3850, the crime scene itself. Gertie II gets out, opens the back door, and pulls me out without the slightest concern over my injuries and throws me down in the dirt. Paula snarls a parting message in my ear: "Maybe you'll realize now that we're a real family," and gives me a swift kick in the leg before they both get back in their car and drive off, mission accomplished.

I lie there, happy to be alive at least. Suddenly I see other people milling about, a few taking photographs of this empty lot. At first I don't believe it, but, yes, these shutterbugs are true-crime buffs. I see somebody else dressed as Gertie, but this time it's the "young Gertie" and I can tell she's really a girl. Another is dressed like poor Sylvia, with those hideous words scratched above her midsection in obviously fake blood. The ingenue Gertie and the imitation Sylvia pose together for the other true-crime groupies. I vow to burn my Gertie portrait if I ever get out of this trip alive. I struggle to my feet. Gertie #3 sees me and yells out in hyperexcitement and disbelief, "John Waters!" I limp away as fast as I can.

BAD RIDE NUMBER FIVE

EUGENE

Great. I'm stuck inside city limits, the worst place to hitchhike. My cuts are sore and the new tattoo is going to get infected, I can tell. I should go to the police, but then what? There'd be big-time publicity and I could never continue the trip and there goes the whole deal. And besides, maybe I did deserve a *little* bit of punishment for that cake, but certainly not this! I look down at my chest and see that the yellow fluid oozing out has turned brown and the letters, especially the A and H of ASSHOLE, are starting to swell. I should go to the hospital, but then again, how do I explain this hideous epitaph scrawled on my chest? "Oh, this? I was just drunk!" I'm sure there are great plastic surgeons once I arrive safely in San Francisco who can help with laser-surgery tattoo removal, *if* I can just get there in one piece.

But nobody picks me up. I keep walking anyway because a few "Basement" buffs are still following me. I pose for cell phone pictures with a couple of them and that seems to do the trick. All except for one persistent African-American Gertie impostor (a man? a woman?) who won't leave me alone and wants to "come along." I try to explain that no one will stop to pick me up hitch-hiking with a Gertie look-alike, but she's persistent. Finally, I show her my chest, and while she thinks it's fake, she's still impressed. An exclusive shot of "Gertie" and me and my horrible new tattoo seems to satisfy her. She retreats happily, adding the photo from her cell phone to her *Basement Are Us* blog.

Just when I think I'm going to pass out, a car stops for me. I'm in luck, I think to myself once I get in the car and painfully put on my seat belt. "Eugene," as he introduces himself, looks like a hippie; he'll be gentle. No funny stuff with this guy. He explains he's going to St. Louis but will let me off at a rest area outside the city on I-70 so I'll have a better chance to get a ride farther west. He explains that he's a vegan and offers me something to eat. I am starved out of my mind. I don't have any food issues—I can eat anything. At least I thought I could. Eugene offers me a raw turnip, which, I guess, is better than nothing. He rants against the evils of any animal products and then continues on against "the criminality of force-feeding hospital patients and prisoners nonvegetarian meals." I agree—what else can I do?—and ask him for another turnip. "Hungry little muvva?" he asks good-naturedly, tossing me one. I notice he is eating what look to be hedge clippings, and when I ask him what he's having, he tells me they are exactly that. "There's free food everywhere!" he brags. "Just eat leaves . . . grass . . . the spirits give you nourishment—it's right before your eyes!" Before I follow up he takes out a baggie and sprinkles some kind of brown seasoning over his hedge salad. "What's that?" I ask, ever the foodie. "Dirt," he replies as if I'd just asked the dumbest question in the world. "You mean, like earth?" I ask, confused. "Well, yes . . . I call it land . . . sod . . . it's all delicious." I hold out my half-eaten raw turnip and he sprinkles a little of the "vegan spice" on it. No matter what he calls this seasoning, it still tastes like dirt to me, and this crust of the earth gets caught in my throat and I gag. "Here," he says, holding out a bottle of what I *thought* was lemonade. I take a big swig and spit it out immediately. The liquid tastes salty, spoiled, disgusting. "What the hell is that?" I demand in between dry-heaving. "Urine," he says matter-of-factly, "nothing better for you than drinking your own wee-wee." "But that's not *my* wee-wee," I sputter. "You're correct," he answers with pride, "it's mine." I retch. "I'm healthier than you," he says, shrugging without concern, "you should be thanking my bladder, not complaining."

I can't believe I just drank this hippie freak's piss. I continue to gag as he drives along, looking at me in food pity. "You poor thing," he tsks-tsks, "it's all those animal parts stuck in your veins that are making you sick. Bristle. You know what that is?" "No," I admit weakly. "That's stiff animal hair left over on pork product." Gag. "Don't be puking in my car," he warns, "and if you do, I would expect you to eat it back up. Consuming one's own vomit is a way to train your digestive system to reject animal-derived substances." "Please," I beg, "do you have anything a little less radical to eat?" He thinks a minute. "Sure, you like tofu?" "Yes!" I yell, practically salivating for something I've at least enjoyed in my culinary past. "Here you go," he offers, taking out a bowl made out of a recycled tin can, "it's raw. The way *tofu* should be eaten." I scarf it down.

He is listening to the ridiculously childish novelty tune "To-furky Song" by Joanie Leeds, but I can tell he sees no humor in the chorus: "Wobble wobble wobble, not gobble gobble gobble." What do I care? At least the recording covers up the sudden rumbling in my stomach. We continue to drive, and much to my humiliation I fart. Eugene looks over at me and says with a straight face, "Reject that suet!" "What is suet?" I ask, anything to divert my embarrassment. "The solid fat prepared from the kidneys of cattle," he deadpans. Suddenly a blast of shit fires in my pants without warning. The stench is overpowering. Oh God, I think, he's going to expect me to eat *this*!?

"That's what you get from eating meat!" he scolds with a savage new fanaticism. "I have food poisoning," I wail. "Why didn't you cook that tofu?" "Cooking is a violation of the natural order of food, you fool!" he lectures with an obnoxiously patronizing tone. "Please pull over," I plead. "Absolutely not," he answers. "You have to learn a lesson about excrement. Your bowels are sending you a vegan message." "No, they're not," I scream in mortification, "I have diarrhea! Please let me stop at a restroom." "I bet you have wiping issues," Eugene suddenly accuses me. "What are you talking about?" I argue in building delirium as another mudslide of shit blasts out and trickles down my pant leg. "You're nuts!" I yell. "I'm sick, pull over." "*I'm* nuts?" he barks. "Me? The healthiest man you've ever met? Do you know what I'm going to die from?" he rants like the fascist he is. "Nothing. That's what I'm going to die from. *Nothing!*"

With that, he veers off Route 70 and pulls into a family rest stop. McDonald's, Pizza Hut, the whole nightmare of fast food right before my eyes. He slams on the brakes and the scabs on my knees break apart, the seat belt cuts into my infected tattoo, and a final logjam of liquid turds detonates out back. "You were born under the astrological sign of Feces, meat pig, and you will die under that sign," Eugene spits out in final judgment. "Now excrete from my car!"

I do. I walk through the parking lot, and the whole world can see I have shit my pants. "Hey, shithead," some brat of a kid yells as both his parents hold their nose and laugh. I don't make eye contact, but just make a beeline for the men's room.

I walk through the packed food court, gagging and farting every time I see or smell food. Wouldn't you know it, the bathroom is crowded. All the stalls are filled. "Oh my God," some man mutters in disgust when he sees my sorry state of affairs. Out of the corners of my eyes, I notice men stopping in their tracks and then scattering in horror. Finally, a stall opens and a college-student type exiting makes direct eye contact with me. "John Waters?!" he cries in surprised happiness. "Yes . . . ," I stupidly answer, pushing past him and slamming the door shut behind me. "Oh my God!" I hear him yell to just about everybody. "Did you see that?! That was John Waters. I'm almost certain he has shit his pants!!" I hear grown men laugh in constipated smugness and digestive superiority.

I hang my jacket on the inside hook and plop my chafed ass down on the toilet, but there is nothing left to come out. I attempt to clean myself up. It was hard outside to take off both my underpants and pants, but here in a rest-area men's room it's downright scary. I'm sure bathroom users can *see* me bottomless through the cracks in the stall door. I roll up my disgusting boxer shorts to ditch upon leaving. I flush a couple of times and use the clean toilet water to wash out my pants. I'm on my hands and knees scrubbing the cloth with all my might. It's a good thing I wasn't wearing white jeans as I usually do in the summer. I flush over and over until someone yells, "You okay in there, buddy?" I freeze. "Yes, I'm fine," I lie, rinsing out my Levi's one last time and hoping they will dry quickly once I'm out in the sun.

Just as I turn around to face the daunting task of slipping into wet pants, I see a hand come over the top of the stall, quick as lightning, and grab my jacket. "Hey, fucker," I yell as I trip over my boots struggling to get one leg into my sopping jeans. "Stop! Thief!" I shout, but all I hear back is the footsteps of the running jacket-snatcher. "Someone just stole my coat!" I scream, but for once, the bathroom seems empty. I run out of the booth in my stocking feet, still zipping up my fly, but all I see is a father and son walking in, eyeing me with alarm. "Did you see somebody run out with my jacket?" I ask, completely beside myself. "How would I know what your jacket looks like?" the father asks with rude sarcasm. "Yeah, moron," spits out the kid to me as I stuff my feet into my unlaced hiking boots and race past them, depositing my diarrhea underpants in the trash can right in front of their suddenly scared-shitless eyes.

I run through the rest area with my laces flapping, tripping over them every few steps. "Thief!" I yell, but people look away and I don't see a security guard in sight. Once outside in the parking lot, I realize whoever swiped my jacket is long gone. No jacket. No bag. No phone. I'm really alone. In St. Louis, for shit's sake.

BAD RIDE NUMBER SIX

WOODY

At least there's an entrance ramp back onto I-70 West, my supposed lifeline for this misadventure. Maybe a freshly fed fat family from the food court will have mercy and pick me up. I stand with my thumb out for over two hours but I don't mind because I'm praying the wind is acting as a deodorizer of my fecal accident. Suddenly I spot a discarded can of Off! insect repellent in the weeds near where I'm standing. I leap over and grab it and spray it all over me. Off! is not a real deodorant but I've always loved the exclamation point included in the brand name, and besides, I don't have any toiletries left, this will have to do. Even the Maybelline eye pencil I keep in my sports-jacket pocket is now gone. I pick up a cigarette butt from the roadside gravel and without a mirror, from memory, try to shade in my graying signature facial hair. Who knows if I colored within the lines? For once, I *do* want to be recognized. I can use all the help my "look" can muster.

Naturally, the next ride's driver has no idea who I am but I learn way too much about him immediately, straining to hear his braggart opinions over the most obnoxious, screaming talk-radio shows that he violently changes back and forth by pushing the channel buttons so hard I'm amazed they don't break.

His name is Woody, and oh yeah, he smokes. Parliament filters. Four packs a day. "Filter, flavor, pack or box," he sings loudly, reminding me of the vintage ad campaign. The car stinks so bad of cigarette smoke that I'm at least sure he can't get a whiff of my rectal troubles. I used to be a heavy smoker, too— five packs of King Kools a day before I quit, so I can't be *too* judgmental. But still. He hot-boxes each cigarette right down to the recessed filter and then lights the next one straight from the butt before he flicks it out the window, possibly starting a forest fire. Thank God I gave up this filthy habit or I'd be dead by now.

"Want one?" he asks, holding out his pack with the Parliaments arranged temptingly like in the old magazine ads. "No, thank you, I quit," I politely declare. "Why would *anybody* quit smoking?" he rudely responds. "Because I don't want cancer," I answer smugly. "Don't you miss it?" he taunts, French-inhaling even more militantly than I did in those mock "No Smoking in This Theatre" announcements filmed for the Landmark Theatre chain.

Good God, I hate this guy, but at least we're covering some ground. We're already in Kansas when he tells me he hasn't been to sleep for thirty-eight hours. "Let me drive, then," I offer, trying not to sound too alarmed. But no, he wants to talk about my least favorite subject, sports. "You know about the baseball curse of the billy goat?" he quizzes me with a newfound urge to chatter. "No, I hate sports," I explain, but he acts as if he doesn't hear me. "It's true!" he shouts, blowing a big mouthful of Parliament smoke in my face, as if I'd argued his point. "In 1945, a Chicago Cubs fan—and I am *not* one of those twats," he rages, "wanted to bring some fucking billy goat to the World Series game." I feel like screaming. I am already so bored with this guy's dumb sports rap, but he doesn't pick up on my disinterest.

"Now, why did this cunt-licker bring a billy goat? I ask you," he demands. "I have no idea of what you're talking about," I try to explain. "Exactly!" he hollers. Exactly *what*, you fool? I shriek in my mind, looking out the window into the vast nothingness of Kansas wheat fields and debating which would be worse, being reincarnated as livestock or having to listen to this colossal blowhard?

"But rightfully so," he continues ranting, "the Wrigley stadium security squad wouldn't let him bring this stupid billy goat on the playing field, so what does this fucker do?" I refuse to participate in this meaningless conversation and instead concentrate on his burning cigarette in the ashtray. Would it hurt if I had just one? As long as it's not menthol? For old times' sake? I think of my now-gone file card in my jacket pocket— the one where I daily list my chores plus the number of days it's been since I last had a cigarette—3,426, if I remember correctly. Do I want to blow my near-ten-year nicotine sobriety and have to start over by quitting again and writing the number 1?

But who can think straight when asshole Woody is still raging? "This dickwad with the goat puts a curse on the Cubs!" he flares up. I grab a Parliament out of the box and light it in a desperate attempt to escape this maddeningly boring conversation. One drag and my head spins. I feel faint, like a teenage girl who has just lit up for the first time. NOOOOOO, I can feel my body yelling back at the first inhalation of cigarette smoke, but Woody's too self-absorbed to even notice. "This ballsack actually curses Wrigley Field," he continues, flying off the handle, "and you know what?" "What?" I finally stammer, between reckless drags of nicotine pulsating into my bloodstream and instantly turning me into a chain-smoker. "What? WHAT!!?" I yell again, grabbing the whole pack of Parliaments out of his hands and actually eating one right out of the box. Unlit. "That motherfucker's curse works!" Woody yells back, not at all troubled by my sobriety slippage. "And there's never been a World Series game played there again," Woody spews before suddenly swerving off the highway to a rest stop. "I gotta take a shit," he announces.

This is one of those unmanned rest stops. No food, no gas. Just a place to go to the bathroom. I notice there seem to be a lot of cars. Maybe too many. Woody charges inside but I linger, chain-smoking and stretching my aching limbs. I notice a man who appears to be jerking off in his parked car. I look away. I figure I might as well take a leak, since my food poisoning seems to have subsided. I go inside and immediately notice there is "activity." A full-scale "tearoom." I don't see Woody but I can hear him *still* talking to himself about sports in a stall between his repellent grunts of defecation. Every urinal has a man standing in front of it, so I wait nervously. I see other guys, some obviously gay, going in and out of the stalls zipping up or down, on the hunt. A guy turns away from the urinal and I see his erect penis is still out. He gives me a lecherous grin but I try to ignore him and take my place at one of the other urinals. The guy next to me—and he's not bad-looking, either—is shaking his semi-hard dick to finish up his last drops. I try not to look. I'm never piss shy, but suddenly I am.

I break away and burst into one of the stalls, and my legs hurt so much, I sit down on the toilet to piss. I don't care. I'm an injured homosexual. Suddenly I look up and see a big uncircumcised dick poking through a glory hole. I am shocked! It is broad daylight and we're in the middle of Kansas! Just as I jump up to flee, the door to my stall is kicked in and an undercover cop (one of the guys I saw cruising) breaks in and flashes his badge. "Vice Squad," he announces as he grabs my arm. Another cop stands on the toilet in the next booth and leans over. "You're under arrest," he warns me as he struggles to put his stiff dick back in his pants on the other side of the glory hole. "For what?" I plead to deaf ears as another cop (the cute one I saw shaking his dick at the urinal) rushes in from the front and, with the help of the first vice cop, handcuffs me. "Entrapment!" I yell as the other gay guys inside run from the restroom like roaches when the lights come on in a slum kitchen.

I see Woody outside, still motormouthing about sports to the driver of an undercover-cop vehicle who seems to be hanging on to his every word over the lyrics of "I'm a Lone Wolf" by Leon Payne blaring from the cop's radio. I used to love this song until I hear both Woody and the vice hog singing along mockingly to the lyrics "I'm footloose and I'm fancy-free, and strictly on the prowl." Woody looks over at me as if I were a stranger. "Them fruit-loops hate sports," Woody blithely informs his latest conversational victim; "serves them right!" The other undercover cop dragging me out agrees: "If they were just home watching the sports channels instead of sucking cock, they wouldn't be in all this trouble." The first outside cop shoves me down in the police-car cage just as in the arrests I've seen on the news. I debate telling the cop Woody's been driving without sleep for days but don't because, well . . . I'm from Baltimore. I'm no snitch.

We peel out and I don't believe my ears. We're in the middle of nowhere and this pig has the siren on. "Is that really necessary?" I ask, trying to be reasonable. "As necessary as protecting families who are trying to take a dump but can't because you Hoover-mouths have turned a clean rest area into a sex pit," he answers with a total lack of sympathy. "I didn't do one thing," I protest like Dawn Davenport. "It was you guys who had your dicks out!" "Everything you say," he recites from memory, "can and will be used against you in a court of law." Fuck. I'm going to jail. "Can I have a cigarette?" I plead, already jonesing in nicotine withdrawal. "Didn't you read the surgeon general's report?" the cop asks unsympathetically. "Smoking's bad for you. So think of the letter *M* and then think of the next two letters in the alphabet and apply them. *N-O* spells *no*! Does that answer your question?"

BAD RIDE NUMBER SEVEN

BUSTED IN KANSAS

"Sodomy is illegal in Kansas," the booking officer blithely tells me as he snaps the most unflattering mug shot of me possible on their outdated police camera inside the tiny Bunker Hill County Jail. "I wasn't committing sodomy," I shout. "I just stopped to use the bathroom!" "Yeah, yeah, yeah," he responds. "Look, we don't go for 'greedy bottoms' here in the Midwest." "Greedy bottoms!?" I yell in full horror. "I don't do that! I'm all about safe sex." "Safe sex is illegal sex here in the Midwest," my jailer announces with final authority.

I try to change tack: "Look, I'm famous, I made that movie *Hairspray*." "With John Travolta?" he smirks. "No, the first one," I try to explain, "with Divine." "Never heard of it, but that don't matter. I hate fag musicals, anyway." "Look, can I call a lawyer?" I ask, knowing I'm allowed one phone call. "No phone service at this little ol' jail. It's a historic place—mostly open for tourists." Before I can challenge the blatant disregard of my legal rights, he orders me to "strip down." "You're kidding," I sputter. "You heard me!" he barks. "Lose your laundry." As I slowly remove my clothes, he notices my cuts and bruises and, after seeing my hideous new tattoo, gives me a wolf whistle. I am completely mortified. I hear some hick announcer on the radio crackling in the background mention my name and I strain to listen. ". . . Mr. Waters, the sixty-six-year-old director of such Hollywood films as *Cry-Baby* and *Hairspray*, was arrested for public lewdness in a public men's room beside the highway in rural Kansas. His attorney had 'no comment' except that he was 'trying to confirm the truth of this breaking story.'" "Lift your nuts. Spread your ass cheeks," orders "Ilsa the He Wolf" of Kansas as I close my eyes, think of my PEN membership, and do as told. "Bend over," he growls. He takes *way* too long to look. I hear "Riot in Cell Block #9" by the Robins start to play on that same radio station, but the only riot "goin' on" here is inside my head. I stand back up in embarrassment and he jerks me around to face him. His breath smells like licorice plaque. "Next time," he snarls, "maybe you won't take the Hershey Highway when you visit our great state." Before I can answer, he buzzes open a gate and shoves me inside a cell. The only cell in the tiny little rural jail.

I've got a cell buddy. His name is Veneer and he's black and he's here for a sodomy charge, too, but unlike mine, he was home with his boyfriend and somebody reported "suspicion of fellatio," and these rotten cops spied through his window and busted him when he and his boyfriend were giving each other head in the privacy of their own home. "'Knob-Gobbler,'" the jailer introduces us, "this is 'Mattress Muncher.'" We look at each other with a shared hatred for this jerk.

"I'm just a normal queer," confides Veneer when we're alone. "Me, too," I say, sort of telling the truth. "Wait till you taste the food in this shithole," he warns. "Chipped beef. Rancid bologna. Mystery meat." We can hear the clinking of the jailer's keys, and this same hog comes back in with our dinner on plastic trays. "Here you go, ladies," he snorts, "time to put on the feed bag!" He plops down the most disgusting meal I've ever seen in my life. "Nutraloaf," explains Veneer; "don't eat it!" "But I'm starving," I admit, yet he's still adamant. "That crap is made from rotten tomatoes, week-old moldy Wonder bread, and the skin of tortured poultry! The opposite of free-range! They keep these pitiful chickens out back in tiny little cages and torture the poor birds with electrical cattle prods until they kill themselves by hurling their skinny carcasses against the cage bars and bleed to death." Yummy, I think as I look down at my plate. I'm so starved, I eat it anyway, retching and choking from the gristle-filled texture of food hell itself. "Oh, yeah," adds Veneer, "they put saltpeter in it, too." Damn! Just when Veneer was starting to look cute.

We try to have sex during the night but Veneer had warned me. I can't get it up and feel so frustrated when he tries to suck my dick. We try several times, and even though I'm always willing, nothing happens. That saltpeter sure is strong! Eventually, we give up and pass out unsatisfied in separate hard metal bunks. The rotting nutraloaf is never removed from our cell, and once the lights are turned off, I can hear some kind of vermin creeping around and chewing it up. I actually hear a rat puke.

We are awakened by the flash of cell phone cameras. The jailer is leading a pack of sightseers on a "historic tour" of this "renovated and restored" onetime-abandoned single-cell jailhouse. "Here are two obvious homosexuals, 'fudge packers,' if you will, who invade our state every year, having illegal 'pricknics' in our rest areas in flagrant violation of Kansas Statute 21-3505—criminal sodomy." "I only gave a blow job!" yells Veneer in defiance as the tourists cover their ears in aural disgust. "Call the Maryland Film Commission," I beg. "I was doing research for my book!" "Skull Pussy and Pillow Biter," the jailer barks, still referring to us, "the two-headed transplants of rear entry."

Later in the day, we are dragged into the only other room in this tiny jailhouse, a miniature courtroom with a judge's bench and three seats for the public. I see the lowest-rent entertainment reporter I vaguely remember from some long-ago movie-press junket. One of those hacks that kept stopping the taping and demanding you call him by his first name in your responses to his extremely unoriginal questions. God, I marvel, if he's a reporter from Smoky Hills Public Television as he claims, his career must be in real trouble. His station is located in this almost abandoned town, Bunker Hill, Kansas. Population: 95.

The judge enters and he looks exactly like the cross-eyed actor who plays the biggest fascist sadist in Pasolini's movie masterpiece *Salò*. Veneer gasps. I gulp. "Court is now in session," our elected official announces in a flat Midwestern accent. The other two reporters, one from the faraway *Wichita Times* and the other from a local flea-market classified giveaway sheet, are allowed to take photos while our TV guy videotapes. "You two ass-bandits are accused of sodomy," the judge announces without looking at us. "Semen demons will not be tolerated anywhere in Kansas, plain and simple. How do you plead?" "Your Honor," Veneer tries to argue as his own attorney, "I am constitutionally guaranteed the right to give oral sex—" "Overruled," the judge yells before turning to me. "And you, homo-hack?" he rudely addresses my humble self. "Judge, I have not been allowed to contact my attorney, which is a flagrant violation of my rights." "You've seen too many bad movies, cream puff," he rules with a hint of hidden nellyism. I suddenly realize this fucker has a little "sugar" in him himself.

But he's not a "brother," believe me. He gives us both two weeks of community service with the understanding that we must be out of Kansas by sunset the day our sentences end. Veneer seems relieved. But I'm not! Two weeks? That's an eternity. I have a flight to catch from San Francisco to Provincetown for the start of the season in eight days. Two weeks in Bunker Hill, Kansas, seems like a life sentence. Our jailer drags us out of the courtroom and we are paraded in a perp walk before the pitiful little press corps. I ignore all their rude questions except two. "Yes, I have seen *Black Mama, White Mama,* and no, I do not identify with this movie in my current situation."

Next stop, the same pitiful rest stop where I was arrested. It's much quieter, not a pervert in sight. I guess by now the word is out that this onetime jumping tearoom is now heaty. "Okay," the jailer announces, "get out. Your job," he says to me with a smart-ass grin, "is to pick up all the used rubbers you may find at this location. And you," he says to Veneer, "you give out these homo-health tips." I see Veneer blush, even though he's black, when he reads the "Rimming and You" flyer filled with graphic descriptions of various strains of hepatitis that can be caused by indiscriminate analingus. Veneer and I look at one another in militant anger but know better than to argue. I find a stick and use it to poke through the bushes. I find a lot of used prophylactics. The semen is mostly dried up but in some it's runny, heated by the sun on this unfortunately warm day. I pick them up with my bare hands and deposit them in a torn Rite Aid plastic bag I find stuck blowing in the wind in a low tree branch. My jailer nods his approval.

Veneer is having a much tougher time. Since most of the drivers who are stopping have to use the bathroom for legitimate purposes, they become enraged when they politely take Veneer's flyer and read the scandalous message. Some don't even know what "rimming" means and ask him innocently. Other men *do* know and are infuriated to think that they have been identified as engaging in such. One guy actually punches Veneer in the mouth. My jailer runs over to try to break it up and I see my chance for freedom. An effeminate, bewigged older gentleman has just driven up. Back in Baltimore, we call this type a nellbox, but never to their faces. I guess he hasn't heard of the police crackdown yet. Before he can even get out to cruise, I approach him, still pretending to look for rubbers, and whisper stealthily,

"Help me. I'm being held prisoner by homophobic authorities." The nellbox looks at me, over at the growing brawl with the jailer and Veneer, and then back to my crotch. "Get in, girl," he whispers in his most exaggerated old-school-queen vernacular. I leap in and immediately lie on the floor. He slowly drives away.

BAD RIDE NUMBER EIGHT

BLOSSOM

"Gay to my hole, Miss Thing," he whispers out of the corner of his mouth as he drives right by my jailer and poor Veneer without their even noticing I'm gone yet. "I beg your pardon?" I answer, for once perplexed at the meaning of his gay slang. "I'm Blossom," this big galoot of a queen answers, not bothering to translate, "and don't you forget it, girl!"

Oh God. Is it wrong to be gay but still have "gay shame," as it's humorously called by hip fags in the U.K.? Embarrassed at the old-school poofs who exaggerate the stereotype and give the new queer generation a gayly incorrect name? It's a tough call. I remember when Divine first saw Richard Simmons and confessed that he felt homophobic. I can identify here. Suddenly Blossom reaches into the backseat and grabs a bakery box, which he hands over to me. "Have some pie, butt plug," he offers with a deranged look in his eyes. "Okay," I mutter, once again hungry after days of irregular meals. My tattoo is hurting. Every time I move I can feel the scabs stretch and break, and you can see pus leaking through my shirt in the front. "You pop your cork?" Blossom asks me with sudden lechery when he notices. "No," I explain in horror, "I have an infection." "Well, let's stop and get some medicine," Blossom clucks like a hovering mother, suddenly pulling off Route 70 and heading south on Route 281, wherever that may lead. "Hey, I need to stay on Route 70," I cry, but he doesn't slow down.

"I gotta be careful," Blossom whispers even though it's only me in the car to hear. "Why?" I ask, almost afraid he'll confide the truth. "Can I tell you a secret, girlfriend?" he asks, and ignoring his gay familiarity, I answer warily, "Maybe you better not." "I'm on a mission, Mary," he continues, disregarding my advice. "These straight fuckers need a payback." "Who?" I ask, having no idea of what he's talking about. "Breeders!" he snorts back. "Oh, come on, some straight people are fine. These days, you can't tell a person's character by his or her sexuality," I argue, not caring if he agrees or not. "Oh, yes, you fucking can!" Blossom suddenly snarls with unassimilated gay fanaticism. "Somebody's gotta pay!" he threatens as he swerves off the road to enter a Rexall drugstore parking lot.

Blossom pulls into a handicapped parking space and slams on the brakes in a decidedly ungirlish way. "I'm mentally handicapped because of heteros," he shouts for the world to hear, even though it's only me in the car. He opens the back door, gets out a can of spray paint, and writes SPAGHETTI IS STRAIGHT UNTIL YOU GET IT HEATED UP! on the next car. At first I don't understand, but when he takes a hammer out from under the front seat and smashes the windshield of another car and snarls, "Make heterosexual divorce illegal," I begin to understand the severity of his twisted militancy. I hate separatism, but I'm too freaked-out at this point to debate sexual politics.

Besides, I feel dizzy. "Come on," Blossom says, dragging me out of the car and toward the drugstore, "you're coming with me." "I don't feel well," I try to explain, hoping to stall him, but telling the truth. What's the matter with me? I feel light-headed, nauseous, not myself. "That's because straight pig-fuckers are around," Blossom rants, suddenly back to his hetero-bashing. "I feel like puking, too, every time I think of them dancing the Electric Slide."

Blossom suddenly changes the subject, all business. "Okay, once we get inside, we're just two trouser-bandits out shopping." My head starts spinning in some kind of weird vertigo and I reach out to hold on to him for support. "If we get busted," he continues, ignoring my frailties, "you don't know me, Girlene, and I don't know you." Suddenly the horizon spins and I fall to my knees. My scabs, just beginning to heal, rip apart. Blossom pulls me back up to my feet with surprising strength.

We both see security guards rushing to investigate Blossom's now-reported vandalism. When he gives me a wink, I realize that was Blossom's point in the first place. We enter the store. Blossom knows the layout. He heads right to the bottled-water department, grabs a large bottle of Evian, looks around to see if he's being observed, unscrews the cap, takes a gulp so there's room, and pours into the bottle some Clorox bleach from a hidden container he pulls from his pocket. "Straight throat!" he mutters, and even if I have no idea what he means, I know it's not good. The whole place is spinning again and I begin to collapse, but Blossom catches me just in time.

I can barely make it back to the car. Blossom, now in high spirits, is mumbling hate-crime threats and giggling insanely as he sees my deteriorating condition and lets me lie down in the backseat. I feel *really* bad. He takes pity on me and feeds me another piece of pie. Just as the first bite goes down my throat, a lightbulb goes off in my brain. This freak is poisoning me, too, only this time it's on purpose. I spit it out. "Why? Blossom, why?" I beg. "I'm a gay guy, too!" "Because you're a traitor," he hisses as he jabs on the CD player and "Strychnine" by the Sonics comes on. I usually love this kind of music, but the lyrics are suddenly not funny. "You're a bisexual sympathizer, an assimilated faggot," Blossom continues. "Worse yet—you're not an outlaw anymore!"

I vaguely remember stopping at two more convenience stores. He went in alone while I lay helpless in the backseat. First it was a Hy-Vee drugstore where he replaced milk of magnesia with ipecac ("so they can feel as sick as I do when I see straight guys sitting in a movie theater together with one empty seat between them so their legs don't accidentally touch"). My memory is foggy on the last one, but I think it was some place named Cheapo Depot, right over the Oklahoma border, where he injected citrus fruit with rat poison ("If leather bars are vanishing, so must straight people"). I finally lose consciousness.

It's early morning when I wake up. I'm in some sort of "adult" hotel with Blossom. Pay-per-view bareback gay porn is playing on the TV. He's completely nude with an erection, and his legs are up and wrapped around his head. His asshole is so overused it resembles a baboon's. Blossom. Now I know where he got his name. He's tied a noose around his neck and strung it tight over the faux rafter overhead all ready to be sprung. He's obviously an autoerotic-asphyxiation enthusiast. Stroking his enlarged cock, he has been waiting for me to wake up and focus on this full horror show. "Gay to my hole, Miss Thing," he announces for the second time today, and this time I think I know what he means. He snaps the cord and the rope flips him around to his feet and hoists him off the ground. He chokes in ecstasy. Maybe he reaches an orgasm. I'm not sure. I run.

BAD RIDE NUMBER NINE

CAPTAIN JACK

It's fucking boiling outside already and, natch, without my bag, I don't have my sunblock or my baseball hat. And Beaver, Oklahoma, is not exactly a hotbed of shopping choices. I stand in the rising sun for a long time. No cars come by. I feel old with my infected tattoo, my achy legs, and a general fatigue from the anxiety of cross-country hitchhiking that has gone so wrong.

The sun gets hotter and I can feel my bald spot burning. I find an old piece of cardboard by the side of the road and I hold it over my head, but every time I reach my arms up, my tattoo scabs seem to rip and pull apart. I'm thirsty. Jesus, I see some sort of bird overhead. I hope it's not a buzzard anticipating more bad luck for me. I'm not roadkill, I am a man.

"Captain Jack" is, beyond a doubt, the most disgusting-looking driver who has picked me up so far, but after several hours of waiting with bleeding sunburn blisters you'll get in any car, believe me. He is of indeterminate age, maybe even younger than me, but the years have not been kind. Grizzled worse than Gabby Hayes, and smelling stronger than the comic-strip character B.O. Plenty, Captain Jack also is a goiter sufferer. He has a huge, hideous one on his neck. I have always feared catching a goiter from a stranger and have voiced such concerns to my assistants in the past, but they just hooted and hollered, "That is medically impossible." I'm not so sure. At first I think the clinging, pungently damp, and horrendous stench in his car is his breath, but then I realize it is goiter odor. Every time he speaks, his repulsive growth rises, falls, and quivers in thyroid-hormone starvation.

Captain Jack claims to be a recycler but he sure ain't "green." He's a hoarder of unrecyclable plastic. The entire interior of his car is filled with dirty deli trays, old #4 prepared-food containers, filthy plastic cups, and moldy take-out containers. This is the first car I have ever been in where I notice roaches. Captain Jack doesn't talk much, but God, he stops his vehicle a lot! At every rest area, manned or unmanned, he pulls over, roots through the trash, and "rescues plastic orphans," as he calls the "unwanted inorganic children" of our garbage. I could run and try to get another ride, but he's going all the way to Colorado Springs, a good distance, and he is at least a safe driver. Besides, the families in Oklahoma don't look friendly. Not one person has recognized me. But by now, without my eyebrow pencil or little scissors, who could? My pencil-thin mustache is in piss-poor shape. You can't see it now unless you're up close, and the odor zone of infection of my tattoo keeps any potential mustache viewer safely at a distance.

Captain Jack has little "friends" in his car, too. It takes me a while to notice "Janice," whom he introduces as "his wife," who's made out of plastic rings from carryout six-packs and some coathanger wire twisted together in some kind of torso with a head fashioned out of an empty paint can with a wig on top made from food-stained paper napkins. He has "children," too. "Myrtle," a baby girl sculpted entirely out of food scraps, who he confides "has disabilities" and rests in a discarded and burned kitchen pot some poor fired short-order cook forgot and left on a burning stove. His "son Arnold" could be considered "outsider art" by some, I imagine. He's lovingly formed out of broken beer bottles with an ugly little face painted on with spilled kitchen messes from soiled paper towels.

"It's not right the State of Oklahoma rejects these unwanted little recyclables," he begins ranting before asking me with true bewilderment, "Why should a tin can feel superior to a take-out container? Junk mail is okay to be picked up, while plastic wrap is rejected? How could that not be called discrimination?" "Well," I try to reason, "those are inanimate objects, they're not human, so their feelings can't really be hurt." "That's what you think!" he suddenly rages. "I'm tired of aluminum cans feeling uppity around Styrofoam cups, they're all equal!" "Waste and recycling," I argue, "are gray areas still being worked out by environmentalists. In California, many of these items you have in your car *are* recyclable—it just costs more to do so." That really sets him off. "States' rights? Is that what you're arguing?" he debates with an unhinged passion. "Why does Oklahoma get off the hook? Why should a salad-bar container be trash in this state and a valuable citizen in California?" he screams, his goiter going up and down with each rant. "It *is* a federal case! Spray aerosol cans are fucking better than dirty tinfoil?" he yells, banging the steering wheel on every other word. "How could that be? Somebody's got to stick up for take-out containers. Plastic-bottle supremacists will not be tolerated!" I watch with growing alarm as his goiter turns deep red, then purple, and finally almost black.

Suddenly his goiter explodes. Not only am I covered in a thin coat of pus but so is he. Oh my God! I pray I haven't caught goiter germs! "See," Captain Jack shouts in agony to me, "see what recycling discrimination can do to a man!?" Much to my relief, Captain Jack continues driving safely despite the fact that the steering wheel is also covered with slime from his exploded growth.

In a panic, I turn on the radio without asking permission and am relieved to hear that incredibly beautiful, melancholic "Lonesome Drifter" by Jericho Brown playing. But Captain Jack scowls at the lyrics because he obviously doesn't feel that way. "I'm sorry, Janice," he sobs to his recycled "wife," flicking off the radio in contempt. "I've tried to be a garbage integrationist," he explains to his spouse, "but society fights me every step of the way." "Change takes time," I soothe him, but he doesn't even hear me; he's in another world by now—a recycled state of mind. "Arnold? Myrtle?" he blubbers, completely ignoring my human presence, "I have never refused refuse, have I?" They don't answer as far as I can tell, but he seems unfazed. "I don't waste waste, do I?" he continues to plead to his pitiful little family of garbage talismans, and somehow he seems solaced by their silence.

All I know is that I feel a little bump in my neck, and at first I think it's just my imagination. When I grab the rearview mirror over so I can look, I almost don't recognize myself. I appear so exhausted and weary. And no, it's not just my lunacy, I *do* have something growing and it's no pimple. I can't wait to tell Susan and Trish they were wrong. I knew it! Goiters *are* contagious. "Garbage diversity is a right!" Captain Jack continues crusading without the slightest notice of my goiter concern. The skin around his erupted neck volcano is hanging in flaps, its hole in the center gaping in expulsion, yet he's suddenly upbeat, on a new roll, but I don't even listen. I'm too worried about this thing right below my Adam's apple. Maybe it's just acne; some kind of callus caused by the sun? Even a tumor!? Please, God, anything but a goiter!

"I'm coming, little babies," Captain Jack shouts to the residents of the next trash can as we pull in, unscheduled, to yet another rest area. I know that we're near Colorado Springs, and while I'm quite aware this city has a formidable conservative reputation, I *did* have a show there once at the Colorado Springs Fine Arts Center; maybe they would give me some help? But then I remember my new outgrowth—could the art mob ever accept me now? I run, but it's hard with this fucking thing flapping on my neck. Captain Jack looks up from picking through the filthy, bee-ridden, overripe trash and holds up a large bunch of rusted, discarded wire coat hangers. "See?" he screams to me in the distance. "See how cruel people are?"

I stick out my thumb. But who on earth is going to pick me up when I'm featuring a fresh goiter puckering on my neck for the whole world to see?

BAD RIDE NUMBER TEN

BRISTOL

Bristol, that's who. I get in and immediately regret my decision to not just jump out and run. She's a slightly butch Grace Metalious look-alike dressed in that same red-checkered shirt the novelist wore in her *Peyton Place* author photo (*and* the same greasy ponytail to boot) and has the heat inside her van turned on full blast despite the outside temperature of seventy-five degrees. A dead dog is in the backseat, and the rest of the vehicle is loaded with cages filled with snarling canines in all states of ill health.

She is an "animal rescuer." The problem is, no one *asked* her to rescue these animals; she just felt like the "chosen one." Bristol started her own "doggie underground" where she would kidnap animals from "kill shelters" or other "atrocity centers" such as bankrupt pet stores, puppy mills, or even homes of pet owners (reported by "other furry-friend lovers") who supposedly didn't spend enough time with their animals. Some had daytime jobs, which was totally unacceptable to Bristol. Even being involved in a "love relationship" with another human being was "animal cruelty" in her opinion.

Bristol actually looks kind of like a dog herself. Not an ugly one, just a plain dog: elongated chin, large ears, and a nose that seems to be sniffing for something she will never find. As soon as she pulls off, a cat leaps from out of nowhere and bites me right on my tender goiter. "Ow!" I scream in both pain and surprise. "Don't mind Catnip," Bristol says with a smirk, "she's got ringworm!" Oh, perfect! I'm trapped with an insane pet kidnapper in a car that smells like the worst cage at a zoo. *And* she's got a cat who is giving off bad vibes about me to the other animals in the car. I can see Catnip mewing some lie about me to a dog and I know that sounds like paranoia, but it's true!

All pets hate me. "Oh, he won't hurt you," pet owners coo to me when they see my fear. *"Heel!"* I always shout to the animal, but it never seems to work. Their pets *do* try to bite me. Even goldfish seem hostile when they get a glimpse of my frightened face through the bowl. I don't hate animals. I just have no desire to touch one. I'm not lonely.

But before you call PETA, let me explain. I think *all* dogs should be off leashes, biting people! That's what they *want* to be doing, running in packs like the wild canines I saw in Bucharest that seem so happy to attack you, snarling and yapping when you get out of a cab. Dogs don't want to be home with their owners stuck in some sort of sick S&M relationship, sentenced to a lifetime of human caresses! How would you like to take a shit with someone following you around, waiting to pick it up with a plastic newspaper bag? Talk about humiliating! Also, I hate to tell you this, but can't you see? Your cat hates you.

But naturally I don't tell Bristol any of this because I can see she is one of those maniacs who supposedly "love" animals but always seem to hate people. "Snake bite your neck?" she asks rudely. "No . . . I seem to have developed some kind of goiter," I weakly try to explain.

Suddenly, as if cued by Lucifer himself, the dogs in their cages *all* begin to bark. And Bristol swerves to miss something in the road. I look back and see a mangy dog eating the roadkill of a fox that has obviously been flattened by a speeding vehicle. Her dogs inside the car start wailing in pack mentality. Bristol pulls over, jumps from the car, and grabs some sort of animal tranquilizer gun from the trunk. God knows what else she's got in there because I stay inside the car, but her dogs wail in agonized excitement at the possible pet drama.

I watch Bristol in amazement as she coaxes the insane-looking animal away from his maggot-infested lunch by barking and growling herself in some sort of faux dog communication. Suddenly Bristol fires the dart from the gun like a seasoned veterinarian. The rabid dog flips over and goes limp immediately. The other dogs in the car let out growls of approval and Bristol barks back in dog celebration.

She drags the unconscious dog over and much to my shock throws it in the front seat with me. I can see the stringy shreds of putrefied fox meat still caught in the beast's teeth. "Oh my God," I hear Bristol cry out, suddenly speaking in English, "the poor creature hasn't been neutered!" Well, at least she's not pro-life, I think in the only optimistic moment of the ride. "We'll fix that!" she announces with sudden purpose. To my utmost horror, I see her grab a box cutter from the glove compartment, flip over the mutt's limp body, and slit the skin by the testicles. I look away in horror. "Watch this!" she orders. "Or you can walk to San Francisco." I sheepishly turn my eyes back. "One day you may have to do this yourself," she sternly warns like some kind of veterinarian leader. I doubt that, I want to scream, but then look ahead to the empty highway and keep my mouth shut. Like a skilled surgeon working on the battlefield, she ligates the testicles, and closes up the incision surgically with a pitiful stapler and a tube of Super Glue.

I guess the operation is a success, because Bristol pulls away and all her dogs start barking, almost in song, like that horrible version of "Jingle Bells" recorded by the Singing Dogs. I can't tell what the new dog song *is*, but Bristol starts barking along with them, too, so I just sit there. Musically alone. With my scabs itching, my sunburn peeling, my tattoo oozing, and my goiter throbbing.

Then I see that fucking cat again, eyeing me as it pukes up furballs or something on the floor. Bristol doesn't seem to notice. It looks as if she suddenly has digestive problems of her own. Bristol starts gagging. The cat is retching, and what comes out looks worse than fur. I turn to Bristol in alarm, but she signals me with her hands that she's okay. But she's not. She keeps driving and at the same time starts frantically gesturing for me to get something from under my seat. She can't talk because she's retching and heaving, so I frantically reach under and find a glass bottle of milk. Bristol starts shaking her head in affirmation and I take off the bottle cap and hand it to her. But instead of chugging it down, she holds it just outside her mouth and opens wide. Nothing happens at first, but then I think I see something white dart out of her mouth and then go right back in. The dogs go berserk in the cages. The cat starts hissing and making ungodly noises. Suddenly I see the white head of a tapeworm poke out from her mouth again, drawn by the bait of the milk. Bristol grabs the head of the tapeworm as quick as lightning and starts pulling it out of her throat through her mouth. The cat's back goes up in a hump and it pukes its own whole load of tapeworms. But Bristol doesn't give up. She keeps pulling the tapeworm up from the bowels of her gullet, gagging and choking, heaving and spewing phlegm until finally the tail is disgorged. I watch in complete horror. Bristol, suddenly calm, heaves the carcass of the now-dead tapeworm out the window. The dogs quiet down. I kick off some regurgitated worm remains from my boots. My good boots that I paid a pretty penny for!

We pull into Bristol's "forever home," her animal sanctuary surrounded by chain-link fencing, outside Grand Junction, Colorado. It's night. She offers me a place to stay, and what can I say? I have no money or credit cards or phone; this will have to do. I see thousands of dogs everywhere. A new circle of hell.

Her car comes to a stop and the outside canines go wild to see their leader, jumping up on the hood of her car, licking the windshield, jumping up to the side windows, snarling at me in jealousy. I am terrified but see that the cat is completely nonchalant. When Bristol steps out of the car, all the dogs immediately go silent but begin slurping her everywhere on her body with slavish adoration. Some lick her on the lips, others actually lap her shoes. It's truly sickening.

I relock the doors but Bristol opens them back up with her key-ring remote and tells me, "It's fine." Since she is now covered in dog slobber, which she makes no move to clean up, I'm not sure what "fine" is. I slowly get out of the vehicle, and thank God, the dogs don't attack, they just watch me with the same cold rage the birds had for Tippi Hedren at the end of that Hitchcock movie.

Bristol releases her dogs from the cages in the car and they are immediately welcomed by other snarling packs of frightening mongrels. I am especially unnerved to see the unconscious, now neutered dog begin to come to and then with a rabid ferocity leap right past me to join his fellow curs in pack rule. Bristol smiles in animal lunacy. The infected cat jumps out of the front seat, and Bristol takes a dead mouse out of her purse and flips it in the air directly to the puss's mouth. I thought a cat wouldn't eat an already dead mouse, but I guess I was wrong.

My hostess asks me if I'm hungry and I stupidly say yes. You'd think by now I'd realize that she eats the same food scraps her animals do and expects me to do the same. I'm so hungry, I eat them. When it's time for beddy-bye, she walks me out back and points to a doghouse. It's a human-size one, so I don't complain. Just as I'm about to close my eyes in exhaustion, the overhead clouds part and a full moon shines through. Thousands of dogs howl. I'm not exactly sure, but I think I hear Bristol join in.

BAD RIDE NUMBER ELEVEN

HOGWASH

I get up early. Out of the doghouse for real. Luckily, I still re-member which direction is west. Please, dear God, get me out of Colorado. My goiter has actually subsided a little. Real scabs have formed on all my injuries. The certain tightness of nature's healing invites picking, but I know better. Even my tattoo has stopped oozing, so can I take that as some sort of good sign?

I guess not. I stand there at an entrance ramp to Route 70 West, my aorta of misery, for hours. Knowing better, but at a loss for a better plan, I walk down *to* the highway and give it a try, but alas, it's worse. Cars do come by, but by now I'm looking really rough. Nobody even glances toward me, much less slows down to consider picking me up. I walk for a mile or two and then a miracle. I see a partially crushed, run-over felt-tip marker by the side of the road. Again, I pray. Please, God, let it work. I unscrew the cap and test it on my hand. Thank the Lord above! It's not dried out. I scan the area for anything to make a sign out of but see nothing. I continue walking and glimpse part of a cardboard box that has blown from somewhere caught in a storm-drainage ditch. Maybe heaven itself? I scramble over the brush and grab the potential hitchhike sign like the lifeboat it may be. In desperation, I write out in big, bold letters HELP! I MADE HAIRSPRAY! On the flip side, over the logo of some generic paper-towel label, I am even more shameless and scrawl I'M JOHN WATERS. It doesn't work.

Hours more go by. Out of boredom I walk more. Still no dice. Cars. Trucks. Vans. They all ignore me and my sign. Finally, a motorcycle stops. My one rule: Never get on a motorcycle while hitchhiking. This guy wears the colors of the Sundowners, a biker club I am unfamiliar with. But God knows, he looks like the real thing. Almost like the Hells Angels. Which makes me feel warm and fuzzy because I'm a real sucker for these guys. Well, not literally, because they're all old now. I know you're never supposed to say the words Hells Angels out loud unless you *are* one of them and I try to respect this outsider law. I agree with Quentin Crisp, who called Hells Angels "naturally superior beings." They are. I genuflect to their infamy. I've met some of the Maryland Angels in Baltimore and once took two of them to the Ottobar, a great punk-rock club in town. You should have seen the faces of the tattooed new-wavers and their goth girl-friends when I strolled in with these bikers in full colors. Later that same night I was taken to the Hells Angels clubhouse by them, which is, of course, beyond impressive. Lots of couches. Axes lining the wall. "For what?" I stupidly asked. "In case, John," the Angel answered; "just in case." I see.

This biker who has stopped is named Hogwash, but he's actually better-looking than his name. "Get on, bro," he says with a growl, and instantly that nasty butch fifties instrumental "Cross-Ties," by Dale Hawkins, plays in my head as his musical cue, but before I can enjoy this new imagined score, he snorts, "John Waters, what the hell are you doing out here hitchhiking?" I am so relieved. I try to thank him politely but explain I feel unsafe and too inexperienced to ride on the back of this monster Harley, especially with a member of an outlaw biker gang to whom I've never had the pleasure of being introduced. "When a Sundowner asks a man to mount his hog, only a fool turns him down," he snarls in a steely voice, "unless he wants to go down. And I don't mean head," he explains, suddenly all business, "I mean dead!"

Gulp. I notice Hogwash isn't wearing a helmet and I certainly don't see an extra one for me. "Okay," I say meekly, "but please go slowly," I beg as I straddle the seat and wrap both arms around him tightly. "Ooh, that feels good," he taunts me in a mock little-girl's voice before gunning the engine and peeling out, leaving rubber for quite a distance down the highway.

I am immediately terrified. I see the speedometer climb to fifty, sixty, seventy, almost eighty miles an hour. I yell for him to slow down but he answers by doing a full wheelie. I scream like a pussy. The wind is ripping through my thin hair and flattens my goiter painfully against my Adam's apple. My tattoo pops open and I can feel leakage spreading across my T-shirt. Sonny Barger I am definitely not.

"Please! Please! Please! Let me off!" I beg into the void. But instead this imbecile goes into a "circle wheelie" right in the middle of the fast lane as the cars' and trucks' drivers lean on their horns and swerve away in the nick of time. I know I am going to die.

Suddenly he is putting his legs over the handlebars! "No, don't," I scream. "A high chair," he shouts like a banshee on crack. With that, the front of the motorcycle lifts off the ground from speed yet he still keeps his legs dangling over the front. "I'll sleep when I'm dead," he howls just as we go beyond a "twelve o'clock wheelie," where the bike has gone past balancing straight up and tips over backward in the air. I am thrown off midspin and land hard on the hood of a car before bouncing off and being thrown into the hedgelike highway landscaping. Hogwash is killed instantly as his bike revolves 360 degrees twice before smashing to the asphalt and bursting into flames. A giant tractor-trailer skids out of control to miss the whole mess and crushes Hogwash's burning corpse. I crawl back to the highway feeling no pain yet, in complete shock. All I can think is, I guess this makes me an official member of the Sundowner biker gang.

BAD RIDE NUMBER TWELVE

WARREN AND TARANTULA

Somehow, I'm alive. I'm sure at least one bone is broken some-where in my body, but before I can even fully begin to feel any pain, a car pulls over. I'm not even hitchhiking yet! The guy looks okay, normal enough. A baby in the front seat is crying. I notice that it isn't strapped in a car seat in the back the way it should be for both safety and legal reasons.

"You okay?" he asks with what I think is genuine concern. "I don't know," I truthfully answer. "Get in, I'll take you to the hospital," he offers. "Maybe I shouldn't move," I argue, "maybe I should just wait for the ambulance to arrive?" The infant starts screaming hysterically with a lung power I thought not possible. "Hold the baby," the driver suddenly commands me. "Huh?" I mumble in confusion, in no shape to hold anything, much less a shrieking tyke. "Help me," he begs in a sudden emotional plea. I'm so confused and injured I don't know what I'm doing and get in the vehicle.

As soon as I close the door, he peels out and the baby falls on the floor. I can't believe my eyes. It goes ballistic. "Pick him up!" he yells, and I'm so stunned I freeze. "Shut up, Tarantula!" he screams like a maniac. "Tarantula?!" I say out loud in disbelief. "That's the baby's name?" "That's what I call him now!" he shouts. "I have to! His fucking mother is a custody cunt! I gotta be careful!"

Oh God, what have I got myself into now? *Nobody* could have luck this bad! I reach down and pick up the baby and realize that my left shoulder must be broken. Tarantula bites me. I drop him in shock and naively recoil before realizing I'd bite me, too, if I were in the same situation. "Hey, look, mister," I begin to lecture before he cuts me off with "Warren! No use lying about my name when she's got an all-points bulletin out on me. But the kid? I gotta protect this little fucker."

"Little fucker?" Jesus, I reach down again and pick up the little boy, who hardly reacts as if he's being comforted. He howls like a banshee. Warren suddenly pulls a broken-off car aerial out from under the seat and waves it menacingly. "You want another whipping?" he shouts like a madman, just like Dawn Davenport in *Female Trouble*. "Don't you hit this child!" I scream in horror, holding the crazed infant close to my damaged chest. "Stay out of it," Warren threatens me. "You don't know what I've been through. Look!" he yells in a frenzy, pointing up to an AMBER Alert electronic billboard overlooking Route I-70 West. I see the description of his car and the words CHILD ABDUCTION in flashing letters. Jesus Christ, what the fuck do I do?

"You said you were taking me to the hospital!" I stupidly argue, but he just tosses me a couple of jars of baby food and says, "Feed the kid!" I am so overwhelmed with dread that I just do as I'm told. The baby gobbles it down and I suddenly realize all I've had to eat in the last four days is dog scraps. "Can I have some, too?" I feebly ask. Warren nods and I scarf down some stewed prunes. I try to burp the baby, but each time, he spits up his food.

"Look, give yourself up," I try to convince Warren. "Divorce is an emotional issue. The judges are used to this kind of drama in custody cases and they'll understand your actions." "Who said I was married?!" he asks as if I were the stupidest person in the world. "Well . . . you said she was a 'custody cunt' . . . ," I stammer. "She is!" he rages. "But I don't know her! I saw her on the bus with the kid and she was letting him eat sweets. That's just wrong! I couldn't allow little Tarantula to grow up and be a fat slob, so I snatched him and ran. She starts screaming, 'Give him back!' That's a custody cunt in my book."

I look out the window at normal people driving by. Families who have no idea of the hell happening right now in the lane next to them. *"Help,"* I mouth to the driver of a home-pest-control exterminating company. He looks at me blankly, I guess internalizing his own troubles at home. "Call the police," I overenunciate silently to a woman with her own child snugly seat-belted in the back as she talks on the phone, probably illegally. Thinking I'm giving her shit for being on the horn by misinterpreting my lip-rendering of "police," she hangs up guiltily and drops the handheld in her lap and never looks back. I hunt for eye contact from car to car and despair at not seeing a friendly or helpful face.

Suddenly I hear a police siren in the distance. I look over at Warren and I see this sound makes him totally insane. "You drive!" he orders, turning on the radio full volume. I can't believe it. What's playing but the song "Baby Sittin' Boogie" by Buzz Clifford. That crazy tune with the dubbed-in baby's voice gurgling "goo goo dah dah"–type lyrics. But no baby is singing along in this car. Ours is screaming bloody murder. "Give me the child," he barks, taking his hands off the wheel and actually starting to try to change places with me. The car starts swerving wildly from lane to lane, and I painfully grab the wheel from my side with one hand and jerk up Tarantula by the arm with my other. With Warren's foot on the brake we slow down quickly, and cars have to slam on their brakes behind us. I don't look back as I'm switching seats with this madman while the car almost coasts to a stop, but I hear an accident or two happening as a result.

"Floor it!" Warren orders, grabbing the baby as the sirens get louder and I can see a fleet of speeding cop cars approaching us in the rearview mirror. I do as I am told. Tarantula is turning up his own volume now, screaming so loudly that I get a minor nosebleed. Holding the infant, Warren rolls down the window. "I tried to be a good father," he sobs to no one in particular, suddenly flicking off the radio; "I adopted this little boy to protect him!" "Put the baby down!" I tell Warren in a new, calm voice. "America is already fat," he argues back, hoisting the infant up to his opened window. "What are you doing?" I panic, horrified to see that Warren appears to be taking aim with little Tarantula. "Don't throw that baby!" I scream, trying to grab back the child, who is howling again, correctly sensing upcoming insane danger. "Children cannot grow up obesely," Warren rants, his eyes rolling back in his head. "No, Warren, *no!*" I scream—just as he throws the baby out the side window and hits the perfect bull's-eye of an open window of another car, driven by a healthy-looking woman in the next lane. I see the lady scream, but I'm pretty sure little Tarantula landed safely in her lap.

I crane my neck to find a place in the traffic to pull over. Finally, the police will help me. I can tell them everything and end this horrible nightmare of a road trip. To hell with the book. Go back to the movies. I don't have to be behind the camera. I'll work in a movie theater. Anything but this. I'll be an usher!

But before I can stop the car, Warren opens his door while

I'm still speeding along and leaps out into full traffic in what has to be the most selfish suicide ever. Not only does Warren die, so do six others (including two policemen). Fourteen others are injured, some seriously. The pileup of smashed vehicles that crashed trying to avoid his bouncing body on the highway is a sickening sight to behold.

BAD RIDE NUMBER THIRTEEN

RANDY PACKARD

"Hi, I'm Randy Packard and I'm from REACT," says the trucker looking out from his driver's-side window, stalled in this multivehicle-from-hell accident. I'm half pulled over to the side of the road and my whole body is shaking. I see mangled bodies in the road. Traffic is at a complete standstill. One car is overturned. "What's REACT?" I say cautiously, not trusting a soul anymore. "It's a CB emergency-channel organization made up of volunteers, many of us truckers, to assist other motorists in time of disaster." "Call the police, then," I beg, "there's a little baby that's been stolen who's now safe in a brown Toyota. There's an AMBER Alert out for this kid right now!"

I see Randy talking on his CB walkie, and once he gives me the thumbs-up, I feel confident that little Tarantula, or whatever the hell his name is, will be rescued. But what about me? Do I wimp out now and give up? I'm in Utah, for chrissakes. Isn't that just two states away from California? After all I've gone through, don't I want the book to have an ending? One that isn't cowardly? Anticlimactic? I can't give up now.

"I'm just a hitchhiker," I blurt out to Randy honestly, hoping to get all my cards right on the table. "I know you are, John," he answers with kindness and charity, "and I've come to give you your last ride. All the way to San Francisco." "But how did you know I was here?" I shout out in gratitude, suddenly feeling as if a savior has been sent from above. "You've got a lot of fans, including some of the more 'creative types' in REACT," he says with a friendly chuckle. "The CB channels have been abuzz with your sightings since Indiana. Come on, get in. Can you walk or shall I come assist you?"

"I can walk all right," I reply in an adrenaline rush, just thinking of my beautiful apartment waiting for me in San Francisco. I leap out of the car, but my legs give out and I stumble to the ground. "Whoa, cowboy," Randy yells. "I'm okay," I shout, struggling to my knees and hobbling over to the other side of the truck in hope and gratitude. Before I can even climb up, Randy has flung open the passenger door in welcome. I climb in.

He's wearing no pants. Before I can react, the locks go down automatically with a scary metallic finality. I struggle to open my door but I'm locked in. "Gacy lives," mutters Randy with the evil look of Leatherface and Richard Ramirez put together. I look over in fear and can't help but see his disgustingly crooked cock, with some kind of herpes infection, twitching in arousal. "Please," I beg, "just let me out, I won't say anything." When he doesn't answer, I try a different tactic in desperation: "Come on, I'm not your type!"

"Oh, but you *are* my type," he says with a supremely creepy grin as the traffic begins to move. I yell "Help!" to the driver of the car next to us, but nobody's helping anybody—they all want to escape this accident mayhem. "I hate all cult-film directors," Randy announces with bone-chilling seriousness. "But why? We just want to surprise audiences," I cry. "I'd like to kill David Lynch," he seethes like a snake about ready to strike. "But I know David . . . he's a really nice guy *and* an amazing director," I plead.

Before I can go further, Randy blurts out a confession that freezes all words in my throat. "I just killed the entire midnight cast of *Rocky Horror* in Salt Lake City last night. You're next."

Oh God, this can't be true. I can't write my own death. Michel Houellebecq, one of my favorite writers, already did that! Readers will think I'm copying! Randy Packard drives like a professional, unfortunately, so there's little chance we'll be pulled over by the cops for speeding. I grow even more alarmed when I see we're headed toward Las Vegas. I don't want to die in Las Vegas. "You know fucking Quentin Tarantino?" he mutters angrily. "Yes," I admit, then clam up, not wanting to give out any more information. "Gonna castrate him," Randy mumbles with delight as I see his repulsive dick grow an inch and vibrate. But he's just getting started. "Cronenberg?" he asks, but I don't want to encourage him, so I don't answer. He grabs a cattle prod and jams it into my arm, giving me a hideous electrical shock. "I met him," I sob, "I don't really know him." "Slit his throat!" Randy announces with premeditation before continuing his little laundry list of future cult murders. "Todd Solondz?" "Great filmmaker," I answer reluctantly. "Behead the freak!" he bellows before slyly asking, "How about your buddy Pedro Almodóvar?" "Yeah, he's the best director there is!" I argue, hoping for Randy's mercy. "I'm gonna blow his brains out," he growls, taking out a revolver from under his seat and aiming it right at me.

"Hold it! Hold it!" I yell, hoping to buy time. "We are just writer-directors trying to do our job. Look, I'm sorry if my films offended you . . ." "You think eating shit is funny?" Randy demands with terrifying hostility. "No! No! I just was commenting on censorship laws at the time of *Deep Throat*," I beg. "Yeah, yeah, yeah," Randy sneers before whipping out a pocketknife and stabbing me in the leg. "*That*," he roars, looking at the blade still stuck in my flesh, "is funny!! Ha ha ha!"

"Just repeat after me," I plead. "It's only a movie. It's only a movie. It's only a movie," but this old catch line from an exploitation ad campaign doesn't do the trick. "And that birth scene in *Female Trouble*," he charges like an obscenity prosecutor, "was absolutely *disgusting*!" Before I can even plead my defense, he shoots me in the other leg. I howl in agony. Randy's dick seems to be leaking some kind of fluid as it grows, and it's definitely not sperm. I scream for my life.

We pull into the Las Vegas city limits. Time flies when you're being tortured. I see the ridiculous skyline of the town—a place filled with tourists I have spent my lifetime trying to avoid. "Look, Randy," I groan through spasms of pain, "just let me out here. I promise I won't make any trash films again—I'll go make mainstream movies, I swear!" "It's too late for a career change," Randy snarls with murderous rage as he pulls his truck off the road into an abandoned drive-in movie theater. It's been a long time since any movies were shown here. There's not even a screen anymore and the concession stand has been burned to the ground. The few remaining poles for the speakers have been stripped clean of working parts. Randy slams on his brakes with a sickening finality.

"Get in the back!" Randy orders. "No, Randy, please," I argue. "Let's go see *The Avengers*. Let's go see Hollywood tent-pole blockbusters!" His answer? A bullet into my right foot. I almost pass out when he grabs me and throws me into the opening he has carved between the truck and the trailer he's pulling. Inside is a cult-movie-director torture chamber. Josie Cotton's cover version of the theme song from *Who Killed Teddy Bear* is playing on some sort of sound system. Beneath movie posters for *El Topo* is the decaying body of Alejandro Jodorowsky, who I *thought* was still alive until Randy tells me differently and takes credit. I see George Romero's amputated head hanging in a basket surrounded by posters for *Night of the Living Dead* and all its sequels. "Enough" is all Randy offers in explanation. Before I can scream, I trip over what appears to be a corpse clawed apart by wild animals. Randy kicks it and I realize that this poor human is still alive. I try to look away, but Randy grabs my head in a choke hold and forces me to gaze upon this nauseating face. Oh my God, it's Herschell Gordon Lewis and he chuckles when he sees me! He's *still* got a sense of humor even as he approaches death.

As Randy pushes me forward into the bloody pit of horror, I realize this is not the barrel of his gun poking me in the back but his erect penis, crusted and disfigured from a new venereal disease that I doubt has been diagnosed by even the most advanced contagious-disease specialists. I can usually talk my way out of anything, but now I'm not so sure. I keep flashing back to the Grim Reaper character in that Ingmar Bergman film, but realize sharing this film-buff memory with Randy Packard would be extremely ill-advised.

Suddenly I am hoisted in the air by a strategically placed bear trap. The clawlike grip of the catch slices into my one ankle and I sway in agonizing helplessness, my head crotch-level to Randy Packard's disgusting unit. He takes an Odorama card out of a drawer and rudely rubs it with his penis, the sores scratching the smell labels, and then pulls out a giant saber from a velvet bag and strokes his blistered hard-on with his callused fingers one last time. "No, Randy," I plead, just as the pimples on his penis pop at the exact moment he shoots a full load of infected, unsafe semen into my eyes. Thank God I barely see the blade slashing forward. It doesn't even hurt when he cuts off my head.

Oh no, I see the long white tunnel. You've *got* to be kidding me! This cliché couldn't be true, but it is! I feel myself elevating up, through the clouds, up, up, up to what? Oh my God—heaven?! It's fucking true? I see God but he gives me the thumbs-down. Over his shoulder I see awful people from my past—mean nuns from Sunday school, ignorant Christian Brothers who discouraged my interests in high school. I see Cardinal Shehan! Mary

Avara, the Maryland film censor! Is that Art Linkletter? Good God—Anita Bryant. All in heaven. God looks at me blankly and then whispers, "Catholics were right."

I scream in horror and feel myself plunging downward, past limbo, where despite updated dogma to the contrary, unbaptized babies *do* cry in frustration over never getting to see God. I plunge into hell and see all my deceased friends, but they can't see me or each other. It's hotter than Baltimore in August. *It's a Wonderful Life* plays on an extended loop on movie screens in every direction. I watch it for eternity.

THE REAL THING

NONFICTION

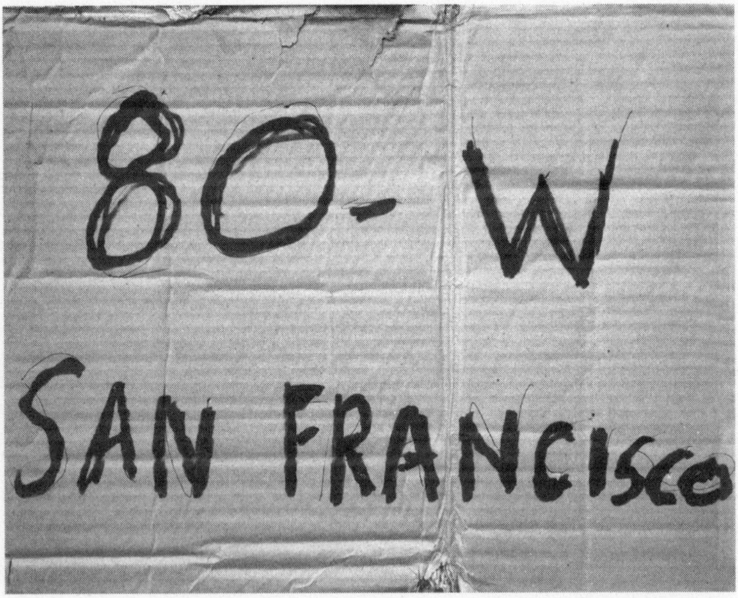
80-W
SAN FRANCISCO

REAL RIDE NUMBER ONE

DAY CARE

Okay, here's what really happened. Real life. May 14, 2012. No more fiction, just the truth.

I notice Susan and Trish have stopped discussing my hitching plans at the office. I can see their shared fear for my safety on their faces. Even my young art assistant, Jill, has caught the "worry" bug, sheepishly suggesting someone follow me on the road "to be sure you're safe," which I, of course, reject immediately. I could tell friends my own age were also concerned. Even my criminal buddies were appalled! "Carry a gun," one warned. "Take Mace," another ordered, and even the closest of my Baltimore convict friends sent me a handwritten graffiti drawing from jail that read *B-More Careful*.

As the day of my departure approaches, everybody's anxiety starts getting on my nerves. I have just written my fictitious death a few days ago, but nobody knows that yet. "Come on, be positive," I argue in exasperation. But truth be known, I am starting to get nervous myself.

On Mother's Day, twenty-four hours before I leave, I try not to show my fear, kissing my mom goodbye after dinner. She has no idea why I'm vanishing, just something vague about "research for a book." I figure she'd be horrified and worried if she knew I was hitchhiking, so I tell only my sisters the truth in case they need to reach me in an emergency. Will I ever see my mother again? I wonder as I walk out her door.

Sunday night at my house it's all quiet. My medium-size fake-crocodile-skin plastic tote bag is packed—five old pairs of boxer shorts, one of which I plan to discard each day after wearing; a pair of black 501 Levi's jeans; five Gap T-shirts; a *Scum of the Earth* movie-logo baseball cap; a label-free dark blue wool scarf some guest left behind at my Christmas party and never reclaimed; a Brooks Brothers dark blue wool turtleneck in case it gets chilly; a Patagonia orange nylon hooded rain jacket; and a pair of blue Japanese-brand Sunny Sports slip-on tennis shoes illustrated with pirate ships. Supplies include a Redline tactical flashlight, a fold-up umbrella, BlackBerry wall and car chargers, an Olympus digital tape recorder and batteries, a large felt-tip marker for making hitchhiking signs, a backup pair of reading and distance glasses, sunblock, and travel-size toiletries (including sample-size jars of La Mer Moisture Cream and Eye Concentrate). Susan has made me purchase a SPOT satellite GPS device, which supposedly tracks me anywhere, even in remote areas where cell phone coverage is nonexistent. How I am supposed to get this out of my pocket and push the emergency button if someone pulls a gun on me or the car is upside down in a ditch remains unanswered. I also take a bag of raw almonds, some trail mix, and two little bottles of Evian water for nourishment, a "fame kit" to prove to cops that I'm not just homeless, a stack of autographed, embossed PS: THANKS FOR THE LIFT business cards that a fan had sent me years ago that I recently discovered in my studio, and, of course, my TripTik booklet, prepared by AAA, whose employees thought I was *driving* across the country, not begging rides.

I wake up without the alarm five minutes before it's supposed to go off at 6:00 a.m. Oh God, it looks as if it's going to rain, but mercifully it hasn't started yet. I take a hot bath, drink some Tazo Awake tea (the most delicious brand, which I fear will be unavailable on the road), and get dressed, putting on my new REI hiking boots (that I'll never wear *after* this trip), waterproof gray socks (*so* unlike the Paul Smith ones I usually wear), maroon jeans from MAC (the best clothing store in San Francisco), a striped Agnes B. long-sleeved T-shirt, and a faux-bleached-out-black cotton Issey Miyake sports jacket. I'm not totally Comme des Garçons–deprived; my black belt was definitely designed by Rei Kawakubo. I slip my heavily edited wallet (in case I'm robbed), containing just a couple hundred dollars of cash, two credit cards, only one bank card, and my photo ID, into my inside coat pocket. I grab my key ring with the Saint Christopher medal an old friend has given me for this trip and the compass attached, which Susan forced on me, and realize in my new life on the road I only need one of my keys—the one to my San Francisco apartment, my final destination. I turn on my SPOT tracking device, throw caution to the wind, and walk out the front door carrying my bag and one other, smaller canvas tote (from Maggs Bros Ltd, a U.K. bookshop I love), containing my different hitchhiking signs.

It's completely still out. Thankfully, no neighbors are out for a morning jog. I walk up the street feeling like a troubled teenage runaway. I flash on Divine as Dawn Davenport hitching in her baby-doll pajamas in my film *Female Trouble* and identify with her today. I get to the corner of my road where it intersects Charles Street and begin to hitchhike north toward the Beltway, which will hopefully take me to I-70 West all the way past Denver to Route 6 North to 80 West in Salt Lake City and then straight into the Bay Area. But there's a problem. No cars. It's 6:30 a.m. and commuters are coming *into* Baltimore, not leaving the city. Finally, a few motorists—maybe three in twenty minutes—pass by. I realize Jill has made my I-70 WEST/SAN FRANCISCO hitch-hiking sign so you have to turn it over and around to read it correctly, not just flip it, which makes it harder to flash to oncoming possible rides. The drivers seem to refuse to even look at me. I feel like a complete fool.

I decide to walk up to the traffic light a couple of blocks away; at least here, where St. Paul Street connects, maybe there will be more cars on this well-traveled route. But no. I stand here in silence, alone. Then I feel a fucking raindrop. Then another. I am three blocks from my Baltimore house on the first day of my book expedition and it's raining; something I had imagined for fiction, but in real life it's suddenly impossible to believe. I take out my hooded rain jacket and put it on as my bags begin to get wet. I probably look scarier with my hoodie pulled up, I realize. It's also harder to recognize me and I'm embarrassed to admit I am already hoping this will happen.

Still no rides. I've been here for what? An hour? It continues to pour rain. I take out my umbrella but I soon realize it is impossible to hold a sign you have to flip and turn while it's getting wetter by the second *and* an umbrella in the other hand at the same time. Plus I'm sure I now look like a sopping-wet junkie Mary Poppins. More cars pass me. They probably think I'm one of those homeless men who sometimes stand at this intersection holding cardboard signs begging for money.

Just when I'm seriously considering going home and starting again the next day, when maybe the weather will be better, a car pulls up at the light and I hear an unfamiliar voice yell, "John Waters!" It's my first ride! A young African-American big-and-beautiful Tracy Turnblad–type woman who excitedly cries as I get in, "I loved *Hairspray*!" Strapped in a baby seat in the back is her gorgeous little daughter, who at first gives me a wary look but then breaks into a big smile.

I am so happy to meet such a brave fan. A woman. With a

baby. Amazing. "*Where* are you going?" she stammers in nervous excitement and confusion. When I explain I am hitchhiking to San Francisco, she starts laughing and screaming and waving her hands, apologizing she is "only going to Northern Parkway and turning west" to take her daughter to day care, and "then I have to go to work." I don't care. At least I am in a car headed in the right direction, out of the rain, if only for a few more blocks. I wish I remembered her name, but I was in the car for such a short time and so wet and excited to get picked up that I forgot to tell myself what it was on my tape recorder when I got out of her car. I did remember to give her my first THANKS FOR THE LIFT autographed card. Boy, did she deserve it! The first kind driver who took a risk on me. I salute her!

REAL RIDE NUMBER TWO

MINISTER'S WIFE

Reality check. It's still raining and I'm only about five minutes (at the most) away from my house. But at least I've begun. I stand there for maybe fifteen minutes, wondering if I should throw my original route plan to the wind and walk to the other side of the traffic light, going west to Jones Falls Expressway, and not take a ride from anyone unless they are continuing to I-70 West. But then I see a car do a U-turn going south on Charles Street and pull into a church parking lot just ahead of where I am hitchhiking. "Are you John Waters?" the female driver asks after pulling to a stop beside me and rolling down the passenger window. "Yes, I am," I answer in gratitude. "What do you need?" she asks, maybe thinking I wanted a tow truck or a mental-health practitioner. "Just a ride to I-70 West," I tell her truthfully. "Hop in," she says.

At first, Sarah Finlayson, my fifty-nine-year-old fit and pretty blond driver routinely returning home from her morning workout, *had* thought I was a homeless beggar, just as I feared. But suddenly, as she chatted on the car speakerphone with her twin sister, Mary, who lives in New Jersey, she told me she had blurted out, "I think I see John Waters," and decided to investigate. When I explain I am hoping to get a lift beyond the intersection of Baltimore Beltway and I-70 West, she offers to take me there "because it is raining." I know with rush-hour traffic this could take at least an hour but I just keep my mouth shut and thank her.

Mary stays on speakerphone at first, I'm sure, to be certain I'm not a John Waters impostor, or worse yet, a hacker (the murdering kind). "Be careful with my sister," she timidly orders, and I assure her I will, even though any serial killers would have agreed to the same thing. "Isn't my sister's car cute?" Mary continues, nervous at first, probably just trying to keep the chatter going in a positive direction while she assures herself her sister isn't going to end up a cadaver to be tossed into Baltimore's notorious body-dumping ground, Leakin Park. "It is," I agree, having no real idea if a Lexus is expensive or not. I may have been able to easily fantasize the vehicles driven by my "best" and "worst" drivers, but in real life I'm completely unobservant about cars. Who cares what they're driving as long as they stop and pick me up? "Isn't this exciting?" Sarah enthuses with a smile Mary can't see; "I'm gonna brag tonight at the conference." "My sister is very nice," I hear on the speakerphone; "her husband is a minister." It's a godsend, I realize. Literally.

"Are you married?" Sarah asks with sudden good-natured aggression. "No," I answer quickly before she smiles and continues, "Now, are you gay?" "Sure," I respond, and I get her immediate approval: "Okay, good!" I'm slightly surprised. "Good" because this means I'm not heterosexual and therefore probably not a potential rapist, or "good" because, well . . . she's a cool lady?

"You should have called me first, I'd take you the whole way," Sarah then kindly volunteers as we hit the rush-hour Beltway traffic and I thank her again for going off-route. "I'm very excited to help you out," she graciously responds. We're silent for a moment, but soon the sister gets nervous. "Still there?" Mary asks with a tinge of mild worry. "Sure are," I respond, "and your sister's a good driver, too!"

As we pass a sign for upcoming I-70W, Sarah shows no sign of fatigue or looking for a place to drop me off even though we have gone much farther than I ever imagined she'd take me. We drive by a highway sign reading DENVER—1700 MILES and I gulp as it starts pouring rain again. "How did you meet Divine?" Sarah asks, and I just keep talking like a phone-sex worker desperate to keep a caller on the line. The longer I can keep them entertained, the farther Sarah might take me. I realize I am actually responding to both Sarah's and Mary's questions with real lines from my stand-up act. "You're better than *Imus in the Morning*," the sister cracks. Singing for my supper, once again.

"It's raining, John," Sarah sheepishly points out, and I know she feels bad for me, so I whip out my THANKS FOR THE LIFT card and hand it over. She seems happy. Here's a souvenir that proves this whole morning actually happened. Meanwhile, Mary feels a lull in the conversation and says, "I should wake up my daughter." "Don't!" I beg when I hear that the teenage girl just worked the night shift. Why would she need to talk to me? Mary tries anyway. I hear the daughter's protests mumbled into her pillow over the speakerphone, and finally, much to my relief, Mary gives up. "Okay, I'll let her sleep," she sighs in celebrity-introduction defeat; "I guess she doesn't want to get up."

Sarah is beginning to realize we are pretty far away from her home and finally admits, "I have to use the bathroom." I suggest we stop at a McDonald's I see advertised ahead. "You've given me a really good start," I assure Sarah as she turns off and I rubberneck back and see there is a return entrance ramp to I-70 with enough room for a car to pull over to pick me up hitch-hiking. "We're here," Sarah announces to her sister as we pull into the fast-food parking lot and I say goodbye to Mary over the speakerphone. I take my luggage inside with me, just to be safe. I know Sarah won't take off with my bag, but after all, I used to break into cars myself in the sixties—maybe I've got bad karma that way. You can never be too sure.

Inside the Woodbine, Maryland, McDonald's I think of my late dad—he always liked McDonald's coffee and was a fan of their senior-refill policy, even though as far as I remember he *never* had a second cup. As Sarah heads for the ladies' room, I buy her a cup. Usually I'd be having a java at this time of day myself, but one thing a hitchhiker learns early—being regular can be a tricky thing on the road. So I'm nervous about starting a natural process that is obviously hindered by the randomness of thumbing a ride. I am scared to even eat.

"That's very nice of you," Sarah says as she returns to her cup of coffee and we sit down in a booth. I have my hitch sign out hoping someone will notice and offer me a ride, but nobody does. Sarah even casually asks other customers if they're "headed his way," but they politely make excuses. I can tell she's disappointed I'm not recognized.

The downpour continues, so I slip into my rain gear while I'm still under cover inside, remembering that the umbrella is a real hindrance on the highway. Sarah is hesitant to leave McDonald's, worried about letting me off in such inclement weather, but I know it's time to part. I'm a big boy, I won't melt.

We get in her car and I direct her down the hill to where I want to be dropped—the Exit 73 entrance ramp onto I-70 West. I get out and Sarah reluctantly says goodbye. I know how hard it is for her to pull away and leave me in the torrential rain. I thank her kindly. Before I left, everybody had said, "A woman alone will never pick up a hitchhiker." How wrong they were. Here's a minister's wife who practices what she preaches; not only is she smart and sassy, she's a lovely, funny lady who gives religion a good name. Thank you, Sarah.

REAL RIDE NUMBER THREE

GLEN THE FARMER

I stand on the entrance ramp with the hood of my rain jacket pulled up. I have hope. For the first time I am hitchhiking in a place where I have no idea where I am. It feels authentic. I'm really doing this! Few cars come by, much less turn to go on the interstate. It starts raining harder than ever. There's no cover and I am getting drenched. Even my faux-crocodile bag is gradually becoming soaked by the rain. I'm too afraid to open it to see if my few clothes inside are also getting wet. My cardboard sign starts sagging and I can't hold it up anymore. I despair for the first time. It continues to pour. I wish I were on a movie set and this deluge were coming from a rain machine. But it's not. Nobody yells, "Cut." I try my MIDLIFE CRISIS sign but *still* no one stops. I cannot believe I am standing alone in the middle of nowhere, like a drowned rat, unable to get a ride.

I look down and see the waterline stain rising on my bag, and when I look up, hurray! a pickup has stopped to give me a ride. I jump in and feel so happy. Glen, an eighty-one-year-old farmer, explains he's going to Frederick, which is about forty miles away. I am 100 percent sure he doesn't recognize me, and it only takes me a second to realize he thinks I'm just an old guy down on my luck.

Glen talks about how much he still likes to work. His farm has been in the family for years, but one of his sons, who always wanted to learn to fly as a child, grew up, got his pilot license, and was killed "doing what he loved most" in a plane accident. Glen is not sure if the rest of his children will want to continue to deliver hay—what this kind farmer loves to do best. I tell Glen (another safe driver) that I'm a film director and agree with him on how important it is to love your work. "We both will probably die doing what we love best," I say cheerily. He doesn't say it, being too gentlemanly and polite, but I can tell he doesn't believe for one second that I'm a film director. He tells me if hay gets wet and you don't dry it out before storing it in bales, spontaneous combustion can happen and fire will break out and burn down the barn. I start to talk more about movies again, hoping to convince him I really am a director, but then realize, what's the point? He's got his own dramatic real-life scenes, why should he need cinema? Especially mine.

Glen even knows a good place to drop me off—an I-70 entrance ramp beside a strip mall in Frederick, Maryland. He pulls into a parking lot out front of the Fractured Prune, a donut shop, so he can let me out safely in the rain. I thank him profusely and am dumbfounded to see him suddenly take out his wallet and try to hand me a $10 bill. I stammer my gratitude further but try to explain, "I really don't need it. I have money and credit cards. I'm hitchhiking so I can write a book about it, but that is so kind and thoughtful of you!" I can see by his merciful but indulgent smile that he doesn't buy a word of this either, but he reluctantly puts the money back in his pocket. I am shocked and incredibly moved by this man's generosity. It's still pouring rain, but as I exit his truck, I'm filled with goodwill. I look back at this real-life gracious hay farmer and he waves goodbye with a warm, grandfatherly smile. "Old MacDonald had a farm, EE-I-EE-I-O."

REAL RIDE NUMBER FOUR

BIKER

This rain is getting on my nerves. It can't continue forever. I go into the Fractured Prune and get a hot cup of tea. Nobody is inside except the girl behind the counter, who may have glimpsed my hitchhiking sign but shows no reaction. At least there's a bathroom I can use. After all, I *am* a paying customer. The men's room is perfectly clean, but I can't help feeling like the Crackers character in *Pink Flamingos* when at the end he says to Divine, "Let's sleep in gas station lavatories this time, Mama. Fuck permanent residences. It'll strengthen our filthiness."

The rain still hasn't let up. I finish my tea and don't want to be accused of loitering, so I walk back outside. It's a great ramp for hitchhiking. Lots of cars. Lots of rain. Nobody stops but I'm still a little upbeat because I realize I can always go back inside the donut shop if I need to use the bathroom again after that morning tea. My sign is getting drenched now. Water is dripping off my rain-jacket hood down onto my face. I try to make eye contact with drivers but realize many are local and my sign saying SAN FRANCISCO is too far for them to even consider.

Just when I don't think it could possibly rain any harder, it does. I can't believe it. My sign is so waterlogged it is becoming useless. Please, God, make a car stop, I catch myself praying, feeling like a complete hypocrite. But no, another forty-five minutes and *still* no one stops. I go back into the Fractured Prune with my tail between my legs. The manager is now out front doing chores with the same girl behind the counter, ending the breakfast shift and getting ready for the lunch crowd. I ask him if he has any cardboard I can use to make a new hitchhiking sign. He's pleasant and without commenting begins to break down a cardboard box and sadly warns me, "It's supposed to rain all day, you know." I just nod and take out my industrial-size felt-tip marker and start making a new sign that is a little more reasonable: END OF I-70W with the same S.F. on the reverse, this time flippable *without* having to turn around the whole sign horizontally. Sheepishly, I use the bathroom again. I piss when I know I can.

Okay, coward, I tell myself, get back out there and get a ride! Rolling up my waterlogged pant cuffs, I trudge back out to the exact same hitchhiking spot and hold up my sign. One thing I can say, these waterproof boots I bought sure do work. But the sign's message doesn't. No one stops. I change tactics—ad campaigns really—and see if humor in advertising has any effect. I try my backup I'M NOT PSYCHO sign to see if that gets any results. I see a couple of male drivers laugh as they read it, but none put on their brakes. Maybe hitchhiking is *not* the time to be a comedian, I suddenly realize. I go back to my more generic version, but that doesn't work either. Big puddles are forming where I'm standing. Passing cars start to splash me and my poor bag. Thank God it's *not* real crocodile. Police cars go right past me. At least they don't stop and give me any trouble. At least that.

It's always a shock when someone actually stops for you. It takes a second to sink in, and then you panic, grabbing your stuff, afraid people will change their mind and pull off. I jump in the van and see a blue-collar guy, maybe forty years old, who looks friendly enough. He's "not goin' that far," he apologizes, but promises to drop me off at an I-70 West exit that has "services." I like him. He reminds me of all the real bikers I know and love from the Holiday House, a bar in Baltimore I've been hanging out in for decades, where I filmed a big scene for my concussion–sex addict comedy, *A Dirty Shame*. Turns out he *is* a biker. So was his father. So was his grandfather. A long line of bikers! Almost like the flip side of the Daughters of the American Revolution. Generation after generation. Debutante types and bikers. Aren't they both kind of the same? Rarefied? A secret club that few are eligible to join? Their own never-changing fashions? Their coded language? Even severe body types?

I notice the biker who picked me up is missing a couple of front teeth, but he's *still* kind of cute. He tells me he's married to a lady surgeon and speaks highly of her. She keeps him in line. He seems to like that. We talk about how the biker identity is fading fast today with young people, and how a bad white boy is more apt to copy the black gangster style if he wants to be a rebel. I can tell this rubs him the wrong way. "Why would they do this?" he wonders, and before he can answer himself in a way I feel could be racist, he stops himself and smiles. He knows it's a losing argument. I bet his great wife has taught him that racism is not only wrong—he *likes* being wrong—but stupid. He's too sweet and nice to be stupid anymore. Maybe a strong woman with a taste for bad boys has tamed him to a point where he feels relief at not having to be a troublemaker, at least for part of the time. I bet they have a great sex life and a nice relationship. He pulls off at an exit to scout the return entrance ramp for me and, seeing it's a good one, lets me off. I feel happy again. I want to kiss him goodbye on the cheek, but it's only Day One, so I'm still a little sheepish. I think he might have laughed. In a nice way.

REAL RIDE NUMBER FIVE

THE CORVETTE KID

It's gonna get better, I keep telling myself. I'm on a roll. Having no idea where I am is kind of liberating. It's still pouring rain but the biker wasn't lying, there *are* "services" at this exit. I see a Burger King at the top of the hill in walking distance from where I, once again, have my thumb out. Uh-oh. Almost no cars come down this road either, and the ones that do don't turn onto I-70 West. They're all local rides—what I am beginning to learn is the enemy of successful hitchhiking. A big truck with the motor running is parked right off the road a little way up from me, but I don't see any driver. Maybe he's sleeping in the back and maybe . . . just maybe he'll pick me up.

I stand there for at least forty-five minutes. A wall of water pours down on me and it doesn't let up. Then it gets windy. My most recently drawn sign is now sopping wet again. I feel like crying. I wish the truck driver would wake up and see me standing there helplessly, but I guess he's still sawing wood. At this rate my trip will take ten years, and that's if I'm lucky. I can't stand it anymore. I have to wait it out somewhere—the downpour can't continue at this strength forever.

I hoof it up the hill to the Burger King. No customers are inside, except for one weird-looking guy, but he refuses to even make eye contact. I ask the young girl behind the counter if she has some cardboard, and she nicely gets me a box and I attempt to break it down. What would be a simple task for most men is, for me, as always, problematic. I rip the corners incorrectly, tearing into the sides, and end up with only two usable pieces of cardboard. I write the 1-70w message again but make the letters too small to read from a distance and have to do it over. Oh, well, one dry sign is better than none.

I decide since this is an almost-empty fast-food restaurant now would be a good time to try to eliminate. As long as that weird guy doesn't try to follow me inside. Oh, good! It's a single toilet with a lock on the door. And it's clean. I sit down on the toilet and remember I haven't eaten a thing. What do I expect? Shit or get off the pot. I get off. Mission canceled.

Back in the restaurant, I'm not sure if I'm relieved or disappointed to see the one weird guy is gone. He might have given me a ride! Then again, he might have killed me. Oh well. I look outside and sheets of rain are pounding the glass windows of the Burger King. I feel like such a vagrant standing inside here without a purpose. I force myself to leave.

I slog back down the hill, in what *must* be flooding conditions, to my hitchhiking spot. The truck is gone. That's who the weird guy was—the driver! Maybe the other backup trucker was asleep in the bunk, snoring, getting on the other driver's nerves. I'll never know.

I fucking stand there in the rain for another half hour. You can't imagine the misery of waiting for a ride in the endless pouring rain. Because of the limited peripheral vision caused by my having my rain-slicker hoodie up, I don't even see the miracle suddenly happen. I just look up and there is a 1999 red Corvette ending a U-turn right in front of me. The driver, a cute, stocky blond guy, rolls down the passenger window and asks, "How far do you need to go?" I feel like Francine Fishpaw in *Polyester* when Tab Hunter pulls up in a Corvette and the Odorama Number 8 smell "new car" begs to be scratched and sniffed. "San Francisco," I say as I climb in, and "The Corvette Kid," as I immediately christened him in my mind, doesn't seem to blink. "I'll take you as far as I can."

From Myersville, Maryland, he's a twenty-year-old sandy-haired Republican town councilman (the youngest in the state), who, dressed in T-shirt, cargo shorts, and white leather Nike sneakers, is on his way to pick up his lunch at the local Subway sandwich shop. He tells me he stopped because he "feels guilty." "Two weeks ago I saw a hitchhiker standing right where you are and I didn't pick him up." We chat. He has no idea who I am even after I tell him. He has never seen any of my films. I don't ask him how far he's going and he doesn't say. I just keep talking. We both realize we'd probably head-butt on some social issues, so we wisely avoid politics. And as he puts it, "potholes and how to fill them" was more a subject a town councilman like himself would deal with and those are "not exactly Republican or Democrat issues." We cross the state line into Pennsylvania. A twenty-year-old transporting a senior citizen across state lines for hitchhiking fun. "Is this a federal offense?" I say out loud. We both laugh.

His mother starts texting frequently, and while I don't see how he answers, he admits she's alarmed. After all, her son borrowed her car to go to lunch and now is in another state with a supposed John Waters (whoever the hell that is), whom he picked up hitchhiking. Imagine the red flags going off in that house! I try to picture her Googling me. Great. What would come up first? That I was just awarded the Outfest Gay Award and would be performing my one-man show, *This Filthy World: Gayer and Filthier*, in two months? Or my friendship with ex–Manson Family member Leslie Van Houten? Or the dogshit-eating scene in *Pink*

Flamingos? "Plus, how do you know it's really him?" I can imagine Dad butting in, "How do you know it's not some 'Crockafeller'-type impostor serial killer or robber who's gonna steal your mother's car and murder you!?" "Is there an AMBER Alert out for you now?" I ask The Corvette Kid, nervously recalling the Tarantula "worst ride" chapter I'd already written. He laughs again. I guess that means there's not. We keep going.

We're now on an adventure. And why not? I think. What twenty-year-old *wouldn't* want to go on such a crazy spur-of-the-moment trip? How often could this unlikely scenario repeat itself? If The Kid is worried about running off with a gay cult-film director, he sure isn't showing it. We talk about small-town life versus the big city. Youth. Dating. A girl he wants to hook up with later in the month when he goes to Joplin, Missouri, to help tornado victims rebuild their homes. Drugs. Show business. And taking chances in life.

We see a sign in western Pennsylvania saying LAST FOOD AND GAS FOR 123 MILES, so we stop and I fill up the tank. He accepts with gratitude and makes no mention of turning back. We have been traveling for hours. We get back in the car and drive a short way to New Stanton Plaza and go in this Quiznos sandwich restaurant for lunch, which isn't so bad. I trust The Kid but make some excuse about bringing in my bags and signs because "I have to find something inside," but the real reason is that you never know—he could get cold feet and drive off while I'm in the men's room. I buy us lunch. At first he protests, but I tell him it's the least I can do since "we're now Thelma and Louise." He chuckles and says his mom and her friends always call each other that.

But I can see by The Kid's nervous glances to his cell phone that his mom ain't laughing now. Why is her son 160 miles away with "The Prince of Puke"? Have I kidnapped him? Is he fighting me off? She must really be upset because when he finally gives in and calls home, she doesn't even recognize his voice. "Who is this?" I can hear her suspiciously ask. "It's your son!" The Kid sputters in exasperation. Does she think it's me on the phone impersonating him and he's locked in the trunk? I offer to speak to her, but he acts as if he doesn't hear me and gets off the phone.

He keeps driving. His mom keeps calling back. Finally I hear him tell her, "I'll be home by seven o'clock," which I know is impossible, but I don't butt in. We go through West Virginia but just the northern tip. Another state of runaway fun! Wheeeee! I can't believe this kid is such a daredevil. Good God, we're in Ohio. We've been driving for four and a half hours. Even I know our little folly has to end soon. I tell him to start looking for a good exit off of I-70 West to drop me off where there are gas stations and motels.

We pull off on one and both realize this is a lousy exit for hitchhiking—a big shopping center—all local rides, no cross-country travelers. He doubles back to the exit before, which is smaller; a gas station, a convenience store, and one motel. I fill up his tank again, take his photo with my BlackBerry camera, and we shake goodbye. I take out another THANKS FOR THE LIFT card and hand it over. I know The Kid won't regret picking me up on the l-o-o-o-n-n-g-g drive home, but I can imagine him thinking, what the hell just happened? "Come back and go to California with me," I joke, and tell him if he ever needs to contact me to go through Atomic Books, where I receive mail without having to give out my personal address. I'm not sure why I just don't give out my business card. After all, he is my new best friend; the only Republican I'd ever vote for. Why on earth am I nervous to tell him where I live? We'll both remember this day forever, won't we?

It's still only four o'clock, plenty of daylight left. Why not keep going? I see a sign in the distance for a Days Inn, so if I ever get stuck here, at least there's a place to stay. I'm feeling cocky; the rest of this trip is going to be a piece of cake. I set up shop right between two gas stations (one with a Food Mart, the other with an advertised ATM machine inside) in St. Clairsville, Ohio, where The Corvette Kid has left me. I figure most cars going by here are headed to the I-70W entrance that is, according to a sign I walked past, right up the hill. I couldn't see the ramp but I have faith it is there just waiting to welcome me west. Lots of cars come by but none stop. One nice biker-type lady pulls out of the front gas station, rolls down her passenger window, and says, "Come on, honey, I'll take you up two exits," but I turn her down politely, explaining I am "in a pretty-well-set-up hitchhiking spot and want to try and catch an interstate ride." But nobody stops. I amuse myself by watching these two gearhead guys in a pickup race back and forth between the gas stations. Why don't they just walk? I wonder. I fantasize all sorts of illegal scenarios—drugs, stolen car parts—but I guess their activities could be totally mundane. One is very cute, but neither ever makes eye contact with me despite the fact that they practically have to run over me every time they drive back and forth. I imagine running off with them.

By now, the evening rush hour is in full swing. All these cars headed to I-70 West and no one is driving cross-country who wants an infamous companion? I've been standing here now for more than two hours. Has my roadside charm disappeared? A cop slowly drives by, looks me over, but keeps going. Phew. I remember that ridiculous song "Ohio" sung by Doris Day, but feel the opposite of its geographically proud lyrics. "Why oh why oh why oh, why can't I get *out* of Ohio," I want to sing out for the world to hear. Endless string of traffic. No rides. No eye contact from drivers. "All you need is *one* ride!" I chant over and over, and suddenly, lo and behold, someone stops. I'm so excited, I fumble picking up my bags and packing up my signs. I rush to the car and see the driver peering out through the rolled-down passenger window. He's not bad-looking. Maybe this will be a great ride. But just as I'm about to get in he says, "Never mind, I'm not going that far," and pulls off. Well! Why did you stop, then? I want to scream after him. Rejected! I know it's been a long day, but do I look *that* bad? Soaked. Then dried out. Old. I take it personally.

Just when I couldn't feel much worse, the cop comes back, does a U-turn, pulls right over into the second gas station, and drives to the edge of the parking lot near where I am standing. "You can't hitchhike," he tells me after getting out of his vehicle. "But I'm writing a book about hitchhiking across America," I tell him. "I'm also a film director." This throws him, I can tell. He hadn't been expecting that answer, and I guess he believes me. He hesitates and finally says, "Okay, but don't stand in the actual road itself and never go down to the interstate!" I agree to his terms, kind of surprised he's this lenient.

It's getting late. Not dark yet, but still. I hope the only reason I got rides today wasn't just because it was raining and people felt sorry for me. I'm suddenly worried the one hotel I'm anywhere near might have no vacancies. I give up for the day, sure I'll have better luck bright and early tomorrow morning.

I plod across a bridge that goes over I-70 and look west in optimistic but shaky confidence. These bags are kind of heavy, I realize as I climb up, up, up a steep incline, seeing only the Days Inn sign, which was erected to be visible from the highway below. I notice a couple of giant trucks parked on the side of the incline. Rounding a bend and feeling like a weary and weak Elmer Gantry, I huff and puff to the parking lot and finally into the Days Inn lobby. Thank God they have a room. The lady at the desk doesn't blink when I tell her I have no vehicle. I walk to my motel-style room, past many trucks, some with their motors running. I'm too tired to think dirty.

The room is actually fine. At least there's decent lighting, something many hotels (even fancy ones) neglect to consider. Not everybody fucks in the motel rooms—some people read! For the first time today I check my e-mails. Good God. Hundreds. That's what you get when you ignore your business. I go through and only read personal ones. Even though it is after office hours I call my assistants at home to check in, something that will have to continue through the trip and I know gets on their nerves. "But I can only talk to you at night now," I explain. "I can't read e-mails standing by the side of the road in that sunlight, and I certainly can't be doing business inside a car when I am trying to talk my way to San Francisco." Susan and Trish seem to understand and are relieved I'm somewhere safe for the first night at least.

I'm surprised to realize Days Inn has no room service. I'm not being a snob here, but I thought I could at least get a hamburger or some sort of crummy pizza. But no, only "complimentary breakfast between 6:30 and 9:00 a.m." I go back out in the lobby to see if there are any dinner alternatives, but the local take-out menus for restaurants that will deliver here seem too depressing. Nosing around, always looking for inspiration, I see there *is* a bar in the motel. A big one with a disco ball! Only one couple is inside, but it looks kind of amazing. A set from a low-budget *Convoy* meets a *Stayin' Alive* sequel. On any other night I'd be in there in a Baltimore second, making friends. But tonight I'll pass. Hitchhiking with a hangover would be unthinkable.

I'm not hungry anymore anyway. I go back to my room and get out my map and realize I'm only three hundred miles from my house in Baltimore. It's gonna be a long trip. I eat a little bit of the "trail mix" I brought with me, some of which has spilled out into the bottom of my still-damp bag. I feel like a homeless hamster. It's the end of Day One. I guess if you're this tired, you can sleep anywhere. Nighty-night.

I wake up early. Day Two. That I'm actually going to walk outside this motel room and stick out my thumb again seems even
more shocking to me now that I'm past the point of no return. I
peek through the curtains and see it's not raining outside, but it
is incredibly foggy. Great! My fear of multiple car and truck pile-
ups on the highway accelerates. I throw away my first pair of
worn underwear and leave a $5 tip for the maid, wondering if
such gratuities are even customary at the Days Inn.

I go into the breakfast room for my complimentary meal, hoping some cross-country driver will see me and offer me a ride.
But no. It's a hideously lit area with a TV blaring. The six or seven
grizzled men inside don't make eye contact with one another,
much less me. They look stunned by the grim routine of their
lives. I feel the unfriendly vibes immediately, and with one look
at the pitiful breakfast choices this place offers—white bread,
packaged donuts—not even instant bad scrambled eggs or micro-
waved greasy bacon—I lose my appetite. Instead, I gulp down a
cup of tea and immediately go to the bathroom and try to pee

again, still filled with future lack-of-facility concerns. I check out of the motel quickly. Nobody makes small talk.

Alone in the dense fog, I walk down the big hill in nervous silence toward my same hitchhiking spot from yesterday. It is scary foggy. I mean the kind where they could shut down the interstate. A truck or two pass me by leaving the motel and I hold my sign up, but I'm afraid with zero visibility that they'll actually run me over. I march back onto the overpass that crosses I-70W and look off into the pea soup and hope against hope that today will be easier.

But it's not. Same spot. Same deal. Lots of cars. No one stops. I wonder if I should walk up the hill to where the real I-70 entrance ramp is. Nah, probably nowhere to pull over there. Besides, it's engulfed in even thicker fog. Better stay here. All it takes is one car. But that one car doesn't stop. I stand here for hours.

The fog finally starts to burn off and it gets hot. I put down my sign and apply sunblock, which I'm always afraid will look like bird shit if I smear it on without looking in a mirror to see if it's rubbed in thoroughly. I put on my *Scum of the Earth* baseball hat to protect my bald spot. No one will recognize me now, but that's better than sun poisoning. I slip on my sunglasses, too. Now I really look like a loony tune. A different cop drives by and gives me the eye but doesn't stop. I'm surprised.

I see one of the cute gearheads from yesterday in his pickup pull into the gas station. He's still racing around, hopping in his truck, peeling out to drive the short distance to the other gas station. What on earth is he doing? He must have seen me by now, too! I've been hitching out front of where he works for two days, but he still resists any greeting. I'm so bored and frustrated I pretend I have a crush on him in an inappropriate Jane Bowles kind of way.

It's getting to be lunchtime, I gotta do something. This is

definitely not working. Then I see somebody walk up toward me on the shoulder of the road. Oh, no! Not another hitchhiker, I fear. Hey, buddy, I was here first, I imagine arguing, remembering those 1960s hippie turf hitchhiking wars that always erupted in either New Haven, Connecticut, or Santa Barbara, California—two hot spots for interstate-ride begging. As he gets closer, I realize he is a real homeless person. He passes me by and says hello. The first local who has actually spoken to me since I was dropped off in this godforsaken town! I say hi back.

Giving up here, I finally tread up the hill, and when I get to the top, I see the problem. Yes, the entrance ramp to I-70W is here (and it has an okay place to stand), but the real reason no one was stopping is almost none of the traffic is turning onto the interstate. I've been standing on a big local route leading to a large shopping center and a lot of the town's business and retail locations, so nobody's been going my way. They were just going to the mall. Fuckers!

I stand in my new spot, figuring now I'll get a ride. Not sure why I think that. Same tiny percentage of cars swerve off onto I-70 West. The same cop comes cruising back and I see him eyeing me, but he keeps going. It's getting really hot. I don't have much water left. I see a woman who looks straight out of one of my movies walking up the hill toward me. Again I pray it's not another hitchhiker. She looks mean, too. Maybe a hooker? But this hardly looks like a sex hot spot to me. She passes me by. Maybe she's just going to work. Why do you have to turn everybody into a tawdry character? I chastise myself.

The ball of hell known as the sun is rising fast and is now almost directly overhead. I could pass out. I notice one tiny area of shade across the street on somebody's property. Whoever lives in that house above couldn't see me if I sat there for a moment just to rest my weary bones, could they? I plod over to the shady spot of grass and sit down. I don't look at my BlackBerry messages—

it's a world too far away. Instead I call my office and whine to my assistants. They are patient, even though I know they'd like to yell, "We told you not to do it, fool," but instead offer the encouragement that "someone will come along." "Yeah, but suppose they don't?" I argue, and then realizing they couldn't possibly have an answer to that question, we hang up. I just sit there. The first gnat I feel on my skin gets me back on my feet.

I go back to my across-the-street spot, but still nobody stops. St. Clairsville, Ohio, I hate you. I guzzle my last drops of water and decide I've got to walk back down the hill and get some supplies. I can live on trail mix alone, but I do need liquids. Maybe I can talk someone in the first gas-station convenience store into either giving me a ride or letting me pay to be taken to a better area with more cross-country drivers. I pass the second gas station with the gearhead. He doesn't look up but he's still there, so our possible affair is not totally out of the question, I guess.

I go into the convenience store in the first gas station and buy water. Now that Coke distributes Evian, I am always pleasantly surprised to find it available in places like this. The guy behind the counter sees my hitchhiking sign—he must have noticed me out front, too—and doesn't look away. I ask him if there's a better rest area down the road and he says, "Yeah. There's a truck stop about a half hour away," and I inquire, pitifully, "Know anyone I could pay to drive me there?" Silence for a second. "Yeah, me," he answers, "when I get off work at two o'clock." "How much?" I demand, all perked up and instantly relieved. After giving it a moment's thought he says, "Twenty dollars." "Deal," I answer, thinking to myself I would have said okay if he'd asked for a hundred! "I'll go back out and hitchhike, and if I'm still there when your shift ends, let's do it," I negotiate. "Okay," he agrees, and I feel optimistic. Otherwise I might have to ask him for a job. I feel like I live here already.

Back in my first hitchhiking spot between the two gas stations, I feel as if I am in *Groundhog Day*. I hope the gearhead doesn't think I'm stalking him. Same old story. Lots of cars. No rides. Then I see the same cop coming back down the hill, only this time he pulls right over to me. I can't tell if he's a mean cop or not. He asks me for ID. I show him my license and explain I'm writing a book on hitchhiking. He doesn't show his hand but goes back to his vehicle and calls in my info. Satisfied there's no warrant against me, he comes back and gives me my license. I explain that "an officer told me yesterday in this exact same spot" that I "could hitchhike here" if I didn't "stand in the road." "Oh, yeah," he answers, "what did he look like?" "A blond," I answer, conjuring up idealized Tom of Finland visions. I figure now may be the time for my "fame kit," so I take it out, tell him I'm a film director, drop the H-word (*Hairspray*), and offer him a look. He silently reads my whole bio—"film director, writer, actor," etc., and then he looks up at me and says with a straight face, "It doesn't say anything here about you being a professional hitch-hiker." I laugh. He does, too. "You could give me a ride," I suggest brazenly. "Okay," he says, "I will."

I can't believe it. I get in the "cage" in the back and it's the exact opposite experience of what I imagined in the "worst" chapter. This time I wish he *would* put on the siren, but I keep my mouth shut as we peel out. I quickly forget the guy in the convenience store I had hired to give me a ride. Oh well. I told him if I *didn't* get a ride. Besides, I just saved myself $20.

"I can only take you to the end of my county," the officer explains. "This is a sheriff's police car, not a state trooper's, and in Ohio each county has sheriff cop cars that do all the work even though state troopers have all the power." Just as I'm thinking how relieved I am *not* to be with those lazy state troopers, he offers to "call ahead and see if I can find another officer to take you further into Ohio. The exit I'm thinking of is okay," he advises, "it's got a filling station and restaurant, but the second one, outside of my county, is a truck stop with a hotel and it's bigger and probably better for getting a ride." Either all the other cops think he's crazy or they *are* busy because my protector and real-life peace officer can't find any fellow sheriffs to help me out.

"Sorry, I'll have to drop you off at the first one," he says as he exits I-70W and pulls into a giant travel plaza that also is a diesel-truck stop located next door to a McDonald's. We're only seven miles from where he picked me up, but I am so grateful. Maybe I could stay and be his deputy and we could hang out in cop bars after work and get drunk together, I fantasize. "You should have luck here," he says cheerfully; "lots of cars enter and exit on these ramps." He waves to the lone gas-station attendant and highway workmen entering the fast-food restaurant, obviously familiar with the locals. "I'll come back and check on you," he says as I get out, "and if I find another officer who can take you to the next truck stop, I'll have him come get you." Wow. Public service at its finest. I suddenly like Ohio again.

REAL RIDE NUMBER SEVEN

MALE NURSE

I go into McDonald's. People look up at me, I hope in recognition, but I can't be sure. Maybe it's just because I look like an unidentified flying oddball. What to order? I decide on the plainest thing I see on the overhead menu. A Quarter Pounder. It's not bad. At least I've finally eaten something. I try making eye contact with the diners seated around me, but nobody seems to want to chat even though my hitchhiking sign is in full view and you'd think that might be a conversation piece. Not here.

I go outside and stroll through the trucker gas station, hoping someone will see my sign. If they do, it doesn't help. I walk up the lonely highway toward the entrance ramp. I pass a lot displaying sample chicken coops with a sign directing interested buyers where to call. Will I have to sleep in one tonight?

The entrance ramp is a good one with plenty of space for a driver to pull over before the high-speed merge onto Route 70 West. I stick out my thumb once again. It's very hot. Lots of bikers are on the road because it's maybe the first summery-type weather of the year. They always give me the thumbs-up sign when they see me hitching, and I return the gesture. Once again

I'm stuck. Nobody stops. I stand here for four more hours. What the fuck am I gonna do? Maybe no one will ever pick me up! Susan texts me, "Are you okay? Looks like you're still in the same place." No, I'm not okay, I think. I can tell I'm getting dehydrated. I see a nonchain, local-diner-type joint back where I was, across the street from McDonald's. Maybe I'd better take a break, stroll over there to get some shade, and see if any friendly drivers are inside.

I walk back past those now-even-more-threatening chicken coops. I can't help myself—I pick one out just in case that has to be my lodging for the night. I go into the diner and am disappointed to see it's almost empty. Lunch hour is long over so I blatantly ask the table of guys sitting together if they're "going my way?" They politely say no. Then I order a large Coke, something I would *never* do! I haven't had a Coca-Cola in twenty years but I'm about to faint, and when I was a kid, my mom always used to give us a Coke if we were feeling queasy. The waitress eyes me a little suspiciously, but maybe I'm just being paranoid. I use the bathroom like any other paying customer and think of that rude *TMZ* segment I saw where they tailed Larry David and Jeff Garlin into a gas station, and when Jeff Garlin exited the men's room, the reporter had the nerve to ask him if it was number one or number two. Just number one for me. Especially here.

When I return, the waitress delivers my order and I ask her if she knows "anyone I could pay to take me down the road to that bigger truck stop" that the cop had told me about. She doesn't know anyone. Sigh. I drink the giant Coca-Cola and it hits the spot. Any calories I get here *have* to be canceled by the anxiety of this godforsaken day. I leave a 50¢ tip on a $1 check and feel like a fool.

I go back out in the heat and once again plod my way back up to the entrance ramp. Again no one stops. Then I see a cop car pull over, but instead of feeling paranoid I am praying (once again!) that it will be my mythical "cop from the next county" who was originally contacted by the first cop and is now free to give me a ride. But no, it's the first cop! "You still didn't get a ride?!" he marvels. I am mortified. "It's mostly local traffic," I offer as a flimsy excuse. "Well, shake your sign or something," he advises with exasperation. I feel like such a loser; a lazy hitchhiker who can't even hustle a ride properly. He waves goodbye and heads back in the opposite direction from where I'm going. I'm amazed I never imagined waiting this long in any of my "worst" ride chapters. I have been hitchhiking today for about nine hours and have been inside a car for less than ten minutes. And it's only Day Two! I will never get to San Francisco.

Then it happens—as always, when you least expect it. A ride. I bet a cheer goes up in my office when they see by the SPOT tracking device that I finally get a lift. Any driver who picks up a hitchhiker wants to talk, and today I'm especially willing to listen. He's a lovely guy in his thirties, working-class, with a girlfriend at home. He immediately tells me his "life-changing" tale of how his grandmother, after a long illness, had to have her legs amputated, and how he was so greatly impressed by the care she got in the hospital that he wanted to take up nursing for a living. Good. He can nurse me.

He had been divorced and said he got a lot of tattoos to punish himself but was "now better." He has a kid of his own and more children with his new girlfriend, of whom he speaks kindly. He isn't going far, he explains, he has just gotten carryout, at the same McDonald's where I had lunch, to take home for dinner to his family. I ask him about that truck stop down the road I had heard about, and he explains that it has recently gone out of business. All that is open there now is a trucker gas station. My heart sinks; I guess the cop didn't know that. I tell the kindly and not-unbutch nurse what I do for a living, but in a nice way he doesn't seem much interested. I explain my fear of being dropped off so late in the day at an exit without a motel. He says, "After I eat dinner I'll drive back down to this freeway exit and check on you to see if you got a ride." Wow! What a great offer! But what exactly is the offer? If I'm still standing there, do I get to go to his house, meet the little woman, and sleep on the couch? Do I get to nibble on his family's leftover McDonald's dinner? I guess I'm a little less worried when my male nurse pulls off the interstate to let me off. Of course I give him my thank-you card. Maybe he *will* come back if I'm stuck. Grasping at straws is beginning to feel normal.

REAL RIDE NUMBER EIGHT

COAL MINER

Just as I feared, there is no lodging at this exit. Up the street from where I'm standing, partially hidden by tree branches, is a gas station, and from the sign I can see, I gather some sort of convenience store is inside. But how late this place stays open I have no idea. To the right (past a bridge I could sleep under if I had to) I glimpse in the distance giant trucks pulling away after refueling. Visible farther up on the other side of the freeway is the sign for the now-defunct "trucker plaza," the one place I could have spent the night *if* it had been open. But it isn't, John, it isn't.

The only cars that seem to be on the road here are rush-hour types, and they pass with the usual indifference. I sadly realize I'm at an even worse place to thumb a ride than I was when I was last picked up, but at least it's a *different* worse place. I stand there with my thumb out forever. I'm dying here. I call my office and vent my fears. Susan and Trish don't know what to do or how to help because I can't even give them my location. I don't know where the hell I am myself! My BlackBerry and SPOT tracker can tell them a fairly close geographical position, but not exact. I beg them to find a local car-company phone number just in case I'm stuck here in the dark. Susan and Trish can hear the panic in my voice when I realize the workday is ending and they'll soon be leaving the office. They promise me they'll try.

We hang up, and I can see the sun is quickly going down. Terror. I realize I need a new sign that is way more direct—one that *could* work for local riders and at least get me to an exit with a motel. But I am afraid to leave my hitchhiking spot to search for cardboard, because suppose the male nurse comes back? What time *was* he eating dinner, anyway? He must be finished by now! Was he lying about returning? Did he look up my name on his home computer and suddenly get cold feet? No, megalomaniac, he probably threw away your card, you self-important shithead. *I want him to come back right now!*

But he doesn't. I realize I must act or it will be total night-fall. I walk over to the gas-station convenience store and ask the woman behind the counter if I could have some cardboard to make a sign. "You know it's illegal to hitchhike on the freeway," she sniffs. Bitch. "Yes, I know, but I'm on the entrance ramp and the Ohio police have already told me that was okay," I answer with suppressed haughtiness. "In that shed outside to the left of the store is where all the empty boxes are kept," she offers with a hint of class condescension. "You'll have to break them down." I begrudgingly thank her and wonder if she'll call the cops when I leave.

Inside the hot shed I grab a few boxes—all too large—and rip them apart with my hands in my usual clumsy-at-physical-labor kind of way. Ow! I scrape my hand on a staple and now I'm bleeding. Once again, I wonder why I can't do the simple physical things most other men can do easily. Am I *that* gay? So queer I can't flatten a cardboard box properly without ripping it in the middle and making it impossible to be used as a potential sign?

Finally I find a smaller box, and miracle of miracles, the seams flatten properly and I tear off two sides that are the perfect size. I take out my trusty marker and start to scrawl my new plea, NEXT MOTEL, but hesitate, wondering if that message will somehow sound sexual. Instead I write NEXT HOTEL, which is ridiculous—certainly there are no real *hotels* anywhere near these freeway exits, but what the hell? I'd rather sound highfalutin than cheap.

Guess what? The sign works. A coal miner picks me up. A real one. Midthirties. Covered in coal dust like in a comic strip. Coming home from work. And yes, he'll take me to an exit in Cambridge, Ohio, where there are motels. It's only ten minutes away from where he picked me up (Old Wilmington, Ohio, he tells me), but at least I don't have to sleep outside. Yay!

I don't even bother telling him what I do for a living and he doesn't ask. Not the nosy type, I guess. Just a good guy helping out a fellow man down on his luck. I ask him about that Chilean coal-mining disaster and how it was for him to watch that harrowing-rescue news footage and he says he "purposely never looked at it because I have three little girls and have to go to work in the coal mines here anyway, so why upset myself?" He's had a past, just like most of the men who've picked me up hitchhiking so far. He had gone north from this part of Ohio "because it was dull," but became a meth addict before turning his life around and coming back home. Just like the male nurse and the biker before him, the coal miner speaks lovingly about his wife. Usually at home I meet straight guys who bitch about their spouses and complain about the lack of blow jobs they get, but here is another heterosexual man who *does* love women and gives his wife great credit for steering him in the right direction. He seems happy. Heterosexuals can feel good about themselves, too.

Even though Cambridge, Ohio, is past his exit, he takes me there anyway and even checks out the entrance ramp for my tomorrow morning's hitching. It looks good. He asks me which of the several motels we could see I'd like to stay in. I am already a Days Inn man, so I choose what I know. I give him my THANKS FOR THE LIFT card and he takes it politely. He bids me farewell with a smile and pulls off toward home after an honest day's work.

REAL RIDE NUMBER NINE

HERE WE GO MAGIC

I check in, and lo and behold, the clerk recognizes me. I tell him I'm hitching cross-country and writing a book and how hard it is to get a ride. I see him Googling me at the same time he's taking my credit card info. A fat man waiting to check in behind me overhears and says, "I used to be a trucker and there's a lot of truckers who stay at this exit, so you ought to have luck." I tell him truckers can never pick up hitchhikers these days because of all the restrictive new rules, but he says without missing a beat, "Well, believe me, they'd pick you up if you had a vagina."

I go to my room, and as soon as I enter, the phone is ringing. It's the clerk. "Can you come down and do an autograph?" he asks. "Sure," I respond, "as long as you try and hustle me a ride west tomorrow morning." As I sign at the desk, he assures me he'll ask around and leave me a note in the morning if he's had any luck before his shift ends. I have hope.

I go back upstairs and text Susan and Trish at their homes that "a nice coal miner—in the outfit" gave me an eight-mile ride to a Days Inn. I explain about the clerk in the lobby, how he might find me a ride, etc. Susan e-mails me back, "Tomorrow will be better."

I see by checking the day's e-mails that my office tried earlier, without any luck, to find me a taxi or car service when I was whining and panicking. I read the e-mail incorrectly in my usual impatient way and assume when they write that they even "called a local VFW bar" and tried to "talk to a sober enough person to act as a hack" that they were setting up a "fake" ride to pick me up. I write them a blowhard e-mail back saying, "This makes me insane. Please do not do this!" But then I realize they weren't trying to manipulate my story, just doing what I had asked—find me a paid ride to a hotel if I got stuck. I write back with my tail between my legs, "I see this was preventative planning. Thanks."

I continue scrolling down on my phone and read that The Corvette Kid e-mailed me at Atomic Books the very night he left me off. The owner, Benn Ray, doesn't know about my hitchhiking trip so is baffled. He forwards The Kid's day-old initial e-mail to my office, which explains how he picked me up in Frederick County, Maryland, and drove me to Ohio, what a great time we had, and then asks Atomic Books for my e-mail address so he could offer to give me a lift again on his upcoming trip to Missouri.

Not having any idea what The Kid was referring to, Benn sent back the standard line to fans who e-mail there, "I'm sorry, we only accept mail for John Waters," and gave him the address. But The Kid wasn't having any of that and answered, "Okay, he did say to reach him by e-mailing him there . . . If this isn't true and he lied to me, so be it. But I spent 4 hours driving him to Ohio today. All I'm asking is for you to forward the e-mail to him so I can touch base." Susan had seen this forwarded e-mail at work and answered, politely explaining to The Kid the situation with Atomic Books and adding, "Thank you for driving John yesterday. He told us it was a great ride and he really appreciated it. He's checking in with us very infrequently, but we'll be sure he sees your e-mail and thank you for extending such a nice offer. I think he'll be beyond Missouri in a few days but it sure is generous to offer a backup plan." The Kid answered quickly, thanking her, and joking about my having told him one of my assistants was also a Republican, "Glad to hear of a fellow 'R' . . . hopefully John doesn't give you too much grief for that." He doesn't seem put off by Susan's pooh-poohing the possibility of his coming back to get me. "What a great adventure," The Kid writes her back. I immediately e-mail him my cell phone number. You never know.

I feel a little more upbeat. And for the first time on the trip, I am starved. I walk outside into the hub of motels, fast-food restaurants, even a giant tractor-supply warehouse. Truckers are everywhere, and yes, a few of them are incredibly cute, but in real, unporn life most of them are, well, ugly. Just like film directors, I guess. Here is a world I have never been in, in my life. I feel excited! I go in a Starfire convenience store and buy more water, then I head over to Ruby Tuesday for dinner. Another first for me. I sit at the counter and try to appear friendly to the other trucker types who are also eating, but nobody takes the bait. I order tilapia and it's actually delicious. I like Ruby Tuesday, I decide, feeling that I'm almost passing for a normal person. Maybe regular people don't talk to strangers. Maybe that's why I've made no friends here.

I walk back to the motel and make sure the clerk sees me again. He waves. I'm disappointed he doesn't mention anything about a ride tomorrow, but I decide I can't be a nag. Maybe he's still working on it.

Up in my room I look at my AAA TripTik and get depressed. I hitchhiked about ten hours today but only was in cars for a total of about fifty minutes. Day Two has been awful. I have a long, long way to go. Escape to sleep.

I wake up at 6:00 a.m., as usual. Thank God, Days Inn has bathtubs. Showers are too violent for me unless it's really hot outside. I debate throwing away my second pair of underpants. Nope. This trip's definitely going to take longer than five days. I wear my second day's boxers again. I realize I have forgotten one of the main tools of my mustache maintenance—the cuticle scissors I use to trim unruly long or gray hairs. Oh well, for now it's not that scraggly; it will pass for the day.

I go to "work." It's not a far walk to the entrance ramp and it looks like an okay spot. Lots of traffic. But Susan was wrong, it *isn't* "better tomorrow." I stand there with my thumb out. The cop from yesterday would be proud—I shake my sign and make eye contact with drivers but still no luck. Cop cars pass me several times and I know they see me, but none of them gives me any grief. Four hours pass. I try different signs—END OF 70 WEST; the one Susan suggested: WRITING HITCHHIKING BOOK; even just SAN FRANCISCO—but still strike out. Ohio will be the death of me yet. Death by tedium.

Again when a ride stops there is a split second of unreality. Fear they'll take off without me. It's a van pulling a small trailer. The door slides open and I see a whole gang of hipsters. "It's the Manson Family!" I humorously greet them. Each is staring at me in amazement. "Where are you coming from?" a handsome guy asks from the second row of seats. "Baltimore," I answer. "Get in, sir," he says, and I see the friendliest group of smiles I have ever seen break out on all their faces. They are an indie band called Here We Go Magic, which I stupidly and unhiply have not heard of. So much for thinking I'm up-to-date on new music. Driving is the sound guy, Matt Littlejohn. Next to him is drummer Peter Hale. Next row, Mike Bloch, the guitar player who first greeted me, and Avtar Khalsa, the on-the-road tour manager. Next to me in the second row of seats is the sexy and cool Jen Turner, bass player, and behind, in the last row, lead singer and guitar player Luke Temple. All their musical equipment is in the trailer being pulled behind us. They are headed to a gig in Bloomington, Indiana, and offer to drive me to Indianapolis. *Yay! A long ride!*

I am thrilled, no, exhilarated to be in a van with such a hip group. "It only takes one ride" was becoming truer and truer each day. They explain that they passed me once as they entered the freeway but didn't stop. Arguing back and forth if it "really was John Waters," some were sure, others were not, so they decided to come back and see. "He'd never wear that hat!" Peter had argued. I guess he never saw the *Scum of the Earth* movie.

I struggle to fasten my seat belt and quickly bond with Jen, who has full-tilt bad-girl beauty and style to burn. Mike and Avtar, seated in front of us, quickly join in on comparing sexual slang words: *blouse* (a gay man who is a feminine top), *trendsexual* (gay for political reasons), and *heteroflexible* (mostly straight but known to occasionally fall off that wagon). Luke just listens silently from the last row, softly strumming his guitar, as Peter and Matt shout out other rude-vocabulary lessons from the front of the van. We talk about endless touring (they have been on the road for almost two years straight), drugs, Patty Hearst, Divine, and their own hitchhiking adventures from their pasts. This is complete heaven for me—great new showbiz comrades who drive safely *and we are covering a lot of miles!*

We stop for lunch at Giacomo's in Zanesville, Ohio, and I treat. It is the least I could do—a sugar-daddy road warrior! Ha! It is fun to be part of a youth gang again. Not wanting to lose time—they have a show to make that night, after all—we head back onto Route 70 and eat as we travel. I think I surprise them by pulling out my hitchhiking-music compilation CD I had prepared when writing the "best" and "worst" chapters of my book. I mean, what other hitchhiker brings his personal soundtrack with him? They laugh and seem to love all my vintage novelty and country songs about being lonely on the road, and in turn they give me their new CD, *A Different Ship*, which totally coincidentally just came out this week. I can't wait to listen to it in private. Mike asks if he can tweet that they have picked me up, and I say, "Sure." My rule had always been I would never start the publicity or confirm I was hitchhiking until after I was done, but whoever picked me up could do as they liked. Mike tweets on the Here We Go Magic official site, "Just picked up John Waters hitchhiking in the middle of Ohio. No joke. Waters in the car." Jen follows up with her own announcement, "We really picked up John Waters hitchhiking." Both include a snapshot of me with Jen happily riding along in the van and Luke relaxing in the backseat. Proof.

The story goes viral almost immediately. Twitter. Facebook. "Pinkie swear?" was one of the first reactions to Mike. "It is 100% pinkie swear true," he answers happily. *Spin* magazine immediately calls the band's manager and the rest of the music press quickly follows. I can see by Mike's shocked face as he checks his e-mails on his computer that the shit is hitting the publicity fan in a completely unplanned, lovely, and insane way.

I have been with Here We Go Magic for about six hours now, and as we enter the suburbs of Indianapolis, where the band has to go south, they try to find a good drop-off spot for me— one with hotels and restaurants. I can tell that as much as they want to help me find the perfect hitchhiking spot, they will be late for their show if they dawdle. We leave I-70W and I say, "This exit will be fine," even though I can see it isn't. A high-speed, heavily traveled main highway with an entrance ramp to I-70 West would be impossible to pull over on. But the band members have been so wonderful to me that I don't want to hold them up. It's time to say goodbye. We stop at a convenience store parking lot and get out. I ask a stranger to take a photo of all of us together, with me in the middle holding my END OF I-70 WEST cardboard sign. Here We Go Magic drives off into their show-business life and I go back to being a bum.

REAL RIDE NUMBER TEN

SHAUTA

La Quinta Inn has a room. Already stewing about the impossible morning hitchhiking spot I am facing, I confide in the lady who is checking me in. She doesn't raise an eyebrow when I tell her I'm thumbing my way across the country and points out back behind the hotel, where Route 70 West itself runs quite near the property. "You could climb over the fence," she suggests.

The room's okay—not as nice as Days Inn, though, and the lighting is piss-poor for reading. Suddenly I realize I've lost my reading glasses. Oh God, I bet I left them in the Here We Go Magic van. I e-mail Jen immediately. Luckily, I have my backup pair for exactly this occasion; otherwise I'd be unable to read a thing, a torture worse than death. I check my e-mails and see the Here We Go Magic story has crossed over even more. First a site called DCist, then Gawker, quickly followed by Jill Rosen of the *Baltimore Sun*. Gulp. My office's official response to all inquiries has been "We neither confirm nor deny the story," which I realize sounds a little grand. Jen has been especially sweet in her more recent tweets, not revealing where they had dropped me off, "maybe the wild blue yonder." She even has sent me a farewell message: "JW, be safe out there." The band e-mails me back, yes, they have my glasses, and a friend who is at their show, who is based in Indianapolis, from Joyful Noise Recordings, will bring them back to my hotel tonight after their gig and drop them off at the desk. Talk about a ride that keeps on giving!

I look out the window of my room, and indeed I have a perfect, hellish view of Route 70W rush-hour traffic. The whizzing sounds of cars and trucks are starting to feel like the soundtrack of my new life. Climbing over the fence would be a ridiculously extreme act, plus I'd be right on I-70, where no one would stop. I go outside and walk through this suburban shopping-type area and know I'm too near the city. I try walking up to where the nearest ramp is but see this would be a terrible place—nowhere to stand, endless traffic, mostly all local. I panic. What the hell am I going to do?

Yesterday Susan had suggested I call Shauta Marsh, who once booked my *This Filthy World* spoken-word show for the Indianapolis Museum of Contemporary Art. Maybe she could give me a lift to a better hitch spot. At first I dismissed this idea with bluster. "No! That would be cheating," I raved, still the fake-ride reactionary. But once I got back in my room, I was suddenly a little more open to "cheating." After all, wasn't I going to offer a stranger money to get me to a better spot in Ohio? Is it *that* different to call a friend? Actually, yes. It would be sort of cheating, but what the hell, hadn't I mentioned in the prologue that I would "call a limousine" if I had to? It's not *that* bad.

Shauta is surprised to hear from me out of the blue, and I imagine even more startled to hear that I am in her town, hitch-hiking, and needing a ride in the morning. She doesn't balk when I mention, "I like to start early." Not having the nerve to give her my usual starting time of 6:30 a.m., I sheepishly mention 7:00 a.m. She seems fine with that but adds she has to take her two kids to school, so they'll be in the car. "Great!" I say. "Children need to know about hitchhiking." I tell Shauta I'll be out in front of the motel waiting eagerly for her arrival. What an absolute sweetheart!

I e-mail my office that Shauta is good to go, and they are relieved. Trish stays late after work hours, though, and comes up with some good possible locations to be dropped off in the morning. She e-mails directions and descriptions of the areas to both me and Shauta. One has a McDonald's and a "truck center" and is about fifteen miles west, and the other is a rest area ten miles farther that has no restaurants but vending machines and bathrooms and separate parking lots for cars and trucks. I feel better. I e-mail both my sisters that the hitch story has gone public and they should be ready to explain to our mom and calm her down if she should hear. I tell them I am in Indianapolis and am fine.

I guess I'm hungry. By now I have eliminated successfully and feel relieved to be able to do so on the road. Let's see— where shall I fine-dine tonight? I see the usual chain outlets to ignore. Hmmmm . . . the Outback Steakhouse? Looks less corporate than the others, plus I've never heard of it. I'm doing new stuff every day! I enter and sit at the bar and a nice waiter takes my order. I choose a steak. The filet is kind of gristly, certainly nothing to write home about. Nobody looks at me or talks to me despite the fact that two men are on either side of me, also eating alone. They stare at the overhead TVs as if they have never *not* eaten a meal in their lives in front of the tube. I tip more than 20 percent, remembering Nora Ephron's great line that "over-tipping only costs a few dollars more." Here, less than a dollar.

Back at the hotel room, online, I see the Here We Go Magic story is continuing to get an unbelievably high number of hits.

I'm secretly pleased, even though I can't for the life of me think how this could possibly make it any easier for me to get rides. I forward the *Spin* website on Here We Go Magic picking me up to The Corvette Kid and tell him where I am. He e-mails me back, "Okay. Sounds good. I plan to head west in a few days. I hope you don't go too far now." Does this mean there's really a possibility he'll be back? As I curl up to go to sleep, I realize Day Three started off terribly but ended on the upswing. Could my newfound hitchhiking luck last into the next day? How could I possibly get a cooler ride than with Here We Go Magic?

I wake up and am still shocked I am doing this trip. When I hear a message on my voice mail from an old friend who has read online about me hitchhiking, I'm touched but have to chuckle that he's seriously concerned that I have dementia and am wandering around the highways lost and out of my skull. He offers to come pick me up no matter where I may be even though he lives in Los Angeles. I text him back I'm okay. I check my e-mail and see even Baltimore local TV and radio stations are now reporting my hitchhiking. I e-mail my sisters and tell them they'd better tell our mom now—she will definitely hear today. I'm still too frightened over the possible length of this trip to throw away underwear, but at least I put on a fresh pair. Plus a clean Gap T-shirt. Pink. What was I thinking when I packed? I'm getting a little sick of wearing the same Issey Miyake sports coat every day. Usually I'd be more like the Donna Dasher character in *Female Trouble* sniffing, "I really should be changing my outfit anyway, I've had it on nearly five hours," but refrain from acting like her when I, by habit, go down to the free-breakfast room.

The food selection is just as awful as always: white bread, frozen bagels a starving-to-death New Yorker would still turn down, and sugarcoated high-calorie cereal. Same trucker types.

Same uncuteness. Same gloomy lack of social interaction. God, I miss newspapers! Luckily I swiped a *Wall Street Journal* from that lunch place yesterday in Ohio, so I have something to read while I fight the awful fear that Shauta won't show up. Actually, I know she *will* be here, but I'm a worrywart and always need a backup plan. Like crying.

I check out at the front desk and am thrilled to see that the friend of Here We Go Magic did actually drop off my reading glasses. Another kind soul! Shauta's early and so am I. Her two kids, Vivian and Max, in the backseat are adorable and stare at me with friendly but quizzical expressions as I climb in the front. I can't imagine how their mom has prepped them for this preschool adventure, but she's done a good job. Shauta's game to take me to either of Trish's recommended hitchhiking spots but imagines the second one will be better. Always taking the word of the local, I'm sure she's right and relieved she has the time to take me the extra miles. I offer her gas money but she laughs and turns me down kindly. The first exit, on South Holt Road, looks so ominous I tell her not to even bother pulling off to scout. Still inner-city and industrial—the exact opposite of a place a cross-country traveler would stop for services.

We continue on to the farther rest area and I see we are finally out of Indianapolis. She exits and I'm unsure because there are so few cars, but it's a pretty setting. Woods. Nice bathrooms. A separate truck parking lot I can see in the distance. Few travelers compared with an entrance ramp, but I get the feeling everybody who stops here is going a long way. I get out at the end of the rest area right where all the trucks and cars would have to reenter I-70 West. It is a beautiful, even slightly chilly morning. Holding my hitchhiking sign, I pose with Shauta's two great kids, and we all give her the thumbs-up for the picture. I hug her and thank her so much for disrupting her life on such quick notice. Boy, does she deserve the hitchhiking thanks card I hand over with gratitude. They jump back in the car, and right as they pull up beside me to leave, Shauta takes, through the passenger-side window, a final photo of me hitchhiking. Bye, Shauta! Bye, kids! Once again, I'm on my own.

REAL RIDE NUMBER ELEVEN

VIETNAM VET

I stand there. It's quiet for once. Actually cold. I put on my wool scarf for the first time. The sun's coming up causes a big glare, and when the first one or two vehicles exit the lot, I see the drivers have to squint and lower their visors to see at all. Not even sure they can actually see *me* hitchhiking, so I move back into the shade closer inside the rest area. It's odd having vehicles drive by at such a slow speed. There are few cars. I realize this is the kind of rest area where late at night it would be scary. No security. No services. Except maybe blow jobs inside as I had imagined in an earlier "bad" chapter, but this time it would be robbers, not cops, shaking down the frisky perverts.

Here in the day it feels safe, though. Couples stop to walk their dogs. Even the few truck drivers pulling out throw up their hands to signal they would pick me up if they could. I stand there feeling both foolish and brave. Silence except for the birds. I'm alive, I think, and so many of my friends are not. I may be nuts to be doing this, but I'm kind of proud of myself. I *am* having an adventure. I like my life. Even if I have to stand here for the rest of it.

But I don't. The next ride is yet another nice guy. Nondescript vehicle. He's sixty-six years old, just like me, but hetero, I'm sure. A Republican, he tells me, who is happy Obama came out for gay marriage because "before, when he said he was 'evolving on the issue,' that was bullshit." He's also a Vietnam vet with a Kentucky-type accent, and I never once feel uncomfortable with him.

Here is yet another straight guy who can't stop praising his wife, bragging proudly how she loves to read and how smart she is. I tell him what I do for a living and he shows no real surprise, just says how happy his daughter would be to hear he picked me up, because she loved *Hairspray*. He starts telling me about his career—providing feed for farm animals and how the business has come a long way on healthy nutrition for cattle and pigs. I learn that baby pigs love M&M's as a treat, and if you feed one in a litter that snack, the baby pig will follow you around every time you appear. Chickens, however, are a whole different story. "They're the worst—all their feed's laced with growth hormones. That's why eight-year-old girls get their period now," he explains, "from eating these chickens that are more science projects than animals." Now there is a sobering thought. I eat chicken. I hope I don't get man tits!

He takes me deep into Indiana and I feel so safe and happy. After about two hours I realize he's going to be turning off Route 70W, so I ask him if he knows a good rest area similar to the one he picked me up at this morning. We start scouting and immediately see a sign for one coming up soon. I know he is actually driving farther west than this, but who knows what the entrance ramp will be like when he has to merge south onto his new route. I ask him if he'll pull off now to inspect hitchhiking spots.

This rest stop looks good. A pretty park. Enough cars stop. Even a few truckers mixed in, presumably taking naps. Bingo! I'll take it. I give him my THANKS FOR THE LIFT card and he chuckles and bids me farewell. I'm on a roll. Next!!

REAL RIDE NUMBER TWELVE

TRUCKER

I stand there for a while. I check more Google Alerts and see the Here We Go Magic story is going absolutely batshit, yet I have never felt more anonymous. Drivers leaving in cars politely nod or make hand signals that they aren't going far. I try to remain positive. I see a Hispanic woman with a bunch of kids in the park, taking a break from driving. She keeps looking at me, and I think, wonderful, she's going to give me a ride! But when she walks over to me at the beginning of the exit ramp, I see she is holding out something in her hand for me. "Please take this," she says with an accent, and I am stunned to see what I think is a $10 bill. "No, really, thank you so much," I plead. "I don't need it. I'm writing a book." Yeah, sure, I can see her thinking, here's a homeless person off his meds. I even take out my trusty fame kit to try to prove who I am, but she refuses to look . . . or leave. "Please, sir, take this!" she again orders with a militant kindness that breaks my heart. I realize she is not going to return to her family until I accept. Giving up, I take the bill and realize it's a twenty, not a ten. I am amazed how generous she is. And how privileged and lucky I am. I feel guilty. Not worthy. Suppose I *were* homeless and off my meds? Hearing voices. Demons. No cash or credit cards. I vow to myself as she walks back to her kids that I will pass along her $20 bill like a good-luck talisman to the next needy traveler. I'm still trying to compute the generous act in my mind. You cheapskate, I berate myself, why don't you go over there and give *her* $500?

But I don't even have time to consider this because her gesture has already brought me incredible luck. A trucker who had been parked by the side of the rest stop the whole time I was there pulls out and hollers from inside the cab, "Come on, I'll take you!" I've never felt gayer as I climb up those three steps on the passenger side of the eighty-thousand-pound Kenworth and jump inside. Eureka! A trucker has actually picked me up hitch-hiking! "The book needed this!" I explain right away to the handsome fifty-year-old driver, who seems to take it all in stride despite, I could tell, having never heard of me when I introduced myself. I blurt out how grateful I am, how I make movies, and how "I promise I won't print your or the truck company's name because I know you aren't allowed to pick up hitchhikers." He agrees with that, telling me that while his company doesn't demand two drivers, they do have a chip in the truck to always tell where he is, and his schedule is highly regulated—he's only allowed to drive a total of seventy hours a week and never more than twelve in one day.

It's so modern up here in the front seat of a truck! High-tech. Computers. So massive a vehicle. So high up. So much more glamorous than a limo or a town car. This is fun! He's even a good driver, yet I'm almost afraid to look over at him for fear he'll think I'm cruising, but then I realize not everybody thinks like a queer man. He's just a good guy.

Yet I can't help thinking, isn't this trucker what every gay "bear" is trying to emulate? Tough but gentle? Sporting a belly but somehow still in shape? Unjudgmental but courageous? Smart but also down-to-earth? A supposed "real" man? I ask him about trucker horror stories, and this gets him going—how he once was in an accident when his whole truck flipped over and there were no air bags and he had to climb out the passenger-side window to safety. Or how he saw a collision recently where a school bus hit a truck but somehow the kids were all right. I could listen forever.

He has no patience for whiners. Sure, he hates the ever-present traffic near cities in Ohio and Texas the worst, but he never listens to "filthy" CB radios anymore. "Filthy?" I ask, perking up over a word so near and dear to my livelihood. "You know," he explains, "complaining, bitching about the rules of trucking. I can't stand hearing that stuff." He has only good things to say about life on the road, especially Petro truck stops. "They've got everything," he enthusiastically tells me, "lounges, you can watch TV, good food." "In other words, the Tiffany's of truck stops?" I ask, prodding him to possibly be their spokesperson in a TV commercial. "You bet," he agrees with a grin.

And yep, here's yet one more heterosexual man who loves his wife. I'm telling you, it's a trend! Women I know who are always complaining they can never meet a good straight man—maybe you're living in the wrong part of the country. Maybe you need to hitchhike. Route 70 West could be the path to a great marriage. Go ahead, stick out your thumb for romance.

Okay, trucker heaven can't last forever. He's going to be turning south to go home soon, so once again I flip back to full unease about where I can be dropped off. I explain my "good rest area" karma and we start looking. Pretty soon one pops up and he pulls off the interstate. I give him my pre-autographed hitchhiking card and wonder if he'll tell his family about me. Probably. But it will be no big deal. He's got a nice life—why should he give a rat's ass about anybody's celebrity?

RENEGADE BUILDERS

I scope out the rest area. Very similar to the last one. Except I see some kind of staff servicing the vending machines inside. Uh-oh. Oh well, I've had no trouble so far, why would I now? I buy non-Evian water and then go outside and take up my usual place at the beginning of the exit ramp from the rest area. It's still a beautiful day. I see many drivers come and go, some taking a walk on the parklike grounds, stretching their backs and just being glad to be out of their vehicle for a moment. I notice a couple who look kind of like druggies walking their huge dog. I hold up my sign to the girl, but she shrugs as if she can't—she's not driving and it's beyond her control.

Then one of the staff of the rest area walks out of the building and heads toward me. "You can't hitchhike," she says flatly. "The cops told me it was okay, and I've been hitchhiking in rest areas all across this state with no problem," I lie, almost with an attitude. I notice this lady has few teeth—maybe the staff is work-release from prison, I think, instantly dentally profiling her. Suddenly her whole face changes in surprise. "Are you John Waters?!" she shouts with sudden friendliness. "Yes," I say, completely shocked that she recognizes me. "Okay, you can stay," she says with a complete law-and-order turnaround. I know I should be mad she was shitty when she didn't know who I am and now practically kisses my ass when she does, but when you're hitch-hiking your usual value system collapses.

I see her go over and start talking to the druggie couple, who are piling into a van. That nosy little busybody, I think, as I keep my thumb out for rides. The van pulls out of the parking space and the back door slides open. I see a packed interior—almost like a hoarder's. The two druggie types sit on a mattress on the floor with the giant dog. There's even some kind of bird in a cage. "We'll take you to Kansas City if you don't mind sitting up here," offers a white guy, about forty years old, in the front passenger seat, who seems to be running the show. He points to a space between himself and his wife, the driver. Not a seat at all, just the center console, but who cares!? I climb in and balance be-tween Ritchie and Aiyana, as they introduce themselves. Kansas City? That's far! I am beyond thrilled.

But should I be worried? The van takes off and everybody starts smoking joints. Ritchie tells me that the toothless rest-stop worker had said to them, "Can you get John Waters out of here?" I could tell she had mentioned something about who I was, but I could also feel they hadn't heard of me. I look in the back and marvel at all the personal belongings packed inside the van. Shirley and Jasper, as they shyly announce their names, in-troduce Billyburr, the dog. They remind me of Karen and John, the famous "Needle Park" junkie couple *Life* magazine profiled in 1965 that so obsessed me at the time. Jasper, also about forty, is handsome in an ex-con way, and Shirley's a little younger, pretty, but you can tell she's been through the wringer. I wonder if they're meth-heads.

Ritchie explains that they are on their way to the fracking boom in North Dakota to build temporary housing for the workers. I know little about fracking except it's supposed to be bad and all my liberal friends are against it, but I'm open-minded. Besides, Ritchie isn't a fracker himself; his specialty is building temporary housing in suddenly overpopulated areas. Like war zones. He has done the same thing in Afghanistan, Lebanon, and Iraq. He only has good things to say about the Iraqis he had to deal with: "Great people. Just don't ask them about religion or sex and you're fine. They like Americans; they just don't like our government or press. They see what is reported in the U.S. and it *is* false!" Most recently he has been in northern Pennsylvania and, I gather, is fleeing some sort of illegal-alien-trafficking problem he casually mentions. Ritchie says, "I love Mexican workers" because "they show up and do a better job than the legal ones I can find in this country." Like every man who has picked me up hitchhiking so far, he hates freeloaders. Ritchie picked up Jasper, his old friend he hasn't seen in years, on the way west to help out on the job, and Jasper asked if Shirley could join them. Shirley and Jasper seem to be freshly in love.

I instantly like Ritchie. He's a renegade. A pothead wheeler-dealer who, I could tell, also loves to drink. A pirate. A grifter when he has to be and maybe a bit of a fugitive. Ritchie lost his house to the bank in the last recession. He's broken but not down and still looking for his pot of gold.

Aiyana is a great driver, so I am never nervous perched up here in the middle of the front seats without a seat belt, even though we pass many CLICK IT OR TICKET warning signs. She says they have bad luck—the cops are always stopping them. Ritchie is paranoid whenever she goes even five miles faster than the speed limit. I quickly grow comfortable with all the pot smoke around me but refuse a toke, telling them, "I just can't imagine standing on the side of the road with my thumb out, stoned on weed." Maybe I have a contact high. I hope so. When in Rome . . .

I can tell they are racking their brains trying to figure out what I'm famous for, especially after I give them my thank-you card. But when I list all the movies I have directed, they come up mostly blank. Aiyana had vaguely heard of *Hairspray*, but that was it. "I don't know much about celebrity," Ritchie offers weakly, but keeps tweeting his friends that I'm in the car. They don't know who I am either. Ritchie is extremely proud of his two daughters from another marriage and shows me their pictures, but when he calls them to tell them the news of whom he has picked up, they are tongue-tied, too. Nobody knows what I do until I mention the *Chucky* movie I was in. That does the trick! "Why didn't you say you were in a *Chucky* movie?" I could practically hear them all thinking. Everybody knows *Chucky*.

We pass the Gateway Arch in St. Louis and all marvel at how beautiful it is. It's my favorite public monument in this country. Ritchie delights in telling me that he and Aiyana just celebrated their twentieth wedding anniversary, and when they were younger, they once rode up in one of the little private elevators to the top of the arch and had sex inside. I *knew* I liked these people. I think of the time I had sex in the Bleecker Street Cinema in the mid-sixties with my beatnik boyfriend, Tony, as we watched Marlene Dietrich in *The Blue Angel*, but balk at sharing this story with new friends I have only known for a few hours.

We joke a lot. I keep telling Ritchie I think he's bullshitting me and really he's an arms dealer. The giant dog in the back is incredibly well behaved. He just sits there and never once barks or demands to hang his head out the window. The bird is a blue-and-gold macaw and its name is Biscuit. It's likewise silent, although they assure me the parrot can talk and squawk. I give Aiyana the $20 bill that the nice Mexican lady had given me, and she understands how I want her to pass it along with the proper Native American magic.

We stop for gas at the Pick-A-Dilly gas station and I offer to fill it up. Ritchie and Aiyana make a show of not expecting any such thing, but Ritchie admits it would be a big help, so I happily do so. When I see the bill of $97.86, I am amazed at how big the tank of this van must be! But more shocking is that when I pull out my wallet to get my business credit card, I realize it is missing. I panic. I call home and Susan grills me on where I last used it. When I finally focus enough through my hysteria, I tell her, "That steak house in Indianapolis." I fumble for the restaurant receipt and give her the phone number off it, and she says she'll call when I hang up, and if they don't have it, she'll cancel that MasterCard and I should just use my personal one. Then I realize somehow, just standing here at the pump, I've lost my personal credit card, too. I act like an insane person, searching my clothes over and over. Ritchie urges me to "calm down, it has to be here." I'm getting more and more frazzled, looking under the car near the pumps. I can tell all the crew in the van is thinking "I didn't do it" as I'm sweating and freaking out. Susan, still on the line, tells me, "Just use your ATM card, that's also a debit card and you can pay with that!" "Here it is!" I scream to the world, amazed to find the second "lost" credit card I had somehow misplaced in alarm in my wallet in the wrong compartment. I calm down. I feel like a complete fool. I apologize to my new friends for my crazy behavior, pay up, and we pull away, back onto Route 70 West again. Phew.

I check my BlackBerry and see my office has e-mailed me that *The New York Times* has even contacted us wanting to know about my hitchhiking journey. I am shocked. I e-mail my office back to say "No comment" and feel just like Henry Kissinger. Even the gang I'm with seems impressed that *The New York Times* is interested. But then I get the slight impression that maybe they're relieved I'm refusing comment. After all, press attention is definitely not what these maybe, maybe-not shady capitalists are seeking.

Nobody ever brings up the question of my sexual preference.

Duh, I imagine they'd reply if I had asked if they'd been wondering if I'm gay. I keep seeing all these big "porn outlets" in the middle of nowhere alongside the highway, just like the one I'd imagined for my UFO-sex chapter, and wonder out loud, "Are these stores for interstate travelers or locals?" Ritchie totally surprises me by answering matter-of-factly, "Well, I think that is where truckers who are gay blow each other in the parking lot." I laugh out loud and say, "I don't think so!" He shrugs, still sure of his position.

As we get nearer to Kansas City, Missouri, where they have a house to stay in, they debate where to stop to get "a real meal." Ritchie asks if I'd like to come downtown with them to eat some ribs. I explain how afraid I am to go off Route 70 or anywhere near a city because I'll never get the next ride. They offer to take me back past Kansas City to a good exit after dinner before they go to where they plan to sleep. I try to decline, knowing that this would be out of their way, but Ritchie won't hear of it—I paid for gas, it is the least they can do. Shirley surprises me by saying she is a vegetarian and only eats nutritiously. We talk a little about how hard it is to eat in an unfattening way unless you can cook for yourself. She has a lot of health food packed with her—maybe I was judging her wrongly. But no, when we stop, she asks if I ever saw the filmed-in-Baltimore TV show about junkies *The Corner*. "Sure did," I say, "a great program." "I lived the life of *The Corner*," she says flatly. I see.

We pile out of the van in the parking lot of Rosedale Bar-B-Q and sit on the ground and stretch. Even the dog and the bird are brought out for some fresh air. I feel so excited to be with this gang of outsiders. These days *everybody* thinks he or she is an outsider, but here is the real deal. Probably the only members of the fracking community I'll ever meet. Maybe I'll become a fracking hag when this whole trip is over.

I ask them if I can take their picture. Ritchie and Aiyana

pose with the dog. Shirley and Jasper tell me politely they'd prefer not to. Jasper is a gentleman, though. He says, "Since I was seated in the back of the van with Shirley, I am sorry I didn't get to know you as well as Ritchie and Aiyana did up front, but you all sure were laughing a lot!" Billyburr drinks hungrily from a bowl they set up, and Biscuit actually squawks, but not too loudly. Even the bird knows too much attention could mean trouble.

We have a delicious greasy meal of ribs, baked beans, chili, and Royal Crown Colas. They have beer but I stick to my teetotaler ways. Everybody is beat. We drove 460 miles together and they had been driving all night *before* they picked me up. We pile back into the van and Ritchie gives Aiyana directions on how to get back on I-70 West to go past the city. We keep driving. The exit they thought would be the best, the Kansas Speedway one, isn't. Still local. Not a good ramp. I can tell Jasper and Shirley want me to find a place to get out *now* so they can go crash. We keep driving to the final exit before the Kansas Turnpike begins, Bonner Springs. I don't know. It doesn't look good to me either. The entrance ramp is quite a hike from where the meager choice of motels is located. But what can I do? To go farther they'd have to pay to enter the freeway. I'll get out here anyway and figure out what to do tomorrow. Since there's no Days Inn, I pick Holiday Inn. Ritchie is so considerate that he waits in the van while I go in to check on vacancy. There is one. I come back out and say goodbye to my new buddies. I hope they find their pot of gold. They deserve it.

REAL RIDE NUMBER FOURTEEN

MAYOR

I hate the Holiday Inn. The woman behind the desk is unfriendly and suspicious when she sees me checking in carrying my cardboard sign. The hotel room has the worst lighting so far. I can't even see to unpack my bag, much less read. I am exhausted. My office is long closed for the day, so I e-mail Susan at her home and give her my hotel phone number and tell her to call me. I'm beyond tired, delirious. I check my e-mails and see that my credit card was discovered at that steak house in Indianapolis and is already on its way via FedEx to my Baltimore office. At least I don't have to go through the hassle of canceling and getting a new one.

Susan e-mails me back that she tried the hotel number but "nobody answers." I call her back to confirm the number but she doesn't pick up. I keep calling and not getting through and she keeps e-mailing back, "No one is answering at hotel" or "It just rings and rings." I'm flipping out and leave the most pitiful message I've ever left begging her to pick up. Finally my cell phone rings. It's Susan. I'm so tired I've been calling my office number, not her home number, so she's received none of my messages.

But the reality of the situation is, the rotten Holiday Inn operator isn't answering the main line. I want to run down to the lobby and, if there's anybody behind the desk, scream, "Gone fishing?!" but I can't make hotel enemies, I may need their help.

Susan and I review the day, talk about how my SPOT device stopped working for much of the time inside the van. I argue that it's a falsely advertised instrument, but Susan tells me it's because I had it in my pocket and not "with a clear view of the sky in all directions," as the instruction book demands. "How would that be possible if I were an extreme skier trapped in an avalanche?" I bluster, having never trusted this tracking tool in the first place. I calm down. We hang up. I guess I'm feeling better. Aren't I about halfway there?

I go back down to the lobby to go out front and scope out the distance to the entrance ramp to I-70W. It's far. The new woman behind the desk is a tad friendlier, so I don't accuse her of not answering the phone. I ask her if she knows anybody I could pay to give me a ride on the turnpike to a better exit in the morning. She says to "talk to Floyd, who works the night shift, maybe he'd be willing when he gets off at seven a.m." He's not in yet but I tell her thanks and I'll be back down at eleven, when his shift starts, to ask.

Back in my *dark* motel room, I see from new e-mails that my sisters have told my mother that I'm hitchhiking across America. She was "glad to be informed." She "didn't seem too shocked," my sister Kathy tells me. Maybe my mom's been "broken down into submission" by my public life, as Susan comments when I tell her. Maybe nothing could shock my mother anymore.

I miss hearing from The Corvette Kid, so I e-mail him, "Got three rides today—one was in a huge truck." He answers, "Oh Wow! Way to go! Don't go too far now u hear. Haha." Mmm, not sure what this means. Is he back home, bored, itching for more travel? Nah, just e-mail teasing, I figure. Not even vague enough to be a backup plan. I go back downstairs and Floyd is finally behind the desk. He looks totally mystified when I ask if I can pay him (plus tolls) to take me to the first turnpike exit with services inside the state of Kansas in the morning. I show him the online Here We Go Magic story. I name-drop the titles of my films. He is nonresponsive but says, "Maybe, I'll have to ask my wife." "Okay," I tell him, "I'll check in with you first thing in the morning." Doesn't sound promising. I sulk my way back upstairs. It's late. I turn off the one or two dim lights and uneasily try to go to sleep. Maybe Floyd will come through for me.

But he doesn't. I wait to go downstairs until right before 7:00 a.m. when he gets off. I don't even bother going into the hideous breakfast room. I'm sure bad lighting equals even worse breakfast selections. Floyd tells me he can't take me onto the Kansas Turnpike because his wife needs the car "right when I get home to go to a job interview." "Well, can I give you twenty dollars just to take me up to the entrance ramp?" I beg. He hems and haws but can't think of any excuses so says okay. I tell him I'll wait. I sit outside with my hitchhiking sign and talk to a nice lady who seems interested but doesn't offer me a ride. I look back in and see a new woman is behind the desk, but where is Floyd? It's 7:10 and I don't see him. Has he snuck out the back door to escape me? I panic. I wave my sign to a man pulling out of the motel parking lot in his car, but he ignores me. Suddenly the new check-in lady comes out and says, "Sir, if you continue to flag our guests, I'm calling the police." "I'm sorry," I fib, stalling for time so Floyd can rescue me, "he looked like the type who would have picked me up." "Yeah, well, that was my husband!" she responds with a bit of a sneer. "I won't do it again," I agree, and she goes back in. Bonner Springs bitch. "Where is that goddamn Floyd?" I stew. It's 7:15—I know he's ditched me! But no, here he comes. I'm relieved. I don't mention the trouble and just climb in his vehicle, hand him the money, and make small talk until he drops me off at the freeway entrance.

It's a bright, hot morning and there's not a tree around. I can see the sun rising quickly in the sky. I put on more sunblock. I think, well, this spot is okay. Lots of cars coming from the left and trucks coming from the right. The big problem is that every time a truck turns onto my entrance ramp, it has to make a wide turn and almost crushes my bag. I move it back and then jump out of the way as another rig almost runs over my feet.

I stand there forever. I start to ration my Evian water. My back hurts from standing up straight for such a long time, so I walk down the exit a little and lean up on the NO PEDESTRIANS BEYOND THIS POINT blah blah blah sign. It's wobbly, though, and the more I lean, the looser in the ground the sign gets. A FedEx Ground transportation truck whizzes by and I wish I were a package inside. Cops pass both ways but ignore me. I'm starting to sweat. I have been here five hours. I'm getting dehydrated. I call my office in misery and tell Susan, "Pretty soon I'm going to have to drink my own urine." She sort of laughs but hears the despondency in my voice. I tell her if she sees on the Spotter I'm going backward, it's just that I can't take the heat anymore and I didn't get a reverse ride, I'm just a homeless man walking back to the motel area to get supplies.

Come on, people! Pick me up! I take the last drink of water and really start to worry. I haven't eaten a thing all day. Okay, now's the time. Walk back. Swallow your pride and lug that bag and sign with you through the nearby construction site, across the field, over the main road to the service area. I do so and feel exactly like Wanda in the great Barbara Loden film of the same name where she trudges through a Pennsylvania coal mine in a stunning, long, *very* long tracking shot. Poor Wanda. Poor me.

I see the dreaded Holiday Inn but don't go near it. I stumble into a convenience store and buy two giant bottles of Gatorade and another bottle of Evian. Exiting, I spot a Taco Bell, the only fast-food joint I'm ever tempted to patronize in my real life. I enter, plop down my even heavier bags now that the liquids are inside, and get in line to order. I flash on Lana Turner, who, her daughter Cheryl Crane once told me, was an early financial backer of Taco Bell, and think how I couldn't be any further away from Hollywood glamour than right now. All the normal people on their lunch break look like aliens to me. I'm almost jealous of their lives. I order two tacos and sit by myself in a booth awaiting my number to be called, hoping to be recognized, but customers just stare back at me blankly. I guzzle down an entire bottle of Gatorade, then another. I feel like sobbing as I walk up to get my order but control myself, sit back down, and eat my tacos. With lots of hot sauce, they're pretty tasty. I hope Lana Turner's estate made a small profit.

I go in the men's room. Now I *am* Crackers in *Pink Flamingos* for real, living in public lavatories! Only I don't feel "much filthier," I feel much older. I look in the mirror and expect it to scream just like the joke-shop hand mirror on my desk at home does when you pick it up to look at your reflection. God, I look ugly. Weather-beaten, like in a Walker Evans photo.

I trudge back out, over the highway, back through the field, and onto the construction site. At least there're no guard dogs. I feel like Isabel Sarli in that other great Armando Bó–directed sexploitation film I forgot to mention to my long-ago fictitious good ride Harris, the film backer. The one entitled *Carne*, where she's employed in a rendering plant and gets raped every day walking through the woods to work and yet never changes her path.

I go back to the exact same hitchhiking spot. I lean back on the highway sign but stand right back up in embarrassment because it's so loose by now that I'm half reclining. More cops drive by. They ignore me. Everybody does. In desperation I think of

The Corvette Kid again. Suddenly he's my knight in shining armor. "Stuck in Bonner Springs, Missouri—last exit before Kansas toll highway," I e-mail him. "I'm still looking for your ride Part 2." A man can hope, can't he? "Leaving tomorrow!" he Kid responds. "Hang in there and don't go too much further. LOL." Yeah, sure. And don't worry, Corvette Kid, I'm not laughing out loud! I'm fucking stuck!

But. Still. Yet. Chant again. "It only takes one car to equal a ride," I tell myself. I almost feel as if it were a hallucination when one finally does. I would get in any vehicle, even if it were Ted Bundy driving a Volkswagen with his arm in a sling. See you later, Bonner Springs! I'm outta here.

The agony of waiting for a ride turns into a sheer exuberance once you're inside a new, strange vehicle. My driver is a middle-aged man who at first I think might be gay. But I'm wrong, I guess. He's another politician—the mayor of a small town in the Southwest and married. I don't ask him if he's a Republican. He's an odd one. When I quiz him on how far he's going, he says, "Wichita." I ask him where he'll be turning off Route 70 and he just points to his GPS and says, "When that tells me to turn," which isn't much help to me, but right now I don't even care. I'm out of Bonner Springs and I pray I never go back.

We enter the Kansas Turnpike and make small talk; he, about being the mayor of a little town, and I . . . well, I try to tell him I'm a film director, but I can see that he totally thinks I'm delusional. He ignores every line I try to work in the conversation about my life and then returns the chitchat to his. When I drop the names of my films, he reacts as if I just told him I am Napoleon. After about ten minutes or so of his blank stares to any detail of my career, I give up. So what if he thinks I'm a homeless lunatic. He is still giving me a ride and I couldn't be more grateful.

Suddenly the voice of the GPS orders him to turn off Route 70 toward Wichita and I panic. I got Wichita, which is south, mixed up with Topeka, which is west and where I am headed. I explain how I need to find an exit where there's a good entrance ramp back on where I can stand and how his turnoff ramp to Route 335 South will be high-speed and impossible. He offers nicely to take me past his exit to find a place. We see a sign promising services that are about twenty miles away, and he agrees to take me that far, which is really beyond the call of duty. But as we drive, I see he's getting impatient and he suggests the exit before "would be just as good." I can't really argue, so I say, "I guess so, let's see." He pulls off at the next exit and yes, there's a gas station and some strip malls up the road, but my heart sinks when I realize Topeka isn't far into Kansas at all, and worse yet, I'm in a shabby suburban neighborhood right *before* this city— the worst place possible to get a long-distance ride. But at least it's not Bonner Springs! I thank him and fumble in my pocket to give him my THANKS FOR THE LIFT hitchhiking card. He takes it. I wonder if he will later throw it away. I can't really blame him for not taking me as far as he had promised. I guess.

REAL RIDE NUMBER FIFTEEN

KITTY AND JUPITER

I stand there hitchhiking for a long time. I don't know where I am, but the mayor didn't take me that far—maybe sixty miles. It's already 3:00 p.m. and I've been hitching since almost 7:30 a.m. I've only been in a car for an hour total all day. It's windy. Really windy. I have to hold my hitching sign with both hands or it will be torn apart by the elements. That's when I notice my sunburned knuckles, the only part of my exposed body I didn't coat with sunblock. My stupid hat blows off and I chase it with terror.

For the first time, I notice, most of the drivers entering the freeway are black. They don't stop either. I hastily add on I'M SAFE to my sign, but that doesn't help. I e-mail my office I got a short ride with the mayor, but they already know because of my SPOT tracker and see I haven't made much progress. Trish e-mails back saying, "Your good rides always come in the afternoon." It's true, I never get picked up in the morning. Are early-bird time-manager travelers less willing to take a risk? Make friends with crackpot strangers?

I hitchhike forever. The wind is whipping my face. For the first time ever, I fantasize that I will get a facial and a massage when I get to San Francisco—something I would *never* do in real life. I plunge back into despair again and call my office and beg Susan and Trish to find a taxi, but how can they, they ask, when I can't pinpoint where I am? I grumble and hang up. Stand here longer. Sheer torture! Rush hour is starting. Every driver looks local; they're just coming home from work. I'm gonna have to sleep here! I look over and see some bushes that I try to imagine curling up under. I drink my last drop of Evian water. I'm so discouraged I litter. Throw the empty Evian bottle right on the ground. Take that, nature.

I look back from my selfish deed and there's a van stopped right beside me. The passenger window comes down and a twenty-something Charlie Manson look-alike is grinning at me. Behind him at the wheel is a sexy woman his age thrusting a $10 bill at me. They're not picking me up, they're just trying to help out a poor old guy down on his luck. "Take this, sir," she offers with charitable aggression.

Suddenly she recognizes me and screams at the top of her lungs, "Oh my God, it's John Waters!" I ask if they can give me a ride, and she's waving her hands, practically hyperventilating: "Yes! Yes!" I climb in the back. She pulls off, driving erratically, looking at me in the rearview mirror in shock and excitement, only made worse by her trying to text her friends that she has picked me up. "Charlie Jr." just smiles. They both are incredibly cute. I finally get her to calm down and she admits they are only going two exits, they live nearby. I offer to give them money to take me farther west past Topeka to a rest area. She agrees but says she doesn't want any money. I call Trish in my office and tell her I have a great ride. Since she's my travel-planning expert, I ask her to go online and try to find a good upcoming exit with services, and she agrees to the challenge. My driver struggles to drive and take pictures of me at the same time. I attempt to get her to focus on safe driving by assuring her we can take all the photos she wants when we stop.

Her name is Kitty and his is Jupiter (such a perfect Manson name) and they've been shopping in Wichita. She drives with one hand and starts rooting through her new purchases in the shopping bags with her other. The girl needs a fashion change if there's going to be a photo shoot, I can see that! Jupiter's dressed in hip denim shorts cut off below his knees (almost clamdiggers) and a black T-shirt. He doesn't need a change of clothes; he's devil ready. They both look cool as shit.

She's a disabled vet who, along with many others in the marines, was given a "bad anti-anthrax vaccine" that almost killed her. Kitty claims that the serum "was not kept in a climate-controlled environment. It happened to others, too," she explains. "We were in comas . . . couldn't go to the bathroom . . . had all these steroids [given to her] . . . I couldn't walk . . . I couldn't see peripherally. I wrote President Clinton a letter, and someone from Bethesda wrote back and said the medicine was 'absolutely safe.'" The medical company "had a huge contract [with the armed forces], so I'm pretty sure it was money-related. All bullshit! I got in a class-action lawsuit." "But what happened?" I ask, on the edge of my seat. "We lost," she says with a moan. "It's hard to sue the government."

Jupiter's a roofer. Naturally! Why are roofers always cute? I tell him that he's a dead ringer for a young Manson, and he asks if I'd like some "recreational drugs." They both smoke some pot and offer me a place to stay for the night at either of their pads. I decline with thanks and just tell them how great they both look together. "We're not really together," Kitty admits with what I gather is a tinge of sadness. I try to convince Jupiter that he should try hitchhiking. "Sure"—he laughs—"who's gonna pick up 'Charlie Manson Jr.,' as you call me? You know what they say about Kansas, don't you?" "What?" I bite. "Come on vacation, leave on probation!" I could fall in lust.

We're past Topeka now and suddenly there's nothing—the

real Kansas! Trish has e-mailed me back a possible good exit but it's about fifty miles from where they picked me up. I tell Kitty and Jupiter that I am giving them gas money no matter what they say and they keep driving. *Way* past where they live. We finally pull off where Trish has suggested and I'm kind of shocked. It's a rest area in the middle of nowhere that doesn't even have vending machines, just bathrooms and a parking lot. It's some kind of military museum monument. Trish must have misunderstood. Since it was late in the day, I wanted an exit with motels, but she must have thought because I had some good luck in rest areas with parking rather than fast-food joints, this is what I was looking for. Gulp. Too late now. Only one truck and two cars are in the whole rest area parking lot. Across Route 70 in the distance is a long, long freight train with endless plains stretching behind it. I feel like William Holden in *Picnic*, on his way to the fictitious Kansas town of Inge's play, only in this version I never get there.

We get out and Kitty does a hasty costume change, and we ask the only couple we see if they will snap our picture together. Like all people over twenty years old, the nice lady has trouble taking a cell phone picture but eventually, with instruction from Kitty, figures it out. Our new photographer does the same with my BlackBerry. I give Kitty my business card and ask her to write down her contact information, just in case I'm trapped here tonight and do need to take them up on their sleepover offer. She does so and adds, *Sgt. USMC Retired.* I want to ask Jupiter for his number, too, but it's clear Kitty's in charge. I give her my THANKS FOR THE LIFT card and she seems thrilled. I also make her take cash. It's the least I could do. I wish I could elope with these two. It feels like they saved my life.

REAL RIDE NUMBER SIXTEEN

WALMART GUY

But as soon as they leave, I get nervous quickly. The couple that took our picture pulls off. There's now not one other car in the whole rest area. It's getting late; I can feel the sun going down. I stand there and look around in the silence. I scope out a place where I guess I could sleep if I had to. My NEXT HOTEL sign couldn't be more appropriate right now. Time goes by too quickly. A car comes into the lot; an elderly retired-looking couple uses the facility, exits, and passes me by. I have to get pushy. I see a youngish guy drive in and go to the restroom area. I grab my bag and sign and run back over to the building and go inside. No services here but I wait outside the men's room door, hoping he'll respond to my desperate plea when he exits.

I wait. And wait. And wait. He must have diarrhea, I think— another reason he won't pick me up. A whole family of Muslim women enter, eye me suspiciously, and nervously go into the la- dies' room on the other side. He's *still* in there! I feel like such a pervert waiting for someone who's obviously taking a massive dump. The Muslim ladies come out and I flash them my sign— why, I don't know, they'll never pick me up! They avert their eyes and beat a hasty retreat. The shitter finally exits and looks horri-fied to see me waiting; not that he recognizes me, he clearly doesn't, but he's pissed a beggar is confronting him. He doesn't even stop, just shakes his head and rushes past me.

I go back to my solitary hitchhiking spot, sure somebody will call the vice squad to report a lurking man in the rest area: me. No cars come by. Finally I see the trucker, who must have been sleeping, climb out of his cab, stretch, and scratch his balls. He's a skinny, late-thirties Appalachia type, wearing Bermuda shorts, a T-shirt, and flip-flops. He sees me standing there with my sign and waves. Could I?

I'm thinking this is the night that I have to sleep in the woods for real. I call my office in my usual panic and ask Susan and Trish to try to find me a cab service that can come take me to the next hotel if I'm stuck. They text me back that Junction City is the only town "near" with a cab company, and it would "take an hour and a half" for the driver to come get me, and the same time to go back. Fuck. I really am going to be curling up in the bushes. Maybe there are some poison berries I can nibble.

I realize that Susan and Trish will soon be leaving the office for the day and it's *Friday*! They have plans for the weekend and, of course, are off work. I'm on my own! I freak and call back and ask Susan to see if she can go online and find the name of a gay bar in Junction City—*if* there even is one, maybe a fan inside could be talked into or hired to come and get me, I suggest. I almost never go to gay bars, so I'm not sure why I thought this plan would work or who would believe me. Susan doesn't balk and texts back, "Xcalibur," and the address and phone number. "Help me, gay brothers," I try to imagine myself pleading to the startled bartender who would answer the phone, but luckily I don't have to make that call quite yet. I see a youngish semi-boho type pull into the lot and go inside to the men's room. Maybe I'll wait outside the building this time and try to talk him into giving me a ride to Junction City. I see the trucker is hanging out in the parking lot—maybe I can pitch them both at the same time.

Luckily, he's only a pisser so he's back outside quickly. I approach him with my sign and tell him who I am and that I'm writing a book and hitchhiking across the country and I'm stuck and need a ride to the next exit with a motel. He looks at me skeptically. He's "not going that far," he says, "only to Manhattan, Kansas." I go online and show him on my BlackBerry all the blogs about my hitchhiking trip. He doesn't know my movies, I can tell, but he's beginning to see the humor of the whole situation. The trucker comes over and joins in our conversation and I tell him my story. He laughs and says he'd give me a ride but he's been sleeping here, waiting for his trucking company to give him the go-ahead to proceed, and now they've changed his plans and he has to wait twelve more hours, then turn around and go back to another city in the same direction he just came from. I tell the Kansas hipster that if he doesn't believe me, he can talk to my assistant in my office. Before he can think up another excuse I have Susan on the line and hand him my phone. She explains everything I've told him is all true. He's coming around, I can tell. I say, "If you don't take me, I'm going to have to sleep in the woods here." The skinny trucker butts in and says, "I'll make up a bunk in the back of the truck for you if it comes to that." Hmmm. Is this the first possibility of sex on this real-life trip? Could I? For the book? I mean, he's hardly a Tom of Finland type, but at my age I'm not exactly the big-basket, strong-jawed muscle-stud hitchhiker myself. Maybe he's offering me a bed in complete innocence? From his friendly idiot grin it's hard to tell. Will I miss tarnished magic? I'll never know because Chris, as he finally introduces himself, agrees to give me a ride.

He not only gives me a ride, he offers to take me all the way to Junction City, twenty miles past Manhattan, where he's going to attend his brother's wedding, because he knows I'll have better luck hitchhiking there. Chris is a sweetheart. A student from Lawrence, Kansas, who is also a manager in the local Walmart. I tell him I've never been in a Walmart in my entire life, but that doesn't seem to surprise him. Suddenly he says, "Oh my God, you were in *The Creep*!" "Yes, I was," I tell him proudly, referring to the hip-hop Lonely Island video starring Nicki Minaj, which has 72 million (!) hits on YouTube. Ah, the power of the Internet. To hell with movies. Only old people see them.

Chris tells me that Junction City is a huge military base, and as we pull near, I see the gigantic Fort Riley. Amazing, I think, I bet *this* is where Bobby Garcia, the marine-porn guy I wrote about in *Role Models*, must be hiding out now! Chris is a cool guy, but I don't share this thought with him. He tells me "it's a rough town" and people he knows have been in fights a lot here.

We pull into Junction City Travel Plaza, and the nearest motel to the entrance ramp back on I-70W is the damned Holiday Inn. I go for it. I'd check in anywhere after this day! I fill up Chris's gas tank even though, like all nice guys, he at first protests. Since this is the second driver today who, I feel, saved my life, I insist. Another kind guy. Another happy fella. And I stupidly forget to give him my hitchhiking thank-you card. The only ride so far where I've forgotten. What a fool I am! I will feel guilty forever. Chris, if you ever read these words, contact me through Atomic Books in Baltimore and I promise I will send you yours!

REAL RIDE NUMBER SEVENTEEN

KANSAS COUPLE

In the dark Holiday Inn room I collapse. Was this maybe the worst day yet? It's Friday night—no usual guzzling, no usual fun in the works for me. The Corvette Kid calls and says he wants to come get me. I don't know what to think. I see online he has given an interview to his hometown paper where he tells our hitchhiking story but claims he was on his way to Joplin, Missouri, to help tornado victims when he took me to Ohio, which wasn't exactly true. He was planning on doing that the *next* week. He doesn't mention this article now and neither do I. He did say his mother had admonished him to "never pick up another hitchhiker," yet here he is telling me he wants to come get me *again*. When I'm standing on the side of the road with no one picking me up, I want him to come, but when I get a ride and I'm in somebody else's car, I'm not so sure—will that be cheating again? Would it make for a better or a worse book? He could be sitting in his Maryland bedroom just egging me along when he has no real plans to leave. He could be grounded by his parents, for all I know.

I go through my e-mails and see Susan has written earlier, "I spoke to your mom and told her 'all is well in Kansas.' She said she's gotten so many calls and she just keeps saying 'no comment.'" My mother also mentioned to Susan how my uncle's son had just bicycled across the United States from Chevy Chase. See? I think my mom *still* doesn't think hitchhiking is so bad.

How will it feel to reenter my real life when this is over? I wonder. Walk out the front door in the morning and not have to start scoping out entrance ramps? It's hard to imagine that here in Junction City, Kansas. Susan and Trish e-mail me from their homes, relieved I have arrived safely at a motel for the night. "You have about 300 miles to get out of Kansas and into Colorado," they inform me. "Inch by mother fucking inch," I respond, quoting Oliver Stone's great line about what moviemaking is like.

I'm going out—to Walmart! It's a long walk through the giant travel plaza, but besides snacks and water, I definitely need those cuticle scissors—my mustache is starting to look bushy like that of Bob Turk, Baltimore's longest-running TV weatherman. Good God, everybody is a soldier in this town! It's Bobby Garcia heaven! Ten thousand cute military men in uniforms! I keep trying to think of the porno title for the movie I'm suddenly an extra in—*Function in My Junction*? Imagine me here under the influence of two martinis! I could get in real trouble.

Inside Walmart I feel like a complete trespasser. Is this how normal people shop? It's too fucking big. Where are the salespeople? God, it's got a supermarket, too? I wander around trying not to stare at the soldiers, who all look handsome. None know who I am. I even *try* to be recognized by standing in one place for a while pretending to study signs about special sales, but no dice.

Yay! They *do* have cuticle scissors. Candy and newspapers, too! What's this? Oh God, John Travolta's masseur scandal is on the cover of *People* magazine?! I guiltily buy it even though I know the copy I get by subscription is awaiting me in Baltimore. Maybe soldiers' wives have at least seen the Hollywood remake of *Hairspray* with him in it. When they see me clutching the mag in the checkout line, maybe they'll put two and two together. But they don't.

Back in the dingy Holiday Inn, I eat peanuts, gobble Jujyfruits, and guzzle Evian water, catching up on the media and having my own pathetic version of a Friday night. I think of all those soldiers out there. I try to imagine that gay bar Susan had found me, Xcalibur. Could I have pulled off being a Bobby Jr. there? Or would it have been filled with twinks? I try to fantasize about that hillbilly trucker who offered me a place to sleep in the back of the cab of his truck. Would I have gotten the upper or the lower bunk? Is sex at my age even remotely possible on the road? I fall asleep. Alone. And probably a lot safer.

I wake up way late for me, 7:00 a.m., take a bath, then bravely throw away another pair of underpants. Bravado or stupidity? Today will answer that. I make a new sign on the back of the WRITING HITCHHIKE BOOK one. I set a modest goal: 70 WEST THROUGH KANSAS—and once again add I'M SAFE. I guess I mean sexually, too. I look in the mirror at my freshly groomed and trimmed mustache and hope it does its job for me today—getting me a ride! As always, I leave a tip for the maid.

I should know better but I go down and check out the free-breakfast room. Per usual, no one makes eye contact. I approach a guy who looks like a possible ride and show him my sign, but he looks appalled I'd even ask. I never thought it could be possible, but the food is even worse than at the last hotel. The chipped-beef dish looks like liquefied mucus mixed with Dinty Moore canned stew. I sit at a table and drink tea and text The Corvette Kid that I made it to Junction City, Kansas.

I go outside and walk the short distance to the I-70W entrance ramp, which seems like the most central one in this hub of traveler facilities. There's plenty of room for cars to pull over here, too. It's a nice day. I'm starting a little later but obviously not late enough. Still no rides. Oh well, I've got all day, I think. It only takes one car—blah, blah, blah. Damn, it's windy! My sign keeps ripping. Some goddamned tumbleweed might come out of nowhere and blindside me!

It's still always a shock, but a car stops and I grab my bag. Inside is a laborer-type father with his young son, and I can tell by Dad's expression he thinks I'm homeless. The kid doesn't look scared, like maybe they've picked up hitchhikers before, maybe even taken a bum home for a good hot meal. "I'm only going to the next exit," Dad says, shrugging with apology. I thank him politely but reply, "This is such a good spot to hitchhike, I'm going to stay here." He understands. The son looks at me with actual kindness. Some people just *are* decent. They pull off and already all three of us are better people.

But I'm still here. I see cops go by. They don't stop to harass me. Good. I see military tanks go by, too. I wish I could get a ride in one of them, but I look like a don't-ask-but-I'm-telling insane military deserter who's lost his mind and is running away to meet his meth-head AWOL boyfriend. I stick out my thumb at every approaching army vehicle anyway and during traffic lulls look at my BlackBerry. I am totally shocked to see that The Corvette Kid has texted again: "I'm almost in Missouri. Should I come get you or go to Joplin?"

Before I can answer, I get a ride. The back door opens and I see a pretty middle-aged woman on the floor on a mat with a three-legged little white poodle in her lap. Her husband, a nice-looking man, is in the front seat behind the wheel. They're going all the way to Denver and they tell me they'll take me! Thank you, God! He's Mike, a circuit-court judge in a "very rural" town in Southern Illinois, and he's a fan of Barbra Streisand and Liza Minnelli (the only straight guy in the world with that taste?).

And she's Laura, a Democratic Party chair and an animal rescuer (!) who so reminds me of Linda Grippi, my friend and fellow strong supporter of the parole of Leslie Van Houten. I feel so guilty remembering the horrifying animal rescuer I imagined in a "bad ride" chapter of this book. Here, next to me, is a rarity (from what I've seen)—a woman who militantly loves animals but *also* loves people. Even the three-legged poodle is well behaved after initially freaking me out by jumping in my lap and kissing me on the lips the moment I got in the car. I guess he is grateful he's on an adventure, too!

They are headed to some Colorado state park for a vacation and admit passing me by once standing on the ramp in Junction City, Kansas (where they had stayed the night in the same hotel, but slept later), and debating if it was me for eight miles before turning back to come see. And yes, it was me. I try to be a good rider and tell them stories about meeting Liz Taylor and Kathleen Turner, and they in turn fill me in on their lives and how the animal-rescue deal works. The judge and I even talk about our shared opinion that mandatory life sentences without parole for minors are wrong.

I text The Corvette Kid, "Oh my God, I just got a ride to Colorado." He answers, "You headed to Denver?" I respond, "Yep. Will let you know when I land." We drive for hours. Kansas is an amazing state—both beautiful in its minimalist geography and horrifying in its brutal weather extremes. We see lots of little dust tornadoes on each side of the highway. Kansas is so-o-o-o-o-o long. So boring. Yet so awe-inspiring in its horizontal, hypnotic dullness and threatening lack of population.

After more hours of traveling together and bonding, Laura admits she wouldn't have recognized me or have known who I was if it weren't for her gay son, who has been a fan of mine forever. "Let's call him," I offer, and she dials his number and I hear her ask him about me without revealing anything. He starts telling his mom how he's been reading online that I am hitch-hiking across the country. Unbelievable! He already knows! "Guess who we picked up?" she says with, yes, glee. "John Waters." And she hands me the phone and her son is speechless as first. No wonder. What are the chances of this happening? He's a great guy and even starts quoting lines from *Female Trouble*, but in a cool way, not like that other scary fan I imagined earlier in this book.

We pull off in Bunker Hill, Kansas, to get gas and I offer to fill it up, but they won't hear of it. Instead I buy the snacks, but only because I grab the bill before they can pay. While Mike is using the men's room, I take Laura out back of this big rest-area convenience store to look for cardboard. After all, my 70 WEST THROUGH KANSAS sign will be obsolete when they drop me off in Denver. We actually Dumpster-dive together to get the right-size box and take it around front, back to the car, where Laura thinks Mike has a pocketknife to break down the box. But as we walk through the giant gas-station parking lot, the ever-present howling wind blows open the box, and thousands of Styrofoam "peanuts" pour out and accidentally scatter all across the rest area and into the Kansas plains themselves. Oh well. Not much us litterbuggers can do. Except step on it! Mike does. See ya later, Bunker Hill.

The Corvette Kid has texted back, "Sounds good. I'm in Kansas right now." You gotta be kidding me! That means he has been driving for forty-eight hours straight at eighty miles an hour with no sleep, *not* stopping to help tornado victims in Joplin, Missouri, where his parents think he is going. He's actually coming to get me?! "Don't get arrested for speeding!" I text. "Hey," he writes back, "I'm on Mission Impossible here. LOL. There's no stopping The Corvette Kid, my friend." "Evel Knievel," I answer. "If you leave Denver I may have to smack you by the way. LOL," he adds. I'm starting to really get impressed by this guy. *If* he's telling the truth. Suppose he's still in his bedroom in Maryland playing a game? Well, I'll see soon enough.

An incredibly ferocious rainstorm is approaching as we plow our way across Kansas past signs promising ahead RATTLE-SNAKES, PRAIRIE DOGS AND A SIX LEGGED CAT. I guess this *is* show business here in Kansas. I offer to get in the back on the floor with the dog but Laura wants to stay there, she promises she's comfortable. The black clouds are getting ominous. Naturally we talk about Dorothy, then discuss storm cellars, but never mention there's nowhere for us to go now if there is a tornado. Torrential rain hits. It's actually scary, but Mike is a great driver and we make it through without flying off to some freaky local Oz. I see a junkyard that is exactly like the one I imagined in the "good ride" rave chapter. So perfect. So isolated. Right smack-dab in the middle of nowhere with a trailer on the edge of the property where the owner must live. Wonder if he's cute.

Suddenly the sun is out but it's still raining. Surely there must be a rainbow in these weather conditions, the three of us agree, but after searching the horizon on both sides of the interstate, we come up visually empty-handed. Maybe Kansas is fed up with all this *Wizard of Oz* bullshit. Maybe the state lawmakers have outlawed rainbows. I text The Corvette Kid back that I will wait for him in Denver and "will call from the hotel. If you haven't stopped to sleep, do so." I know he couldn't still be in his Corvette because that was his mother's car, so I add, "I will wait for The Corvette Kid no matter what you are driving," "Will do," he answers, "Kansas is scary long." Good God, he's gaining on us! I tell Mike and Laura about The Corvette Kid, how he picked me up and how now he is coming back, and I see they are too polite to ask, "What the hell's going on here?" I don't know the answer myself. All I know is I'm glad he's coming. It's not cheating—he's still a stranger giving me a ride, he's just picking me up for the second time.

I feel so comfortable with Laura and Mike, even the dog. We pull off at Colby, Kansas, and have lunch at Montana Mike's. God, what a town. The wind is still howling. What could life possibly be like here in the dead of winter? We sit in a booth and Mike and I order a big, fattening meal while Laura is more health conscious in her choice. I use the men's room (no graffiti, dammit) and pass an empty video-game room. Such a Nan Goldin "art" shot. So sad, so lonely, so empty of fun. I try to imagine the bored, angry teens of this town *in* this pitiful room and shudder at the potential hormonal violence this clubhouse from hell might provoke. I insist on paying for lunch.

We keep going. God, this is such a great ride! My new family, Laura and Mike. They decide they'll stay in a motel in Denver, too, rather than keep going to their state park, where they actually aren't sure where they'll be camping. Since The Corvette Kid is picking me up, it doesn't matter to me about exit or entrance ramps, so we all can stay at the same place.

We cross into Colorado. Yay! Mountain time! I've made it to the West. It doesn't look much different from Kansas for a while, though, still sparse. Scary little towns I'd probably get stuck in if I didn't already have a ride. We even pull off and scope out the motels on the outskirts in Limon, Colorado, but they seem spookily uninviting. We don't check in.

Nearer Denver it starts to look just like every other city does—same chain shops and motels—but we don't care, we just need a room at the inn. We pull off and pick a place, the La Quinta Inn, 4460 Peoria Street, which is in the city limits but near the airport. We unload and Laura hides the dog in one of her bags to sneak him in. I know this is Mike and Laura's vacation, so I tell them, "Farewell, my new friends. I'm going to let you have a romantic dinner alone." We ask a stranger to snap our group photo on our respective cell phones and he does happily. I know my undercover travel adventure is still safe when he whispers to Laura, "Is that guy homeless?" Laura laughs and then, as we go inside, asks me, "Were we the most boring people to pick you up?" I honestly answer, "Are you kidding? You were perfect!" And they are. Absolutely, undeniably marvelous people who give me faith in the kindness of strangers *and* the gifted new Saint Christopher medal on my key ring. They rescued a dog *and* me.

REAL RIDE NUMBER EIGHTEEN

CORVETTE KID AGAIN

I check into my room and text The Corvette Kid the exact address of the hotel. He texts back that his own car has a GPS so he can easily find the location and he'll probably sleep before he continues driving. I answer back like a stern dad, "You should." I've got time on my hands: maybe I'll do laundry, wash those dingy underpants I haven't thrown away. I go down to the desk and ask if there's a Laundromat in the hotel. "Yes," the girl behind the counter says, surprising me; I didn't know these kinds of places had washers and dryers available. I go up to where she instructed me and see it's just one room with nothing in it but a washer and a dryer. No change machine. No soap. I race back down and she gives me both and I stomp back up, throw in my underpants and a few T-shirts, sprinkle on the soap, and put in quarters, but the machine jams. Now what? All my pitiful homeless clothes are covered with detergent. I go all the way back down and tell her, and she accompanies me back up with a paper clip. She attempts to jam the stack of quarters through but is unsuccessful, goes back downstairs while I wait, and finally returns with a credit card, which she uses like a professional lock picker, and presto, the coins drop and the machine starts working. I thank her and figure it's safe to leave my clothes in the wash cycle even though I had already fantasized stealing somebody else's laundry in one of the "good ride" chapters in the book. Reality is never as exciting as fiction.

Back in my room, which is okay, better lighting than Holiday Inn but not as good as Days Inn, I try to kill time but get bored and plod back up to the laundry room. This is the exact opposite of glamour. Naturally, the clothes are still sloshing around, so I just wait until they're done. Alone. I don't use dryers because my T-shirts will shrink, but they'll never dry hanging in my bathroom overnight, so I toss them in with my clean underpants and hope for the best.

I wonder if The Corvette Kid pulled over to sleep. Do I pay for a separate room for him or does he just take the other bed in my room? I have no idea what he expects. If I don't offer to pay for the room, does it look as if I'm coming on to him? Or just an innocent sleepover? Who knows, I think, as I gather my still slightly wet T-shirts and boxers and head back to my room.

It's Saturday night in Denver! I'm going out. I go online and find out where *The Dictator* is playing. It just opened today all over America and I purposely didn't read the reviews because I want to see this Sacha Baron Cohen movie first and make up my own mind. The girl at the desk tells me which theater is nearest. At first I think maybe I'll hitchhike *there*, too, but then internally yell at myself, come on! You're off work tonight! This isn't part of your trip, take a cab! I do. It's not far. I feel so alien in the backseat of a taxi. Am I now just a bourgeois passenger from the middle class, too dim-witted to hustle a free ride?

The theater is located in some giant outdoor shopping center filled with young people. I am shocked how many fat teenagers I see. Really fat! Four hundred pounds fat! All with giant plates of alarmingly unhealthy food piled in front of them in outdoor cafés. I'm early, as always, so I search around for a more model-friendly type of eating establishment. I settle on the Euro Café and have a Mediterranean veggie roll and a bottled water. It is screamingly average, and although I am one of the few diners, the service is abysmal. Maybe they don't like thin people.

I go into the movie theater and am happy to see it is crowded. I take a seat on the aisle, and three presumably gay gentlemen pass me taking their seats and recognize me and I say hi back. I like the movie. It's so odd to be doing anything besides standing beside the highway, though, so I'm a bit uneasy throughout. As I file out afterward, I run into the gay guys again and one asks me why I'm in Denver, and I tell him I'm hitchhiking my way across the country. He says, "Well, do you want a ride back to your hotel, then?" and I say, "Yes," with great enthusiasm because technically I'm hitchhiking again, aren't I?

I tell the guys that I am staying at La Quinta Inn nearby, and the driver says he knows where that is. On the way I discover one of my hosts owns a drive-in movie theater in Kansas. We talk about the isolation living in those tiny towns, and he fills me in on how tornadoes, some recently, had devastated many of the same places I had just driven through today.

As he pulls up to La Quinta Inn to drop me off, I am momentarily confused. This doesn't look familiar, but what do I know? I'm in a different motel every night and they all blend together. "I hope this is the right one," I joke as I get out, unsure. "Well, if it's not, you can always hitchhike," the drive-in owner wisecracks innocently. I get out. Fuck! It is the wrong one! I check my hotel-key-folder address, and sure enough, they dropped me off at a different La Quinta Inn. I go inside in complete alarm and the desk clerk calms me down. The one I'm staying in isn't that far away, and he'll get the guy that drives the airport-hotel courtesy van to give me a ride back. I am greatly relieved and, of course, give the nice driver a tip for his kindness.

Imagine my surprise when I play my phone messages and hear The Corvette Kid's already here! He couldn't possibly have slept! I'm amazed he caught up to me this quickly. "Come up to my room," I text. "Damn! I already got a room," he replies. Well, that settles that. He texts he's "going to take a shower first."

I e-mail Susan that The Corvette Kid "is here!" "A new chapter—so bizarre," she responds, "there's definitely something strange about his race across the country. He may be one of those Log Cabin Republicans. The adventure continues," Susan signs off.

"Okay, now I feel better," The Corvette Kid texts again, freshly showered. "I could drive another 2000 miles." "Ah, youth," I text back. "Did you eat yet?" he asks. "Yes, but I'll go with you if you're hungry," I reply. "I'll be right down," he answers. Suddenly I think, "Suppose he's not here at all? Suppose all these texts have been a scam? Suppose no one comes down? No one knocks on the door? He could be laughing at me all the way from Maryland!"

But no, The Corvette Kid delivers. He's here, dressed as wholesome as ever in his khaki shorts, T-shirt, and running shoes, but I can tell he's unsure if his "look" is cool enough for the road. It is, even if he is now driving a red Kia Sorento. I am happy to see him. We go out to look for something to eat but everything is closed this late. We drive around as if we were casing fast-food joints to rob until we finally settle for an open 7-Eleven and he buys the most unappetizing prewrapped sandwich I've ever seen. I can see he's excited to be beginning the next leg of our crazy trip and so am I, but I tell him he must be exhausted. He agrees, and I add that he should sleep as late as he can tomorrow morning. Back at the hotel we split up to go to our separate rooms and I tell him, "You could have slept in the other bed without paying for your room. I'm not going to attack you—I'm too tired." He laughs out loud and goes up toward his new accommodations.

I'm actually glad we have separate rooms. When was the last

time I shared a motel room and wasn't sleeping with the person? Almost never. I decide that I'm going to just go as far as Reno with him, then get out for other rides and give him the keys to my apartment in San Francisco and tell him to drive there and wait for me. He's safe. I can tell.

Even though we are supposed to be sleeping late, I wake up at 5:30 a.m. I'm so relieved I don't have to go outside and beg a ride. I see online on the *Deadline Hollywood* website news alert that Donna Summer has died. It's hard to care about celebrity news from a motel that doesn't even carry *USA Today*. I feel lazy just lolling around the motel room, waiting for The Corvette Kid to wake up. I take a bath and then panic when I realize I am out of La Mer cream! If ever I needed this pricey moisturizer, it's now. I look in the mirror and see I have "hitchhiker face." Almost none of these motels ever offer complimentary body lotions. This one does, thank God, and I pocket it. Reduced to swiping cheap toiletries, all in the name of literature.

It's 10:00 a.m. and The Corvette Kid is ready to go. He's freshly scrubbed, looks rested, and seems even more willing to take on his new role as my on-the-road sidekick. I fill up the tank and we're off. As soon as we get out of Denver, the landscape changes. The Rockies are suddenly so scary and beautiful. The Corvette Kid laughs and admits he thought the Rockies were just one mountain we'd go over. We go through ski resorts with amazing vistas, and as excited as I am to see this kind of scenery again after forty years, it is even more fun to see it through The Corvette Kid's eyes—especially when he's missing in action from his parents' home.

We stop at a rest area and ask other tourists to take our picture. I get recognized and sign autographs. If I had been hitching, I bet it would have been easier to get picked up in Colorado than elsewhere. I like this state. We keep going, laughing, comparing stories about his life in a small town and mine as a filth elder. I immediately feel guilty for imagining anything gay about The Corvette Kid. He's just a curious guy and somehow we're suddenly in a book together. Could life be any better than this?

We pull off in Grand Junction, Colorado, and make the mistake of having lunch in Applebee's. It's Sunday at one-thirty in the afternoon and the eatery is packed with families and elderly people after church. The food is horrible and I tell The Kid that this gets the prize as the worst chain restaurant I've eaten in on the trip so far. I visit the men's room and am shocked to see it's filthy. Middle America never looked so unappealing. We drive off and pass a middle-aged male hitchhiker, the first one I've seen this trip. We don't pick him up. I know, I know.

As soon as we drive across the Utah border, there is nothing. Beautiful nothing. Suddenly, the CHECK ENGINE light comes on. If we break down here, we are incredibly screwed. It is hot as hell. No one is around. I have never even seen a cop. We just pretend that it's not on. Gas stations are few and very far between; as in, there aren't any. The Kid's tank is getting low. Now *that* warning light comes on, too. Check engine *and* no gas. I picture the vultures circling overhead. The Kid suddenly points happily to a sign announcing a gas station coming up. We pull over with great relief to a Shell station in Thompson Springs, Utah. Gas is $4.14 a gallon! It was $3.19 in Kansas, but I guess they've got you by the balls here. There's not another one within hundreds of miles, so what are you gonna do, not pay? The Kid opens the hood to check the engine just as his vehicle has ordered him to do, but I can tell he's no gearhead. "The oil seems okay," he says, perplexed. Don't ask me! I don't even know how to open the hood of my car! We pull out and the CHECK ENGINE light is still on. We try not to talk about it.

Route 70 West ends in about an hour, but Trish and I had mapped out with AAA the more direct route to 80 West by cutting up north on Route 191 to 6. This turnoff is about ten minutes ahead, but looking out the window and at my AAA TripTik and the *Rand McNally Road Atlas*, I realize these roads are almost entirely through the desert. What the hell, let's take a chance.

We turn off on 191 and it's just two lanes, one in each direction, where if you have to pass a car, you risk a head-on collision. The fucking CHECK ENGINE light is still on. It's so bleak that we both are energized by the extreme landscape. We see little baby dust tornadoes, just hoping to become lethal ones. They may call this soil "desert" in these parts, but I thought a desert was sand. This is dirt.

Once you veer west onto Route 6, you are in rattlesnake heaven! We pull through the coal-mining town of Wellington, Utah, and I fall in love with the place. Such a weird little community. Tiny houses. Sheds, really. But painted in gay pastel colors. One little blue one was so sad yet proud, crumbling but imposing, that I wanted to move in. There are so many scary little churches, too. I picture *Marjoe*-type preachers curing leprosy. It may be the best oddball city in America. I want to come back and have a vacation here one day. We stop in some convenience store and feel as if we were in *The Twilight Zone*. The Corvette Kid pays for the snacks. I can tell he wants to get out of here. Fast.

We drive north to Salt Lake City. Slowly, suburban life begins to come into view. We're making good time. Obviously, the CHECK ENGINE light is not warning us of anything dire—we have been driving all day at high speeds and we're still going!

We pull into Salt Lake City, which I know a little about from being here to promote my films. I even recorded the score for *Serial Mom* here. We look around for a motel. It's Sunday, luckily, so except for some Mormon art festival, the city is dead. We check into the Comfort Inn, and without discussing it, I pay for two rooms. I tell him to bring in all his stuff because we're in a city and I'm always nervous someone will break into the car. I see he brought with him a *real* Republican preppy suit and regimental tie. It's hard for me to picture him dressed for his other life.

We go to our separate rooms and agree to meet in the lobby to try to find a place to eat—somewhere that has "real food." I text my office that I'm in SLC and that "The Corvette Kid is totally genuine—a sweet kid seeing America for the first time." I e-mail my sisters, "I'm in Salt Lake City. Send Mom love from the entrance ramps of America."

The Corvette Kid and I aimlessly walk the long blocks of Salt Lake City until we come to what looks like a fairly upscale Chinese restaurant. We enter, I get recognized, and they seat us outside at a nice table. The Kid tells me his mother is absolutely horrified now that he has told her he is back with me. She is "freaking." I again offer to talk with her, but he declines and turns off his phone so he can't see her frantic texts. I tell him I'm going to get out of his car in Reno and continue hitchhiking to San Francisco by myself. I'll give him my apartment keys; he can drive there on his own and stay until I arrive. He smiles in agreement but says he is *not* telling his mom and dad that now. I confront him about that interview he gave to his hometown paper and how it said he was on his way to Joplin to help tornado victims the *first* time he picked me up, which wasn't true. He readily agrees and explains the paper got it mixed up; he had told the reporter he was supposed to go there about a week later. I believe him.

We talk about our "types." He admits the waitress at that Applebee's we ate in who wore tight jeweled pants was "hot." So I mention how this one truck driver we had seen in a rest area looked pretty good to me. Earlier, when we had pulled into the lot of our Salt Lake City motel, he had checked the oil yet again, worrying about that CHECK ENGINE light, and I had cracked "how butch" he looked under the hood. He burst out laughing—he was getting used to my sense of humor. The Corvette Kid picks up the dinner check. I knew he was a classy guy.

As we walk back to the Comfort Inn, I see a lot of student types hanging out and say to The Kid, "Go out by yourself if you want. Have some fun!" I can tell he's been considering just that possibility, but I'm unsure if he actually will. We go to our rooms and promise to meet in the lobby early—a big day ahead of us. Nevada, here we come!

I wake up too early and go down the hall to the dreaded breakfast room and see a DO NOT DISTURB sign on The Corvette Kid's door. Oh God. Hope he didn't pick up a girl. I stop myself on that one. Why not? If he did, I hope she's pretty and smart. At least this breakfast room has some decent cereal. I eat and worry. Wouldn't he come here first to get something to eat before we check out? Oh well. Young people sleep longer.

I take the elevator to the lobby and pace back and forth. As soon as The Kid's one minute late, I picture him dead, cut up by some hooker, but a few seconds later there he is, lugging all his bags back downstairs. He's unharmed, with a big smile on his face, ready to explore America. Yes, he went out but nothing happened. Just "hung out in the street with some skaters and punk types" who were all students. I'm glad he mingled. He's already had coffee in his room.

We stop for gas and I fill it up. We're both revved up. It's Day Eight for me and I'm feeling good. The Kid is rarin' to go. Nevada—get ready! You are about to receive into your community—the filthiest people alive! Hardly. I need to calm down.

As soon as we drive out of town, the geography changes; the Salt Flats, Utah. Endless. Beautiful. GOVERNMENT TRAINING CENTER, the sign says. To train what? we both wonder. Then we see our first mirage—the cheesy cinematic kind where in the long, flat road ahead you see water, yet it disappears as you approach. Nevada must be getting nearer because we see great signs for the first gambling town across the border, West Wendover. $10 LAP DANCES. My God, what could those girls look like? Maybe this town is another future vacation spot for yours truly?

Once we cross the state line into Pacific time, I see the first and possibly the cheesiest gambling casino in the state. Its sign reads THE NUGGET—FREE TRUCKERS—7 DAYS A WEEK. The Kid and I marvel at this offer. Does it mean truckers can stay there without paying forever as long as they gamble? Imagine how exciting and dramatic and terrifying this place would be. A photo op that could raise Diane Arbus straight out of her grave.

We see a sign for a town coming up actually called Oasis, Nevada. When we pull through this, I would imagine, once highly anticipated burg, all that is left off the freeway are about five dilapidated buildings, deserted, rotted, and boarded up. What happened? Who was the last to leave? Are there squatters inside? What a perfect village—its name itself is a lie!

We stop for gas in Valmy, Nevada. Talk about local color. The cashier behind the counter, a tough desert moll if there ever was one, looks as if she just ate a pound of nails for breakfast. The decor seems done by Vincent Peranio, who production-designed all my movies. Two pitiful slot machines are inside. The Kid and I both play and we both lose. Has anyone *ever* won here?

As we're going back to the car with our meager snack purchases, we see one guy and two ladies exiting their vehicle who appear to have stepped straight out of one of my screenplays. Pushing middle age but definitely not settled, they're on their way, you can tell, to some kind of wild fun. Especially the dame with the extremely dyed-blond hair and the stilettos! Are they swingers? They give us a big grin as they pass us in the parking lot, but I'm not sure if they recognize me or are just looking to make friends. The Corvette Kid and I smile back and then look at each other slightly bug-eyed in surprise before I fill up the tank. Gas is $4.69 a gallon—a new high.

I look in the road atlas to see where we are, but Valmy is not on the map. We turn on the radio and not one AM *or* FM radio station comes in. The CHECK ENGINE light continues to add a touch of anxiety, but we've risen above that—just that we're still moving is proof we're okay. I wish there were highway signs that read NO SERVICES. NO NAME. NO SUCH THING, because that is exactly our location.

We're starting to feel starved, but there aren't even bad chain restaurants on this highway. Eventually we see a sign for a town coming up called Lovelock, Nevada. It sounds good to me. Like "Lovelips" or "Liplock." There's a prison there, too, which always makes me feel included. We pull off and instantly feel as if we've been cast in a cowboy movie. Lovelock is like a set for the Wild West, only it's real. We drive around and pass the Cowpoke Café. How can we not stop? A perfect name for a perfect place.

Inside is even better! It's decorated like the Long Branch Saloon in *Gunsmoke*. Home-cooked food, too. I'm shocked when a big, big lady approaches me and asks for an autograph. I pose for a picture with her and The Kid takes it. We sit down to eat and it is delicious! My chicken soup is the best meal I have had on the trip—by far. The Kid and I look startled when the swingers we saw back in Valmy enter for lunch, too! Wow! Are they following us? I wonder, before realizing this is such a great place maybe every traveler on the highway is in on the secret but us.

I go outside to take a phone call from my office and update them on my whereabouts. They are happy I'm with The Kid and inform me that the Kansas Couple have Facebooked pictures from our ride and now these have gone viral, too. I quickly check my Google Alerts and am both horrified and, I guess, flattered to see some company has already manufactured and offered for sale for $19.99 a "hitchhiking bull denim tote bag" with my END OF 70 WEST sign pirated from the Facebook picture. Jesus.

Back inside the Cowpoke Café, The Corvette Kid informs me he's been talking to the swingers, and they did recognize me and he's given them his phone number because they want to get together with us in Reno. I can tell The Kid is flattered by their attention. Maybe he doesn't get hit on back in small-town Maryland. He's shy, I realize, unsure of his sex appeal. I'm happy this trip is building his confidence, but suddenly I feel like the conservative relative. God knows what they have in mind; I wonder, a little granddad-grandson five-way? I roll my eyes and grab the check. "Come on, Kid, we're leaving."

We keep going. Lots of brush fires in the desert and nobody is even there to put them out. Some of them are big, too. Oh well . . . I'm not Smokey the Bear, but obviously no one listened to him. We're getting near Reno, "The Biggest Little City in the World." A place for which I have low expectations. We pull off in Sparks, Nevada, the town before Reno, which seems somehow shabbier than how I had imagined it with Connie Francis. One of the swingers has just texted The Corvette Kid that we should hook up here and party. I am slightly shocked. He gives me a shit-eating grin and chuckles.

We pull back on the highway and continue into Reno, auditioning entrance ramps for dropping me off for the final hitchhike leg in the morning. None look promising—too inner-city. I bet the cops are strict here. We drive around looking for a hotel. It looks depressing; the people in the street seem beaten down, old. We pull into the parking lot of a big-name casino hotel and go in to check prices and see if they have a vacancy.

The stench of cigarette smoke is overpowering. I literally gag from the odor and I'm not even born-again about people who still smoke. Rollo, the middle-aged doorman, sporting giant muttonchops, instantly recognizes me and escorts me to the proper check-in line. He's a gay blade, all right, and says he will take care of anything I need. It's only $29 a night. Good God . . . what could the rooms be like?

I go out and get The Corvette Kid and as usual warn him to take all his bags inside since the parking lot is uncovered. Rollo's eyes light up when he gets a load of my traveling companion, and suddenly I feel like such a chicken queen. When we check in, the clerk doesn't even ask The Corvette Kid's name! What? Do they just write *Trick* on the registration? Naturally I pay for two separate rooms. Like the Daddy Warbucks they think I am.

We walk through endless casinos with Rollo as our guide to find the proper elevator to get to our accommodations. So many old people. So much emphysema. So many cigarettes. So little time. God, it's depressing to see the blank looks of these elderly retirees, yanking down the handles on the slot machines and barely registering any emotion no matter if they win or lose.

Our rooms, down the hall from each other, are not bad. We've asked for nonsmoking but the toxic cigarette smoke is so overwhelming in this hotel that you'd have to hermetically seal off each room and fumigate for a year before you could even begin to promise such a thing. I'll be sleeping in a modernly designed ashtray for the night. The Kid says that before we go down to explore and eat dinner, he has "some city council work to do" and wants to give another interview to a different hometown newspaper. I try to warn him that the fact he has come back to get me may raise a few eyebrows, but he just laughs.

But as soon as I'm back in my room, I get a frantic call from The Corvette Kid on my cell phone. He's locked himself out. Seems ol' Rollo brought up a VIP platter of cheese and fruit but, instead of delivering it to my room, knocked on The Kid's *and* came into his room. Odd, Rollo knew which was my room and which was The Kid's. I rescue The Kid from the hall and he's unnerved. First, he never knew that management often sends up such food items to welcome hotel guests if they are famous in any way. Plus, it's further unsettling that Rollo seemed a little "too familiar" in his in-room patter, never mentioning the curious delivery to the "unfamous" room.

The Kid's even locked his wallet with ID in his room, so I have to call downstairs and get Rollo to bring back up a new key. He returns and asks to take a photo of us holding the VIP tray. The Corvette Kid is now chuckling. Here's the blackmail photo. The two of us in the honeymoon suite of the hotel. I shoo Rollo away after thanking him for keeping such a good eye out for us. The Kid is still laughing, but he tells me his mom is stunned when he informs her that we are now in Reno together. I guess it does look bad. The hotel thinks I've checked in with some boy, and his parents think he's run off with a pornographer. Plus I'm a Democrat. Even The Kid's friends are contacting him nervously about his adventure. "Way to go," one has texted, "you're with a gay man in a hotel room in Reno?" We roar. It's completely innocent but highly troubling to everybody but us. A bromance is not an easy thing to explain.

We walk out of the hotel at a different exit to avoid Rollo. He's a funny guy, but yikes . . . a little overeager. The streets are mostly empty except for the sketchy homeless. Long blocks of nothing except cheapo hotels and tawdry gambling casinos that look understaffed and ready to go out of business. Then we turn the corner and see cop cars with lights flashing and a small crowd of rubberneckers. In the street is a body with a sheet over it. Some kind of shoot-out, I gather. We stroll by.

We enter another casino and try to get change to play the slot machine. I'm amazed to hear the woman in front of me in line say to her female friend, "God, I love it here." I am stunned by this unironic remark. What could she possibly love about it? The smoke? The humiliation of losing? The free watered-down drinks?

The pathetic glamour of a faux richness that even she could certainly not believe?

We start playing one-armed bandits. The Kid loses a few dollars, but every once in a while, I win. How humiliating. Those dreaded sound effects of coins dropping, flashing lights, and the very public display of winning such paltry change. I go back and forth within my $20 limit, getting almost down to zero, when I win again and suddenly have a $20.25 balance. I cash out. Mr. Lucky! I beat this town! Even The Corvette Kid seems shocked at my gambling self-discipline.

We walk back into the disheartened streets of Reno. The dead body is *still* there. We look for a place to eat, but the pickings are slim. A lot of chain places. Finally we stumble upon a restaurant that advertises organic. Campo Restaurant. A jewel among the riffraff. We go inside and see cute people. No cigarette smoke. The hostess recognizes me and seems speechless I've wandered in. We get a nice table and I order skirt steak and The Corvette Kid has organic chicken salad. The owner stops by to say hello and I tell him I'm hitchhiking across the country. The waitress is nice, too; a lovely fan. She asks, "What are you doing after dinner?" and I politely say, "We can't see the good local bars because we have to get up early." I'm now used to saying *we* and forget what she is probably thinking: Christ, John. How old is he!? The Kid and I have promised to have a celebratory martini once we both land safely in San Francisco. We can't do the town now. Not yet.

We stroll back to the hotel. It's dark out now. The dead body is still there—is there some kind of strike at the local police morgue? The streets don't feel exactly dangerous—I am from Baltimore, after all—but neither The Kid nor I feel like exploring any further. We enter the hotel by yet another door, hoping to avoid the services of Rollo.

Alone in my room, I think how safe I've been the whole trip: not one scary ride, not one bad driver, not one car accident, not one incident of police harassment. My AAA TripTik has been very helpful, and the *Rand McNally Road Atlas* is my manual to hitchhiking success. And my BlackBerry. My love! My life! "Will you marry me?" I ask it. Yes? Thank you and good night.

I awake to the stench of the hotel's cigarette smoke and realize today, Day Nine, could be my last day on the road if I'm lucky and get a ride quickly once The Kid lets me out at a new hitchhiking ramp. I've studied the maps and am pretty sure it's a bad idea to try for a ride in Reno. A town called Truckee is about fifteen miles away, right across the California border, which looks promising. Besides, I like the name. Truckee. My kind of town? I'm so optimistic I throw away two more pairs of worn boxer shorts *and* a pair of dirty socks.

I'm excited to see that for once, the hotel I'm staying in has room service. I talk to The Kid on the hotel phone and tell him to order in, too. He surprises me by laughing and telling me that Rollo called his room late last night and asked him if he "needed anything." Like what!? A blow job?! I wonder. "He was still working at that hour?" I marvel. "No, he called me on my cell phone," The Kid answers. "You gave him your cell phone number?" I roar. "Well, yes," he mumbles, realizing how naive he could be. "Let's get the hell out of here," I say to The Kid, and he agrees. We have breakfast (awful!) and check out.

In the car on the way to Truckee, The Kid tells me that he told his mom this morning he was headed to my apartment in San Francisco and he will be staying there even though I will not be arriving until later. Stunned silence on her part. "Repeat what you just said on speakerphone so your father can hear," she managed to sputter, he tells me. The Kid seems bewildered in a humorous way that his family is so concerned. Me too. We're just appearing on a reality show that's not being filmed. Why is everyone not tuned in?

We pull off Route 80 in Truckee and I like what I see. It's ski country. Beautiful. Evergreens, mountains. It's clear and crisp out. Plus there's a bridge right nearby that I could go under if it starts raining. I hand The Corvette Kid my keys. My office has already called ahead and told my doorman in San Francisco to let him in and give him a parking place in the garage. It's weird getting out to hitchhike again after the comfort of being with such a good traveling companion on the highway. We bid farewell and I look forward to seeing him again in San Francisco at our journey's end. He pulls off. I wish I could somehow get there first! I stand there for a while but I don't get that sinking feeling the way I usually do at the start of every hitchhiking morning. I'm in California. The drivers I see look either upscale liberal or hippie-friendly. It's only been about ten minutes but a car has already pulled over. I grab my bag hopefully but instantly realize it's The Corvette Kid again! "I'm sorry!" he yells. "I knew you'd think a new person had stopped, but I forgot to take a picture of you hitchhiking." I could kill him for a second but then laugh and give him my best hitching pose. He snaps the photo, honks affirmatively, and pulls away, totally unafraid to enter phase three of our time together. I had asked The Corvette Kid earlier in the hotel, "If they make a movie out of my book, who do you want to play you?" "Justin Bieber," he announced without even hesitating.

REAL RIDE NUMBER NINETEEN

RESTAURANT OWNER AND WIFE

I don't stand there for long. I get a ride! Behind the wheel is a cool guy wearing sunglasses and beside him is a pregnant woman who is just as sexy and confident. I say, "Hi, I'm John Waters," and he says, "Hi, I'm Mark and this is my wife, Ali, and you ate in my restaurant last night in Reno." Unbelievable! He even remembers what I ordered for dinner! Yes, he had stopped by our table and I had told him I was hitchhiking, but he had no idea I'd be doing so thirty miles outside of town in Truckee, California, at this time or location. What a fluke.

Mark and Ali are on their way to Napa for a week's vacation and agree to take me all the way there. Yay! One hundred sixty miles or so. Their restaurant, Campo, had been the only bright spot in Reno for me, so I feel guilty thinking so negatively of the town as Mark explains, "Reno is on the upswing." He tells me his bistro is all organic and only uses meat from local butchers. Vegetables are grown nearby, too. You can tell he is a real foodie, yet rugged in a Western way. Obviously he is a famous chef here and a community activist anytime farming is mentioned. Ali was originally from the Pacific Heights neighborhood in San Francisco, and you can tell she is a thoroughbred.

We stop in Granite Bay, California, to get gas and I offer to fill it up or buy them lunch, but they decline, saying, "We wouldn't take anything from a normal hitchhiker, so we won't take anything from you." We talk about mountain roads and I mention my obsession with emergency truck "escape ramps," usually located on a steep, sustained downhill grade in elevated areas. The kind of exit lanes that just veer off the interstate and are graded *up* a hill so if a truck's brakes fail going down, the driver, in a last-ditch effort, just aims into this escape lane and prays the upgrade will slow down his rig and soften the impact of the upcoming crash. Mark tells me the story of a friend who built his house on property right on the other side of one of those mountain emergency stops in Incline Village, Nevada. Never having actually seen a truck use one of these lanes, despite living in the Rockies his whole life, Mark's friend figured, what the hell? He'd build a house here on Mt. Rose anyway. Maybe that's why he got such a good deal on the property. But the unthinkable did happen. A runaway truck lost its brakes and the driver veered into the lane hoping for the best. The best didn't happen. The entire truck smashed, flipped over, landed on Mark's friend's house, exploded, and killed all his pets! His daughter *did* see it coming—imagine that horror!—and ran out just in time and lived. Mark said his friend never got over it. No wonder! I'm so excited I almost start belting out the lyrics to "Runaway Truck" by Red Simpson, that wonderfully descriptive hillbilly tune with the chorus "Dangerous curves all around," but decide to spare my host my unmelodious singing voice.

We keep going on Route 80 past their intended turnoff so Mark can find me a good rest area to hitch. We go even farther and I feel guilty they're going so far out of their way, but we finally find the perfect one—Hunter Hill Safety Roadside Rest

Area. *And* it has a view. In the distance I can actually see the Golden Gate Bridge. I can almost taste San Francisco.

Mark and Ali drop me off at the parking-lot-exit hitchhiking spot, and Ali takes a photo of Mark and me. Naturally, I'm holding my prop—the new 80-W SAN FRANCISCO sign that I made in my hotel last night. We wave goodbye and I know I'm going to make it. I'm almost there.

RELUCTANT HEIR

It's a busy rest area and for once I'm not worried; I'm going to get a ride here easily—I can just feel it. From my viewpoint I can see all those who exit their vehicle and walk to the restroom. By their expression you can tell if they are going to shit or piss, and I try to predict the bathroom activity of each and receive the verdict by how long they stay inside.

I don't have time to play my little toilet game long, though. I get a ride right away. In a van packed with camping equipment, a canoe, maybe even a dog in a kennel—I don't look back for long. The reluctant-heir type who picks me up is the perfect Bay Area man. A handsome seemingly onetime hippie; a fifty-six-year-old guy who "spends most of his time camping" and lives "between Washington State and the Bay Area" (in this van?) and is "on the way to pick up my mom at the Oakland airport." You can tell he's been around but has good breeding. Nice cheek-bones. Uses proper grammar. Even though I imagine my ride is straight (a checkered history with both women and mental-health issues, I'd bet), he reminds me of one of my first boyfriends, Tom Houseman, who also at the time was a boyfriend of my best female friend, Pat Moran. Sadly, Tom overdosed in the seventies, but Pat and I are still best friends. My driver confides, "I had a DUI in the past," "I like Ecstasy," and "I still do LSD." God, I think, maybe I should take LSD again. Could that be my next book? I'll retake every drug I ever took, in order (hash, pot, LSD, amphetamine, morning-glory seeds, glue, heroin, MDA, opium, mushrooms, cocaine) and then do bath salts? Maybe not.

Old money, plus drugs, plus manners, equals a man who is compassionate. He tells me about the homeless family he had been talking to in the rest area before he picked me up. A black and white straight couple with two kids who had a meth-head roommate who drove them out of their house and now, even though they had nowhere to go, were having a picnic in the roadside rest area. What great optimists! Why can't we all be this happy in the face of sudden misfortune? Is this what my rider is trying to tell me, or am I just liberally profiling the man behind the steering wheel? How do I know what I'm surmising about this guy is true? Maybe he's planning on killing his mother once he picks her up at the airport. It doesn't really matter, though, because since he's not going into San Francisco, he asks me at which exit I'd like to be dropped. "University Avenue exit in Berkeley," I shout happily. If I can't get a ride there, I ought to shoot myself.

CRAIGSLIST PAUL

Ah, the great Bay Area weather! It's chilly as I walk over to the entrance ramp. I am ecstatic. Will this be my last ride or will I have to actually hitchhike locally once I do get a lift into the city of San Francisco? I put out my best hippie vibes and it works. Another great guy in a van picks me up. He doesn't recognize me until I get in. He explains he hasn't picked up a hitchhiker in ten years and thought at first, like everybody else, that I was a homeless beggar. He was surprised I wasn't standing at the intersection like other panhandlers. "Why would he be begging this far down the ramp?" he debated in the "split-second decision" it took him to pull over and stop.

His name is Paul and he is yet another cool, kind, middle-aged married guy. He is on his way into the city to pick up a table he bought on Craigslist. When I ask him where, he gives me an address two blocks from my apartment. "Yes! You *are* my last ride!" I tell him with excitement. "*If* you're not a killer," he says with a hint of seriousness. "Don't worry, I'm not!" I assure him as we stop at the Bay Bridge tollbooth. I am so happy to pay that I don't even get a receipt.

Paul is English but has been living in this country for twenty years. He says he "used to hitchhike in London myself until people stopped picking me up." I feel incredibly safe as the breathtaking panorama of the San Francisco skyline that no one could ever get sick of comes into view. I immediately visualize that great YouTube clip of Judy Garland singing "San Francisco" on her 1963 TV show, and once you've seen it, you'll understand how crazily focused, insanely optimistic, and spiritually privileged I feel at this exact moment in my life. I call my friend Vincent Fecteau, who had agreed months ago to be on hand to snap the photo of my final ride and me outside my apartment building. Vincent says he's on the way, but when we hang up, I wonder how he'll ever get there first. He travels by bicycle and we are making great time—there's no traffic.

Paul and I pull into the city and drive by the bus stops I use daily here—my training grounds for this finally about-to-be-completed hitchhiking trip. I almost feel giddy. Shocked that I've actually done this. "From my Baltimore house to the door of my San Francisco apartment building"—the book pitch is finally going to be a reality.

We pull up and Vincent is not here yet. That's okay—I'll get the doorman to take the photo. I can't expect Paul, who seems game, to stick around forever for a photo shoot. I barge into the lobby still carrying my sign, and there's a doorman I don't really know as well as the others. I must look unreasonably excited, beyond nuts. He eyes my sign quizzically as I hastily explain, "I've just hitchhiked across the country," and ask, "Would you take my photo outside with my last ride if the guy who was supposed to show up to take it doesn't arrive soon?" The doorman agrees without comment, maybe thinking I'm kidding. I call my office and tell Susan and Trish, "I have arrived!" They seem incredibly relieved and send out an e-mail to all my friends: "He just called from the lobby of his building in San Francisco. He made it!"

I go back outside and no Vincent, so I figure, let poor Paul go pick up his table. His ride was a short but momentous one for me. I can't hold up the gracious, good-humored man's life much longer. I get the doorman, and Paul and I pose beside his van as I hold my 80-W SAN FRANCISCO sign for the final time. The doorman snaps a few different shots and it's done. Paul chuckles at the whole situation and we shake hands goodbye and he pulls off. I walk, stunned, inside my building to the elevator.

The Corvette Kid is safely inside my apartment, sitting in the dark, seemingly too nervous to touch anything, even a light switch. Vincent shows up and laughs at the missed photo opportunity, and I introduce him to The Corvette Kid. It's almost as if I don't know how to act or speak anymore back in my real life. Susan e-mails that "if it was my unknown ass, I'd still be [hitching] in West Virginia." I check my San Francisco answering machine and hear Mink Stole sobbing in relief that I made it. I am moved *and* shocked to realize she was *this* concerned. I weigh myself. I have lost one pound.

Playlist (Go ahead! Find them online and listen.)

1. Hitch Hike — *Marvin Gaye*
2. Transfusion — *Nervous Norvus*
3. Looking at the World Through a Windshield — *Del Reeves*
4. The Giggler — *Pat and the Wildcats*
5. Loco Moto — *Cornbread and Jerry*
6. Witch Doctor — *David Seville and the Chipmunks*
7. Chain Gang — *Bobby Scott*
8. Travelin' Boogie — *Zeb Turner*
9. Swingin' Down the Lane — *Jerry Wallace*
10. Hot Wheels — *Stan Farlow*
11. Flying Saucer Rock and Roll — *Billy Lee Riley*
12. V-A-C-A-T-I-O-N — *Connie Francis*
13. Hitchhiker — *Bobby Curtola*
14. Bumming Around — *Jimmy Dean*
15. There Stands the Glass — *Webb Pierce*
16. Hitchin' and Hikin' — *Johnny Sea*
17. You Are the Finger of God — *The Addicts*
18. Torture — *Everly Brothers*
19. Tofurky Song — *Joanie Leeds*
20. I'm a Lone Wolf — *Leon Payne*
21. Riot in Cell Block #9 — *The Robins*
22. Strychnine — *The Sonics*
23. Lonesome Drifter — *Jericho Brown*
24. Jingle Bells — *The Singing Dogs*
25. Cross-Ties — *Dale Hawkins*
26. Baby Sittin' Boogie — *Buzz Clifford*
27. Who Killed Teddy Bear — *Josie Cotton*
28. Ohio — *Doris Day*
29. Runaway Truck — *Red Simpson*
30. San Francisco — *Judy Garland*

ACKNOWLEDGMENTS

Of course, I would like to thank my two assistants, Susan Allen-back and Trish Schweers, not only for being characters in this book, but also for running Hitchhiker Central in my office for the two and a half years it took to write and live this adventure. They did endless research, sometimes on joyful subjects, but more often on hideous ones, without the blinking of an eye (or at least ones *I* saw). Trish plotted my fictional geographical route better than AAA ever could have, and Susan tracked down devices to safely monitor me and forced me to realize I had to go shopping for sensible hitchhiker supplies before I left *non*fictionally. Once I was out on the highway, they were my lifeline to reality and were there for me in times of despair. Most important, they kept the secret of my hitchhiking trip until after it had been completed.

Both typed the manuscript from my Twombly-esque hand-written first drafts and, most embarrassing for me, had to read the sex parts concerning their own boss. Susan commented it was hard for her "to tell the difference between 'the Best That Could Happen' parts and 'the Worst'" in the fictional sections of the book. Susan and Trish are both incredibly skilled at editing and did so with me endlessly before we turned in the manuscript to the publisher. *Carsick* is their book, too.

The music playlist was also a group effort. Larry Benicewicz, who has helped me find music for all my movies and the *A John Waters Christmas* and *A Date with John Waters* CD compilations, led me to hitchhiking songs I never knew existed. Pauline Fisher and Mike Page also found me tunes that made the final cut. Jill Fannon hunted down all the selections online and made me endless versions of *Carsick*'s soundtrack so I could audition each number.

My literary agent, Bill Clegg, was the first to hear of my hitchhiking idea, but I begged him not to reveal it yet to Farrar, Straus and Giroux because, first, I wanted to be sure I had the nerve to do it. He kept nagging me to at least let him "tease the concept" and I vaguely said yes, and the next day he called to say they wanted to do it. Gulp.

This is my second book with FSG, and I'm spoiled. What a great team! Jonathan Galassi, my editor, never doubted I'd make it, and when I was halfway through the trip, stuck on some god-forsaken entrance ramp, his encouraging texts were all I needed to keep going. Susan Goldfarb is a patient and expert production editor (I challenge you to find even *one* typo in *Role Models*), and working with her again was a privilege. Ellis Levine gave me focused legal advice, and every time I do a book with him I learn. I'd also like to thank him for never mentioning my singing asshole in our discussion in a legal *or* nonlegal way.

But more than anything, I'd like to praise the drivers who picked me up. If I ever hear another elitist jerk use the term *fly-over people*, I'll punch him in the mouth. My riders were brave and open-minded, and their down-to-earth kindness gave me new faith in how decent Americans can be. They are the only heroes in this book.

P.S. Thanks for the lift.